CW00673347

COLEMAN'S DRIVE

*from Buenos Aires to New York
in a vintage Baby Austin*

by

JOHN COLEMAN

NEW EUROPEAN PUBLICATIONS
14-16 Carroun Road
London

Re-published in the United Kingdom in 1996 by
New European Publications Limited
14–16 Carroun Road
London SW8 1JT, England

All rights reserved. No part of this publication may be reproduced, stored
in a retrieval system, or transmitted, in any form or by any means,
electronic, mechanical, photocopying, recording or otherwise, without the
prior permission of New European Publications Limited.

This book is sold subject to the condition that it shall not, by way of trade
or otherwise, be lent, re-sold, hired out or otherwise circulated without
the publisher's prior consent in any form of binding or cover other than
that in which it is published and without a similar condition including this
condition being imposed on the subsequent purchaser.

British Library Cataloguing in Publication Data

A full catalogue record for this book is available from the British Library.

ISBN 1-872410-06-5 paperback

Copyright © 1996 John Coleman

All rights reserved

Originally published by Faber and Faber, London, 1962.

Printed in Great Britain by Biddles Limited, Guildford, Surrey

Contents

Illustrations

Illustrations

Acknowledgements

For years I have been deeply conscious that Arthur and Josephine Pearse, who went to immense trouble to prepare the maps to accompany my text, were omitted from the original acknowledgements. Now I have the chance, with the advantage of hindsight, to say how important I believe the maps have been for readers of the book.

I can only mention a few of the many people who helped me and made the journey and the account possible. First must certainly be the late Alan Pringle of Fabers who was wonderful to work with and whom I regard as one of the very great editors.

Illustrations would have been a real problem – so many of my own pictures were lost through the hazards of the journey – but for several people who produced some remarkable photographs: John Moore, Joan Rodker and David Preston.

Among firms that supported the adventure were Shell, the Austin Motor Company (BMC and now Rover), Dunlop and many others. Mr D. H. Piper of the Cords Piston Ring Company was exceptional. He provided office staff and facilities all through the original preparations for the journey.

Perhaps the most crucial point, the turning point in the preparations, came when a letter arrived from Lord Montagu of Beaulieu saying that his museum would support the project and that he would like the car to bear the name of the Montagu Motor Museum.

The new paperback edition owes much – if not everything – to Barry Carter's enthusiasm for the book and to his invaluable help in restoring the car in his workshop to the condition it was in at the end of the journey.

Foreword

by John Seymour

In an age in which humans, by plundering very effectively their planet, have managed to create surpluses in every desirable thing (and even more in undesirable ones) there is one commodity that is getting in ever and ever shorter supply. And that is Adventure.

Maybe it is a measure of the success of human technology that adventure is in such short supply. If you get lost these days in the most remote of mountain ranges you will probably not have to find your own way out; a helicopter will come and pluck you off and take you to a nice warm casualty ward in the nearest hospital. No doubt to most modern people this seems to be a very good thing. The last thing most modern men and women want is adventure. They want safety, comfort, untrammelled sex and plenty of leisure for looking at the television. They can get, vicariously, all the adventure they want on that. But, perversely, there is still a need for adventure in this world.

Maybe this is because during the millions of years of our evolution before this age we had plenty of it, and are evolved to expect it, to cope with it, and in fact to need it. If it doesn't come our way we are less than whole people. And maybe much of the unhealth of society is caused by its absence.

The story in this book indicates that if you really want adventure, you can get it – even in the second half of the twentieth-century (probably in the second half of the twenty-first century you won't need to look for it; there will be all too much of it!).

In the early 1920s the Austin Motor Company launched the Baby Austin on the astonished world. I remember, as a young child in England, seeing these very cheap – and very unathletic-looking – tiny motor cars taking over the roads. They were the first real 'people's car' and they heralded the era of mass motoring.

After the Second World War, John Coleman found the remains of one of the very first of these (built in 1925) lying in a ditch. He bought it – or at least was given most of it – and restored it. He decided to prove to everybody that this (to be brutally honest) rather sedate little machine was the best motor car in the world and would go where no other car had ever been or could go.

In 1959 he drove it from Buenos Aires with the intention of getting to New York. He was to follow the route taken by Tschiffely some decades before and made famous in the latter's book *Tschiffely's Ride*. By sheer persistence John Coleman made this hitherto believed to be impossible journey – impossible even for the latest brand-new four-wheel drive machine let alone a 'people's car' which one would have thought would have been fully stretched to have travelled from Land's End to John O'Groats. And because of all the trouble he experienced he really <u>saw</u> the countries he travelled through – he really had his nose rubbed in them. South America is t*erra incognita* to me, but I found this book a fascinating travelogue. I have a much better idea of what the continent is like – and feels like. (I particularly like the idea of all those gorgeous senoritas – but if we are to believe our author, he cruised past them with no more interaction than Ulysses had with the Sirens.)

I don't think Coleman proved that an ancient Baby Austin is the ideal vehicle for traversing mighty mountain ranges, great deserts and trackless jungle country but he did prove that English craftsmanship, in the early decades of this century, was pretty good and also that persistence and determination are all that are needed to conquer great obstacles. It will be a sad day for humanity when all dangers and difficulties have been eliminated. It will be a sad day when young people no longer go out and <u>seek</u> adventure – and no longer wish to test themselves and find out what it is like to have to solve difficult problems <u>alone</u> when the situation can be a matter of life or death.

I might add that John still drives a thirty-five year old car. I have been a passenger in it – in South London though, not crossing the Andes – and I am still here to tell the tale.

New Introduction

The world has changed in many ways since I first undertook this journey in 1959. One of the ways is in its attitude to Latin America. In the fifties and sixties the Western world was preoccupied with its own problems and with the Cold War which followed a pretty hot war in Europe and the Far East. That Cold War impinged on the Latin American world through Fidel Castro and was mainly limited to Cuba although the seeds of revolution were quietly germinating underground when I was there.

Not until the violence in Central America and the Falklands War grabbed the world's headlines was it realised that half the American continent was more than just a sleepy backwater which the USA regarded as its backyard.

This changing perception of Latin America may bring it little good but it has aroused the world's interest in its wonders and its wealth and I suppose for that reason, if no other, may have created a fresh interest in my adventures.

Then there is the Austin Seven itself. For many years after the journey it was in Lord Montagu's museum at Beaulieu. Later it went to the Turnpike Centre on the Isle of Wight where the late David Spence became very enthusiastic, not just to display the car but to create a background to illustrate the whole journey. Plans were well underway when a tragic boating accident brought a wonderful and eccentric museum to an end. My own enthusiasm almost died at the same time until it was revived by Barry Carter's infectious response to my book last year.

Now my hope for the Austin Chummy is that it will find a museum with more than just an interest in making vintage cars look like new ones but will understand the lessons that Herbert Austin's "Baby" has to teach the throw-away world about the durable qualities of British workmanship in the earlier part of this century.

I

How I first got the Idea and how I planned the Journey

When I was a schoolboy sixteen or seventeen years ago I was in bed with flu one Christmas holiday. I was given various books to read. I have forgotten the titles of most of them now, but one I will never forget: the famous *Tschiffely's Ride*, which was originally called *Southern Cross to Pole Star*. The pages became vivid to me as I lay in bed reading the simply told, unaffected story of what is probably the greatest ride ever made on horseback. Tschiffely succeeded in travelling with the same two Argentine Creole horses over the whole of the route from Buenos Aires to New York and thus performed a feat which opinion from all quarters had reckoned to be absolutely impossible. His friends and companions laughed at him, the press hinted openly that it was only as a joke that they came to see him off, but most damning of all was the view expressed by the horse experts of both England and Argentina, that he was setting out on a ridiculous venture. Such expressions as 'Absurd!' and 'The man's mad' were ringing in his ears all day long.

Why was the journey believed to be impossible? There were two very good reasons why Tschiffely brought so much ridicule upon himself. Over the long trails that were to lead him up to New York, there were many great and terrible obstacles. First there was the mighty Andes, that long and vast chain of mountains which runs down the western side of South America. They are not quite the highest in the world, but they are certainly the most massive of all the great mountain ranges. When I first read Tschiffely I did not appreciate their size at all, and it was not until I began to make precise inquiries, when I was planning my own journey, that the realization of what their terrific heights meant began to dawn on me. During the journey itself the truth about them was finally driven home to my mind. The traveller faces not only the normal difficulties of climbing, but also a shortage of oxygen which becomes more and more acute as he goes up, and affects men and horses as well as motor-cars. Crossing the Andes from Argentina into Chile, for instance, a car loses between 30 and 40 per cent of its power just at the time when every scrap of energy is needed for the arduous ascents. There are many other peculiar difficulties as well, which people living in lowland countries would never even dream of, but these will emerge as the story proceeds.

It was not the mountains or even the deserts that weighed most in the minds of the horse experts, but the tropical sections of the journey. In the hot, swampy jungle country of South and Central America, it was not only men who died of such deadly diseases as yellow fever; horses too were almost certain to contract equally deadly fevers in lands where members of their species had never been accustomed to living. This fact more than anything else made the great majority of horse experts think that Tschiffely was completely mad. But he had confidence in himself and in his Argentine horses, and he hoped that with exceptional care he could save them from all the dangers of the route and eventually get through to New York. It took him two years to do it and both he and the horses suffered great agonies and faced terrible hazards on certain parts of the journey. They are all to be found in his book and I must return to my own story.

The book about his ride wasn't Tschiffely's only book. He made other journeys and wrote many other books, not so well known it is true, but none the less interesting on that account. In any case I'd made up my mind to search for them after having been so fascinated by his first one. My next discovery was *Coricancha, The Garden of Gold*. It told the amazing story of the conquest of the Inca Kingdom by a small band of Spaniards whose only advantages, against the vast armies of the Inca, were the few guns they carried with them and a legend among the Inca people that one day pure white men would come as messengers of their gods. The Spaniards were able to make considerable use of this to their own advantage. As a result of travelling, reading and a peculiar understanding of the Spanish and Indian mentality, Tschiffely was able to describe how the Inca people lived; he tells of their bravery when they saw for the first time men mounted on horses; he describes the organization of their society in which stealing was almost unknown and the rare instances of it that occurred led to an investigation into the administration rather than imprisonment of the culprit. He goes on to tell of their fabulous temples which were lined with massive quantities of shining gold. The Incas worshipped the sun for, like Ikhnaton in ancient Egypt, they believed that from it came the warmth and energy which brought forth man's life on earth. As such it was a fairly sensible religion, especially as it led to nothing in the way of human sacrifice and little deliberate violence, but produced instead great civil engineering works and a high degree of skill in medicine and surgery.

The fragments of their story can light up a youthful imagination, and it became one of the ambitions of my life that one day I should go myself and see the Inca remains and meet the descendants of the old Inca race. Often it seemed an impossible dream. Peru was such a tremendously long way away, to go there would cost more money than I expected ever to be able to afford, and I assumed that I would merely have to forget the whole idea, which unfortunately is the fate of most of the ambitions of youth. And so I went on reading, and discovered other writers on South America besides Tschiffely.

Tschiffely set out on his ride in the year 1925; that same year, in England, something else had happened that has a bearing on my story. A few years earlier Sir Herbert Austin had designed the most famous of all baby cars ever made, the Austin Seven Chummy, which remained the basic design of all Austin Sevens until 1938. In 1925 the assembly lines for that renowned little car were set up, and the first batch of the first really successful small cars ever made came rolling out of the factory at Longbridge. Among them was the one that was to play so important a part in my life and to give me the idea for fulfilling my seemingly impossible dream.

When I was in the Army and at the University (from 1947 to 1952), I started taking an increasing interest in motor-cars and learning how they worked. In those days one of the most obvious models for a student to possess was one of the many ancient Austin Sevens which had become a familiar and traditional sight on English roads. They used very little petrol and, with a little patience, one could learn to look after them and mend them oneself. In the end I almost became a collector of Austin Sevens, often owning two or three at a time and never able to resist a bargain when it came my way. I spent a lot of time dismantling and reassembling them and often sold them at a substantial profit, which enabled me to add further new members to my collection. I suppose in all I must have owned at least fourteen or fifteen Austin Sevens. People were of course inclined to make remarks and often told me that I spent far too much time messing about with dirty old motor-cars. But I refused to believe that I was really wasting my time when I crawled underneath the old cars in my oily overalls and struggled to make them perform like the latest models. I knew that I was learning worthwhile things, though I never thought at the time that some of that knowledge was later to save my life in certain difficult parts of the Andes and in the Atacama Desert. I believed firmly in the value of practical knowledge, and I thought and still think that such experience is very necessary for people in universities, who spend so much time working out theories in their minds that they forget about the existence of the real world in which theories have to be made to work. I had to work out theories in my mind to repair my car, but it was the car that told me whether they were right or wrong. It wasn't always the cleverest theory that was right, but the one that fitted the facts and made the engine purr away once more.

Most of the Austin Sevens run by students, even at that time, were models of the late twenties and early thirties and so, when I saw a little 1925 Chummy being used by the owner of a boating station to pull rowing-boats out of the Thames at Oxford, it immediately caught my interest. While I was at the University I had made one or two attempts to buy it, but each time its owner refused or asked a price which was beyond my pocket. As I watched it pulling the boats out of the water and tugging them across the bumpy meadows, I realized what a magnificent job it was doing, and felt confident that a car which would stand up to that, would stand up to anything.

It was in 1951 and 1952 that I first saw MO 6320 performing its arduous tasks by the banks of the Thames during the summer months. In the winter its owner seemed to bestow no care whatever on it, and on one occasion I even saw it standing in over a foot of water in the flooded meadows. It looked a poor, bedraggled thing, yet it fascinated me and even then I felt it ought to have some great destiny in front of it. Today, with an air of fulfilment, it stands in the Montagu Motor Museum!

But at that time there were still worse days ahead for the poor car, before I eventually rescued it. I left Oxford in 1952 and started training to be a schoolteacher, but one week-end in the late autumn of 1953 I happened to return on a visit to some friends. On the Sunday afternoon we all went for a walk together through Port Meadow and past the boating station where the little Austin used to live. I had not forgotten it, but I saw no sign of it and assumed it had gone, until I noticed, in a ditch beside one of the sheds at the river's edge, the body of a car. An old car body in those days was an exciting find. Cars and parts were scarce and expensive, and one might discover many useful bits and pieces on such an abandoned body. When I came to look closer, however, I soon identified it as the missing Austin Seven. The bodywork was strong and sound but all the mechanical parts had been removed. I at once began making inquiries, as a result of which I discovered that the owner had finally treated the car too roughly and broken the crown-wheel and pinion in the back axle. He had been unable to obtain a replacement and thought he would make his money by selling the parts. Unfortunately for him, many of them were not quite suitable for fitting on to the later models, and so they were merely packed away with a lot of old junk from boats.

Now my chance to make a deal with him had really arrived. I could have the body for nothing, he said, and suggested that we could come to some arrangement about the machinery. At that moment an idea occurred to me. I had an old boat engine which I'd bought for two pounds ten. I offered to swop it for the mechanical parts of the Austin. The proprietor of the boating station thought for a moment and then decided to accept my offer. The deal excluded the engine which I managed to get from him later.

One day in late November, I set off for Oxford again in the little 1932 Austin Seven Saloon I was running at the time. I was loaded with tools and equipment and all prepared to reassemble the car and tow it away with the help of a friend. In the meantime I had contrived to obtain the necessary back-axle parts, after a tour of several breakers' yards. When I reached Oxford it was pouring with rain and I had to do the whole job out on the meadows in mud and extreme discomfort, and I wasn't as careful as I might have been about tightening up every nut and bolt; my lack of care led to an amusing incident later on. As there was no engine in the car when I had completed the task of reassembly, we towed it up to London. My home was then in South London and at the bottom of the garden was an old coach-house where it was possible to keep three or four cars. There I stored the Austin for some time. After my unpleasant experience of assembling it in the cold and wet, I didn't feel like doing any further work on it during the winter.

The following summer I was short of money, and several times I very nearly decided to sell it, but each time something made me hesitate just at the last moment, for I still had a strong feeling that I ought to do something special with it. As I was thinking of selling it I naturally had to fit an engine in it and get it running. A very strange thing happened the very first time I tried it out on the road. It was impossible to change it from bottom gear to second. For some time I just couldn't think what had happened. Then it occurred to me to try it in reverse. It went backwards. Then I changed it into second gear and it went backwards faster. Then I changed it into top and it went faster still. I had one forward speed and three reverse! I could have driven backwards at forty miles an hour and forwards at not more than five or six! I soon realized that there could be only one explanation. In the rush of assembly on that cold wet day the previous year, I must have accidentally fitted the interior of the back axle the wrong way round. That was exactly what had happened, and now that I knew it, it was only a day's work to rectify it.

Every now and again during the following years I used the car for short periods of time. But now I was much busier with my work and could give the car very little attention. Nevertheless whenever I had leisure to spare I used it to do up parts of the car one at a time. One week-end I remember taking all the wheels off, cleaning off every bit of rust and replacing them. At other times I worked on the engine. That was during 1957 and 1958.

In the very early spring of 1959, I read another book on the Incas of Peru. It was entitled *Incas and Other Men*, and was written by a Canadian called Woodcock, who with his wife had travelled round the Peruvian highlands and visited the Inca remains by any local means of transport available, sometimes in old buses and sometimes on mules. Once again my old ambition to go to those places myself flared up and I envied Woodcock's good fortune in living on the same continent. Then one day as I was standing around in a rather disgruntled mood looking at the half-dismantled Austin, the thought suddenly came to me: 'That's the car I'm going to do my journey in!' In a strange way I felt I'd known it all along. I decided to write to the Austin Motor Company at once. I thought they would certainly be delighted by the idea of someone doing the journey from Buenos Aires to New York in one of their old cars. The reply I received made me realize that the situation was very different from what I'd imagined. It had not occurred to me, for instance, that if the car happened to fall to bits on the rough trails of Chile or Ecuador, it would not help the Austin Company very much. They told me that they were very interested to hear about my plans, but that they received letters every day from people trying to organize expeditions, and they had decided that the company could only support such ventures as they themselves arranged. This was quite a blow, but I was determined that it shouldn't be a fatal blow.

I began casting around elsewhere for support. I wrote to the manufacturers of component parts, but this time I wrote a little differently. I took what I think was a bold step. I had two cars: the antique Austin and a relatively new Morris Minor Tourer which I knew I could sell for approximately three hundred pounds. I decided to sell it and use the money for financing the journey, and so in the next batch of letters I announced that I was intending to finance the journey myself, but that I would be pleased to receive any advice they might have to offer, or any of their products they might care to supply for the final preparation of the car. I now had much more success: boxes of valves and pistons for the engine came rolling in with every post; I was offered new tyres and brake linings and several very big firms promised to give me introductions to their representatives in the countries I was to pass through, and assured me that once I was out there I could rely on a considerable degree of help and support in the main cities. One of the big oil companies promised to write to all their marketing companies *en route*. They didn't actually commit themselves to anything, but they said they felt sure

I would be well looked after so far as petrol and oil were concerned—wherever they might be available! In fact all the oil and petrol used in the journey was paid for by them. Then I was given an official letter to all the British Embassies and Consulates in the territories on my route, for it was officially considered that my journey would help to impress on the Americans, particularly, 'the enduring qualities of British goods and workmanship'. The Embassies were requested to arrange press conferences and to introduce me to television authorities in the Americas.

Things were certainly looking much brighter now. One of my main worries was transporting the car to Buenos Aires. That was a real worry and I feared it might prove a fatal obstacle to my scheme. But there was another kind of worry also. I had to find out what road conditions were like in Latin America. I had read frightening things about them, but now I had to find out exactly. I knew that there was something called the Pan-American Highway which was supposed to run from South America up to North America. First I wrote to the A.A. and from them I learnt that about half of that great highway is not yet built, but still in the planning stage, and that I would have to travel for thousands of miles over rough trails. In addition to this there were four complete gaps in the highway, and on them some of the worst episodes of the journey occurred. Then I received a report from the American A.A. of a journey by two of their representatives, from Panama City to Washington, about half the length of the journey I was intending to undertake. It included a long list of all the things on their car that broke down, some parts such as springs and shock-absorbers being listed several times. It sounded hopeless, especially as the train and ship fares over the gaps were very high, amounting to more money than I was intending to take with me altogether! Still, I thought, if a train can get through, I might be able to bump very slowly along the edge of the line, and although the letter ended: 'Do you still wish to undertake the trip in your 1925 Austin Seven Motor Car?' I decided I would.

Tim Carson of the Vintage Sports Car Club had suggested to me that I should telephone Peter Riviere at the *Autocar*, and ask him about the journey, since he had been on the Oxford and Cambridge Expedition to South America and knew a lot of the route I was intending to travel over. I didn't tell him at first what I was intending to do it in. He seemed surprised enough at the idea of attempting it alone, and assumed that I intended to go in a Jeep or a Land Rover. When I told him I was planning to do it in a 1925 Austin Seven, there was a moment's silence. A friend of his in the same office, whom I spoke to afterwards, gave me a graphic description of how he almost fell over backwards off his chair when I disclosed that I was proposing to go in one of the very first Austin Sevens. After he had recovered, Peter went ahead emphasizing the difficulties which I would encounter in the Andes, described the hundreds of miles of corrugated track in the Atacama Desert, which, he said, would bash any normal car to pieces, and mentioned that I would have to negotiate several long stretches where no road at all existed.

I also wrote to the Editor of the *Geographical Magazine* to ask for further advice. The replies I received were very sceptical indeed. The first letter explained how he himself had struggled over the Andes in a new eight-cylinder Buick, and only just made it. He also mentioned that he had had a new Austin Seven in 1932 and found it quite hard enough to climb Wrotham Hill in that! He considered my venture hopeless and finished by saying: 'I wouldn't be in your shoes for any money.' The second letter came after I had written to say that my Austin had put up remarkable performances on mountain country in England. It simply said: 'There is no mountainous country in England, only a few lowish hills.' It explained that the road in Peru goes up to 18,000 feet, and that the highest peak in the British Isles, Ben Nevis, is only 4,400 feet. That certainly made me think. 'Multiply Porlock by thirty-five,' wrote the Editor of the *Geographical Magazine*, 'and you begin to get an idea!' He also warned me that water boils at very much lower temperatures at such heights and can cause a lot of trouble with the radiator.

It was hard for me to get a true picture of what such heights really meant. I knew some of the mountain passes in Europe, but they only went up to about 7,000 feet in the very highest places. I tried to form some conception of it by working out that there are 5,280 feet in a mile, which is less than a third of the height of the road in Peru, and so I realized that the South American roads can go up to well over three miles high in places! The roads are higher than the peak of Mont Blanc! And heights, of course, were by no means the only problem I would have to face. There were the vast waterless deserts of Chile, Peru and Mexico, one of which turned out to be not so waterless as I'd expected; and there were the jungles of Ecuador where jaguars, head-hunting Indians and many varieties of fatally poisonous snakes were among the hazards that I was told I could expect to meet; and more jungles in Central America, as well as places where bandits abound, from whom, I believe, on one occasion my beard saved me. The prospect was pretty tough with only the thin hood of the little Austin Seven (which might break down at any time under the strain) to protect me, even if I could overcome the first problem of getting enough money to go to South America and get started.

I wrote a letter to Stirling Moss whom I had not seen since we were at school together, informing him of my intention, and he very kindly promised that if he possibly could he would come and see me off, and give a good start to my crazy venture. How refreshing to meet someone who doesn't raise objections to impossibilities! I often thought of him when I was struggling over the roadless parts of the Chilean desert at four or five miles an hour! I decided also to write to the Montagu Motor Museum at Beaulieu, a decision which brought forth excellent results. I found immediate and enthusiastic interest in my scheme. It was decided that I should lend the car to the Museum and make the journey under its auspices. In return for this I was supplied with photographic equipment, a small financial contribution, letters to millionaires interested in antique cars in the United States; and the final preparation of the car was carried out in the Beaulieu workshops, while I rushed round London trying to obtain visas and official documents to travel through a dozen different countries. The A.A. attended to the papers for the car, but three days before leaving I received a letter saying that they believed that the International Carnet was no longer valid in Argentine, so that when I finally departed I was completely unsure if I would even be able to land the car.

I had paid a 10 per cent deposit on my fare to Buenos Aires and the last day for paying the full fare arrived. There was still a horrible question-mark in my mind. Were all those people, who thought I was crazy, right really? I hardly knew what I was doing and perhaps that was fortunate. On the morning when I had to make the final decision the post brought a letter from the Manager of the shipping company, saying that he would like to see me personally and have a talk about my journey. He had a pleasant surprise waiting for me. The company had decided to carry my car the six thousand miles across the Atlantic Ocean for only eighteen pounds. This sealed my fate. Arrangements were also made to give me a send-off party on board the *Highland Princess* the day before leaving, Friday, 2nd October 1959. Stirling was unable to come on the Friday, but the party was attended by Lord Montagu and a goodly gathering of journalists from the newspapers and the motoring magazines. The B.B.C. made various recordings and I was then fully aware that at last my journey was becoming more than a dream.

In the meantime Austin's had changed their attitude towards my journey. I received a letter from the Deputy Chairman of the Company saying that they were prepared to pay for servicing and repairs to the car during the trip and to fly out any spare parts that might be needed. They also provided a car to take me from my home to Tilbury on the Saturday morning, where I had to collect my £300 worth of traveller's cheques before boarding the *Highland Princess*. I called at the bank at Tilbury about half an hour before the ship was due to sail, but the cheques had not arrived and I had almost no money with me. The bank had to phone the Post Office and the package was found and sent out in a special van, which arrived at five minutes to twelve. The driver behaved like Stirling Moss on the road from the bank to the docks and I arrived with only two minutes to spare. The gangplank was lifted but it was not until two o'clock that the ship's sirens sounded and the *Highland Princess* got under way. At that moment I knew there was no longer any chance of getting cold feet and turning back. From then on the only thing to do was to go ahead and hope.

The voyage was calm and pleasant, even in the Bay of Biscay. We stopped for a few hours at Vigo in Spain, and for nearly a day in Lisbon. Only one day was a little rough as we were passing along the Portuguese coast, and saw the valiant little sardine-fishing craft, looking not much bigger than sardines themselves as they made their way out into the choppy seas. I made a number of good friends on board, including two from South America, whom I met later in their homes, and who gave me my first introduction to the Spanish language. I had been intending to study it for several months before leaving, but with the pressure of preparations I never found time until I was actually on the boat. We made another stop at Las Palmas in the Canary Islands, but it was so brief that I hadn't time to travel inland to visit a farm situated right in the cone of an extinct volcano. I could have comforted myself with the thought that I was to see many other interesting things inside volcanoes when I reached Central America, had I but known it. Our evenings were enlivened by the wild and skilful dancing of the Spanish and Portuguese immigrants. I was travelling third class and we had been told to expect them to be sick all over us and to spit around the decks. They behaved much better than we had been led to expect. There was some excitement when far out in the Atlantic someone picked up a repeat transmission of the story of how I had originally obtained the car, and from then on crowds of passengers wanted to join me as I climbed down into the bottom of the boat each day to see that the car was safe and to turn the engine over. It had suddenly become famous.

About ten days later we sighted the coast of Brazil, my very first view of South America. Very early the next morning we steamed into the famous harbour of Rio de Janeiro. The sky was cloudy and it was raining as we passed the grey forms of mountains that run almost straight down into the sea, including the spectacular Sugar Loaf that stands right at the entrance to the harbour, the fabulous Copercobana beach and the airport that reaches so close to the edge of the water that it seems as if every aeroplane taxiing along the runway is bound to land up in the sea! A day or so later we reached Santos, the coffee port farther down the coast of Brazil. We docked for a full day there and some of us travelled by bus along the excellent motorway up the mountains to Sao Paulo, the first of the great new cities of Brazil.

It was now only a matter of a few more days until we entered the River Plate, and docked first at Montevideo and then at Buenos Aires itself, after passing through the waters where the famous battle with the *Graf Spee* had taken place during the war. It was Saturday, 24th October, and just beginning to get light. Three weeks earlier I had been leaving Tilbury and saying goodbye to London and England, and sometimes wondering if I would ever return. But just now I was worried about immediate difficulties: getting through the customs, especially getting the car through without the correct papers.

II

Across Argentina in Rain and Storm

After a long, tense wait with the crowds of passengers, I finally stepped off the boat and entered the customs house to see the little Austin safely unloaded. I breathed a great sigh of relief on that score and surged on among the crowds, anxious about whether the documents I possessed would satisfy the authorities and fearful that I would have to hand out most of my short supply of cash in bribes to get through at all. I breathed a second great sigh of relief when a tall handsome young man made his way towards me and introduced himself as Ricardo Alexander, the representative of the Austin agency. He interpreted my story to the officials and to the newspapermen who had identified me by the odd collection of expeditionary baggage that surrounded me. My carnet for the Austin was accepted, but I had to wait till the following Monday to collect the car with a representative of the Touring Club Argentino.

Ricardo took me to lunch in the beautiful Palermo Park and on the way there I got my first impression of the city. The shapeless forms that hurtled past the windows of the car I estimated to be the traffic of Buenos Aires. Brakes screeched from every direction, and as we shot over some red lights at the intersection of one of the main avenues, Ricardo remarked, 'We've only had these things for a few years and we don't take much notice of them.' 'Don't you take any notice of them either?' I asked hesitatingly, when a policeman blew his whistle and felt my question really to be rather ridiculous. 'I promised my wife that on the day she stops for a policeman's whistle, I'll give her a beating she'll never forget for the rest of her life.'

I would hardly say that all the drivers were quite like Ricardo, but there was a great deal of truth in his contention that the city traffic was the cradle of Argentina's fame in the motor-racing world. I once saw two cars going round a bend both on the wrong side of each other. One had cut the corner rather too fine and the other had reacted instantaneously, swerved out and quickly resumed his normal course as if nothing had happened. On another occasion I was sitting in a restaurant watching the traffic in the street outside. The customary way of entering and leaving a parking-place is by bumping the vehicles in front and behind out of your way. On this occasion a bubble-car was parked in front of a large lorry, the driver of which adopted his usual procedure, and the bubble-car was reduced to half size! This was a graphic lesson for me and I avoided using the Austin in the city as far as possible.

The evening newspapers appeared with my story and picture under this title: 'Red Beard intends to connect Buenos Aires with New York in 1925 Auto.' I was not quite sure how to take it when I learned that Barba Roja, Red Beard, was a notoriously bloodthirsty pirate of the old days in Argentina. Later I heard the story of how a friend of his had once picked a quarrel and asked to borrow his knife to settle the dispute. When the friend was returning the knife the old pirate asked if he had killed his enemy. On hearing that he had not, Red Beard at once ran the knife through his friend saying that it never left his side except to kill. No wonder that he had created an awe-inspiring legend of himself as a killer, and even government ministers trembled at the thought of having to take any action against him.

Buenos Aires, after having recently got rid of the dictator Peron, seemed to me to be in a very democratic mood. Scars from the revolution were still visible on many of the buildings. Peron had consolidated his régime by pandering to the populace, by giving them numerous holidays and a good deal of additional money. He therefore remains very popular even now among large numbers of the poorer people who are unaware of how he dealt with the national economy. After the last war Argentina was one of the countries with the highest gold reserves. Peron used part of this enormous wealth to keep the people happy and the other part he quietly shipped to banks in various parts of the world in readiness for the inevitable rainy day when he would be kicked out. All the while he was making speeches to ignorant people in which he was saying: 'What's the good of gold? Why, it's only what rich people use to fill their teeth with!' I gain the impression from meeting and seeing South American people that no dictator who might contrive to rule them could do more than build a precarious foundation for himself. The constitutions laid down after the Wars of Independence contain remarkable and little-known safeguards of freedom. Latin Americans live and breathe in their own spirit of democracy. If they happen to get temporary totalitarianism it is because their zeal for democracy makes them carry it to the borders of anarchy.

As the days went by, I was gradually getting to know the great city itself, the largest in the Southern Hemisphere. Buenos Aires stands on the southern banks of the River Plate where the vast grass plains of Argentina run down to the water's edge. Not a hill can be seen around the city and within it one can hardly find a street with even a gradual slope. Its streets and avenues, many of which are exceedingly attractive, are arranged in a more or less symmetrical pattern reminiscent of cities in the United States. The diagonal Saens Peña cuts across the regular pattern rather in the same way that Broadway cuts across New York. It is not the main avenue, which is Ninth of July, and which commemorates Argentina's achievement of independence in 1816. The city can pride itself on having the widest street in the world, for this avenue can carry some sixteen lanes of traffic as well as having a small road on either side of it. Trying to cross it at rush hour is like trying to cross a field under machine-gun fire. Buenos Aires also boasts the longest street in the world, Avenida Rivadavia, eighteen miles long and with house numbers going up to twenty thousand. Going to visit a friend down the street can involve quite a substantial journey! Then there is the business quarter where Victorian and Edwardian architectural influence is plainly visible, and Belgrano, the top residential area liberally supplied with trees and elegance. The total effect is of a great cosmopolitan city, lively and alert night and day, not predominantly Spanish and certainly not provincial. In the centre at any rate, the city has received much of its character from England, America and Paris.

I soon learnt to my horror from the Touring Club Argentino that the road over the Andes was badly snowbound and would be closed until long after the normal date for it to be cleared. This was to play havoc with my time schedule, which was carefully

worked out to fit in with the dry seasons in the countries farther
north. There was nothing I could do about it and I decided to
spend three weeks getting to know the great city and its people.
Every morning I made my way to the Austin Agency to supervise
a further complete check-over of the car and to arrange to get
various pieces of special equipment necessary for South American
motoring. Every morning Ricardo pulled a small revolver out of a
drawer of his desk and subjected me to a little lecture on the
importance of carrying a gun. I pointed out that I was not a very
practised shot and that I felt I could get into more trouble with it
than I could get out of. I believed that it was far better to cope
with people psychologically, and quoted examples of men who
had calmed down savage mobs by exposing themselves to their
rage at just the right moment. I had always been interested in the
fact that one of the most savage of all animals, the wolf, becomes
helpless to kill his opponent in the very heat of battle if that
opponent offers his throat under the jaws of the victor. Konrad
Lorenz, the zoologist, points out that there appears to be a built-
in mechanism of this sort in many species, which serves to ensure
survival. I felt sure that the concept of mercy in human beings
was derived from the same kind of emotional mechanism in them.
I believe that it would be hard for even the most savage man to
kill another who approached him with signs and gesticulations of
friendship. I did not suggest that his restraint would necessarily
last for long, but I felt sure that it would work long enough for the
other man to get away. Though, of course, my journey didn't
prove that theory, I did derive great satisfaction from finding it
worked among all the wild people I met, from the Indians in the
jungle in Ecuador to the rough bands of bandits in Central America. Ricardo turned to animals. They would obviously show no
mercy to members of other species. I believed that danger from
animals was a thing that has been greatly exaggerated by people
wishing to make their travellers' tales sound good. This I also
found true.

There were often other people in the office, of course, but I
remember one morning seeing through the glass panel a man
with an extra lively twinkle in his eyes. 'This is Nick Schreiber, a
great oil expert,' said Ricardo as I entered. 'He's driven over the
Andes to Chile and up to the edge of the Atacama Desert.' A most
remarkable monologue ensued as Nick described his experience

of crossing the Andes in a new American car. He told us of how the car was almost pointing up at the sky on the way up, how the road seemed to continue on up for ever and ever, how it was necessary to build up speed at the hairpin bends, to throw the car round almost, and how easy it was to slip back over the edge if the engine happened to stall. The road down into Chile, he claimed, was even more terrifying. He had gulped and merely wanted to close his eyes as he slid along the edges of terrific precipices. The hairs on his head stood on end and the bristles on his unshaven face stiffened up. 'Then you come to the Atacama Desert,' he went on, 'and before you're quarter of the way across your car will have been battered to pieces and you will be dying of thirst. The Andes will seem like child's play to you then—that's, of course, if you get over them. You may also notice the road undulating in front of you. That will mean that one of Chile's daily earthquakes is taking place. They have them at the rate of three to four hundred a year. Then in Peru all will go well. The roads are excellent—if you get to them! Then you'll get into Ecuador and at once you'll be in real trouble. It will either be the rainy season in the jungle and your car will sink up to its middle in mud, or it will be the dry season and you will have to drive along with one wheel in a rut anything up to two feet deep. Then you'll wish for the rocky trails of the Atacama Desert.' 'Shut up,' I said. 'All right then, I won't tell you about Central America.' And every day after that Ricardo would just quietly mention Nick every time he shoved his revolver on the desk in front of me.

One night I went out to dinner at Ricardo's parents' house. His mother was a great enthusiast for Latin America. 'You either fall in love with the Latin Americans or you dislike them and are inclined to fabricate stories about them. We English are especially prone to be irritated by them because they seem to have no idea of time or punctuality. Queen Victoria gave them clocks to try and change them. You saw one of those clocks, I expect, as you were coming into the harbour.' I was interested in this as it seemed to tie up with a comment of Tschiffely's. The Spanish character has always been a peculiar contradiction and many writers, instead of trying to explain it, have found it much easier and more convenient to invent dark legends. Soon I was to meet Latin Americans on a grand scale. On the following day I didn't go into Ricardo's office until rather late in the afternoon. When I arrived I found a group of Argentines who had been waiting half the day to find me. Their spokesman, in his slightly broken English, quickly introduced himself as Pedro Escudero and explained that they were a group of vintage-car enthusiasts and they had been searching everywhere to find me after reading about my venture. 'And now,' said Pedro, 'will you be so gentle as to accompany us to see *our* vintage cars?' They had many varieties of early English cars and Pedro himself had a 1928 Austin Seven, which was undergoing the most fundamental processes of reconstruction.

From then on I was constantly entertained to parties and asados—which are a kind of barbecue springing from the old Gaucho tradition of roasting half an ox over a great fire out of doors, and at which even today a most disturbing mass of entrails is included in the delicacies of the feast. I had quite a delicate problem to avoid eating the knotty stomach of the poor beast chosen for the asado. Then there were indoor dinner parties which began at ten, eleven and even twelve o'clock at night, and conversation about vintage cars, my journey and the new vintage car club they were about to create, which lasted till four or five in the morning. Pedro's wife, they all explained to me (she couldn't speak any English), had suffered fearful neglect since my arrival; and one night Pedro had pushed her out of bed in his sleep and cried out for his Austin Seven! I told them that the way things were going, I thought she was pretty lucky to get into bed at all to be pushed out. This whirlwind of entertainments made it hard for me to find time for the kind English friends who were helping me to prepare for the journey, but I could not refuse to make a little speech about my trip at the Annual Oxford and Cambridge Dinner in Buenos Aires. After a belated yellow fever injection in the afternoon, as it happened . . .

The night before my departure arrived. I was due to leave at 10.30 a.m. on Sunday, 15th November from Kilometre Zero in the Plaza del Congreso in the very centre of Buenos Aires, the point from which all distances in Argentina are measured. Reporters from *The Times*, the *Express*, television news cameras and Argentine motoring correspondents were all due there at that time. I was to leave in a great procession of vintage cars, including a couple of Austin Sevens, Rolls Royces, Alvises, Jaguars and other makes. It was indeed to be a mighty procession and was intended not only to start me off but also to inaugurate the Vintage Car Club Argentino. My car was in the hands of these enthusiasts who had promised to call round for me at 7.30 in the morning, 'Hora Inglesa' as the Latin Americans say when they mean they are not going to be three or four hours late. I was nevertheless nervous on this score for I felt I couldn't quite rely on them. When the spirit moves, however, Argentines are as capable of being punctual and efficient as anyone in the world and their attitude, I must confess, lends an air of adventure to everything they undertake. In England, Europe and the U.S.A. I always feel that there is a slightly deadening demand to fulfil all the requirements of our stations in life with a grave sense of responsibility. In Latin America all is tinged with adventure. Even one's career is a bit of an adventure, a thing you can put aside for a week or two if a foreigner happens to arrive in an old car. One prominent Brazilian journalist I met told me that the difference between South America and the United States was that 'Down here it's eighty per cent heart and twenty per cent business. Up there it's the other way round.'

There were a million and one other incidents like ripe apples falling off trees in the autumn sun, but it is impossible to relate them all. The time in Buenos Aires had had its funny side and its crazy side, but there was a serious side also. I had done much hard work during the days arranging contacts at various points *en route* and getting all possible information, and as I lay in bed on that last night the serious side weighed heavily upon my mind. Nick's story was funny but it was not without an element of truth and I had received a cutting from the *Express*, which said that what Mr. Coleman didn't know was that for a large part of his journey there were no roads at all. It was a gigantic and unknown proposition and I knew that most people thought I was setting out on it without really knowing what I was doing. South America alone is more than twice the size of Australia, and Buenos Aires is well down towards the bottom of the world and New York well on the way towards the top. Was it not after all sheer madness I'd sunk into without really thinking? The unknown prospect grew vivid and gigantic in my mind as I lay motionless in the darkness unable to sleep. What would the mountains really be like? What was the desert really like? Tigers prowled through my mind, jaguars pounced down on to the fabric hood of the Austin from tall jungle trees and poisoned arrows of Indians whizzed across the darkness just about where the ceiling would in reality have been.

As I sat eating my breakfast surrounded by heaps of half-packed baggage, a determined knock made the door vibrate. It was some twenty minutes or so before I had expected the members of the new vintage car club to collect me, but as I looked round and called 'Come in' I saw Pedro Escudero's hefty form in front of my eyes. 'If you please, perhaps you are ready for the expedition to begin.' 'You're early,' I said in a disgruntled tone. 'Well, you see, on important occasions the Argentines are just as capable of being on time as the English.' I congratulated him and swallowed down the rest of my breakfast. 'The vintage cars have been practising all night and we will have to go by some of them that have fallen into trouble when we take you to your Austin.' I instantly sensed trouble and delay, but there was little I could do. We found several vintage cars broken down in various parts of the city and we succeeded in getting one or two of them going. To leave a fair impression of the club, I must point out that they were not intending to start it for another six months or so, with the result that my arrival precipitated a hectic couple of weeks' preparation on half-dismantled cars.

After running out of petrol because the tap had been accidentally turned on the previous day, and after losing the car that was guiding me to the Plaza del Congreso, I eventually arrived on the verge of collapse within a few minutes of the prearranged time. Cars, cameras and reporters duly arrived. After much fuss the procession, and it really was a magnificent one in spite of being gathered together at a moment's notice, began to move off. The plan was that it should be led by a little 1928 Austin Seven of Carlos Ibarra Garcia, and Pedro had organized himself in a standing position in the passenger-seat from which he was guiding the whole procession by flamboyant arm movements. I came second as I didn't know the route. We had hardly gone any distance at all when a frightening incident occurred that brought my cherished journey to within a hair's breadth of a sudden and early end. It was a hot day and the sun was blazing down on the tarred roads. We were going rather too slowly for my top gear at first and I made the horrible error of signalling to Pedro to speed up a little. We must have reached thirty-five to forty miles an hour when my back wheels suddenly skidded in a pool of soft tar. The back of the car slewed round to one side and after a violent jerk was just tipping over. At that very second a fast modern car raced up to overtake me on the near side. Bang! and we'd hit each other. Before I could realize quite what was happening the Austin was upright again and the engine was still purring away. Feeling a little dazed by the suddenness of events, I just kept going, remembering the words of a British businessman in Buenos Aires, who had hammered a piece of what he said was very important advice into my mind: 'If you ever get involved in an accident in South America, drive away from it as fast as you can! That's the finest way there is of keeping out of trouble here.' Not very much farther on, an irate man jumped out of a modern car and waved his hands at me. My Argentine friends soothed him down and promised to have his car repaired on the following day, and the wife of one of the enthusiasts told me how her hands had gone impulsively over her eyes to save her from seeing what seemed certain disaster, and that when she looked up again it seemed like a miracle to see the Austin still upright and running. A dent in the rear wing, which became one of the most prized scars of the journey, was the only damage sustained. Could such good fortune, I wondered, last out all the way to New York?

All our needs were well attended to and the club had arranged for an estate car of one of its members to drive up and down the rows of vintage cars, handing out sandwiches without troubling us to stop. At lunchtime the leader signalled the way down a bumpy lane that led to a typical ranch-type country restaurant where a special feast with lots of good wine had been arranged for the formal beginning of the new club. The lunch took several hours, and I was becoming increasingly worried about how I was supposed to fit in a day's driving before nightfall; but South Americans always advise you to enjoy today, your work can be done tomorrow—'Mañana', they say, 'mañana', probably the most used word in the language and an absolute stumbling-block to anyone with a compulsion neurosis about work. After lunch a few of the cars turned back, but most of them stayed with me for some way, until a storm began to threaten. As a number of the cars had no hoods, the time had come, the drivers thought, for them to return and for me to go on alone. The party of enthusiasts with their wives and children gathered by the roadside and, pretending to weep a little, expressed their sadness at having to say good-bye. A strange sudden sense of being alone at the beginning of a mighty unknown journey came over me. I thought of Tschiffely who at least had Mancha and Gato and I felt a twinge of regret that I was not following in his footsteps for the initial stages of my journey. I had decided to go via Chile instead of via Bolivia.

The road as far as Mendoza was good and incredibly level. The Argentines, who are crazy about road racing, have covered the six hundred miles in under five hours! As I was thinking about how Tschiffely's dog had to be sent back on the first day and remembering how boring Tschiffely himself had found the journey across the Pampas of Argentina, the clouds grew blacker and blacker and large raindrops began to fall out of the sky. I was forced to spend the night at San Antonio de Areco in quite a decent little room in a lodging-place beside a mud-bound petrol station of a well-known English brand, from whom I had been promised help wherever their stations existed. My main memories were of trying to swallow my supper before hoards of ravenous flies concealed it completely from view, and of lorry drivers who took enormous pains to try to understand me and tell me about the roads ahead. As far as language was concerned, I had to learn by being thrown in at the deep end head first. The experience was softened only by the wonderful and patient attitude of the Latin Americans. They regard it as a compliment that a foreigner desires to learn their language and they treat even his most halting and ludicrous attempts with great respect.

The rain continued the next day as I struck across the great plains. Electric storms caused vast sheets of lightning to flash over the endless expanse of grassland. For fifty and sixty miles on end not a house nor a tree was visible. Water seemed to gush in all round the windscreen and the Austin, I felt sure, was the most conspicuous object in the landscape. But in spite of it all the engine purred away satisfactorily, and, as I later realized, preferred it to the blazing sun of the deserts. The wide mud verges were almost like little streams, and where I had expected to see colourful gauchos riding, I saw only descending water. What worried me even more was that it would have been stupid to attempt a journey off the main road along the mud lanes unless it were absolutely vital. I had so many introductions to owners of estancias and all I seemed to be doing was racing along a narrow strip of completely uninteresting tarmac.

Towards evening I reached Venado Tuerto, a very typical town of the campo (country) in the vast farming expanses of Argentina, whose name in English means the boss-eyed stag. I stopped at a garage beside which a new motel had been almost completed. I showed my letter of introduction at the garage and was sent round to the motel which was under the same management. It looks like a night of luxury and expense, I thought to myself, as I began struggling to explain to the girl at the reception desk, the paramount importance of the safety of my little car that had to take me up to New York. Suddenly an English voice interrupted and a man introduced himself as Ken Shaw. Ken was a vet and travelled round the vast estancias testing the cattle and giving his advice. He had been born and brought up in Argentina. The new motel was soon forgotten as Ken insisted that I should come and stay with him. First, however, we had to go on a shopping expedition and then find somewhere to garage the car safely. There was no point in driving it through twenty miles of mud, and Ken had a four-wheel-drive vehicle and had just come past many stranded trucks and cars.

Loudspeakers mounted on old-fashioned cars were making a hideous row advertising various goods as we passed along one side of the central plaza of Venado Tuerto and made our way to the first shop, a well-stocked chemist's of slightly old-fashioned aspect, where we were served by one of those beautiful Argentine girls, who would have been a film star anywhere else in the world. Then we went to a large multiple store which sold nearly everything, including quantities of the plastic goods that Argentina's new industries are turning out. Ken remarked, as many Argentines also are prone to remark, that the goods are not of the same quality as those they used to import from England. Nevertheless in spite of rather poor appearances I found all the things I bought in Argentina extremely durable. Lastly we went to a wonderful old-fashioned ironmonger's. Horse brasses, fine hinges for gates wrought by real blacksmiths, and a great variety of sturdy goods made it a peculiar pleasure for a vintage car enthusiast to be in that shop. My Chummy must have remembered shops like that in its young days. Ken was a great admirer of Fangio, so he told me, as he set the nose of his vehicle towards the swimming mud track off the main road and we hurtled along it skidding from side to side. It was not long before we saw a little cluster of trees illuminated by the light coming from the window of his bunga-low. After a fine supper Ken poured out a glass of whisky for me as I relaxed in a big soft armchair. 'That', he said, as I started to sip it, 'is what we call "roughing it in Argentina" '; and on the following morning I was woken by Ken's wife bringing in a tray on which was laid out a traditional English breakfast with one or two Argentine delicacies thrown in for good measure.

After breakfast the sun came out and Ken suggested that I should accompany him to one of the big estancias, and if I didn't mind waiting while he inspected some cattle, he'd show me round. I gladly agreed. I had feared that the rain might cut me off from this opportunity before I reached the end of the pampas. The estancias or farms are simply enormous, miles and miles of flat grassland without a tree or a house. Wire fences divide off the fields and between them run earth or grass lanes. After driving along such lanes for some distance, we cut diagonally across a couple of fields where armadillos the size of rabbits scuttled about fearlessly, and finally reached the corral where the gauchos had the cattle ready for Ken. I had been curious to know why the armadillos were so bold when men were around. Ken explained their value in ridding the land of insect pests, for which reason the estancieros enforce strong rules for their protection. The gauchos raced around among the cattle dressed in their soft felt hats, wide baggy trousers, their ponchos slung over their shoul-ders and their bright-coloured scarves which, in dry weather, they would pull up over their mouths when galloping along the long dusty tracks between the fields. Their faces showed the mixture of Spanish and Indian in their blood, and the strange yells they let out are handed down directly from their ancestors before the Spanish invasion. These uncanny noises seem to be filled with primitive meaning which the cattle understand at once.

The estancia house itself is usually a large and luxuriously appointed structure without much of special interest to the visitor. The owners, who were in this case on holiday, had their own airstrip and a magnificent workshop, managed by a German en-gineer, which caught my fancy. Without the Austin I felt rather like a fish out of water. Talk was almost impossible for I knew no German and the little car was needed to inspire conversation in

Spanish. Later the gauchos and peones (poorer farm workers) tramped in from the fields to brew their maté. About a cupful of water is poured on to some herbs in a small container. The brew is then sucked up through a tube called a bombilla. The host usually takes the first brew which is supposed to be inferior and is sometimes spat out. Then each guest in turn sucks his brew through the same bombilla. Unfortunately it is regarded as particularly impolite to refuse a maté, but I had been advised that the one acceptable excuse is stomach trouble, to which I resorted in this instance as the bombilla looked particularly filthy.

Very early on the following morning Ken drove me back into Venado Tuerto to collect the Austin. After a little trouble starting, a strange whirring noise emerged from the vicinity of the engine. I diagnosed it as the starter motor fouling slightly the flywheel, a trivial fault that I had met on many an old Austin Seven. As the noise merely died out I dismissed it quickly from my mind. Little did I realize then that fearful things were happening inside the magneto, and it was not until many weeks later, in the middle of the Atacama Desert, that the real cause became apparent and almost proved fatal to my journey. The sun shone at first that morning but soon the great black clouds appeared again and even heavier storms than on the previous days began to descend from the skies. I simply drove on through the rain past the towns of Rio Cuarto and Villa Mercedes, and finally that evening, after travelling over three hundred miles, reached the border of the province of San Luis, where the grass plains of Argentina fade out and arid semi-desert country begins. At last the rain had stopped. The road began to undulate and the whole shape of the landscape began to change. Something seems to tell you that you are drawing closer to the mighty Andes, and when I saw a gaucho racing across one of the dusty fields, I got a sudden and impelling sense that I was really in the South America of my imagination. By the roadside one can frequently see huge spiders whose bodies are the size of a penny and which will raise up their front tentacles like a boxer as you approach them, but in this part of Argentina most of them are not poisonous and not very dangerous. As far as poisonous snakes and spiders were concerned, I had little to worry about until I reached Peru.

San Luis, the capital of the province, is an old-fashioned Spanish colonial-style town. As I wandered round it in the evening, its central plaza was lit by highly ornate antique street lamps, and rows of horse-drawn cabs with tough and equally ancient leather hoods lined one side of the square. Even the little Austin seemed far too modern for the atmosphere of this almost Dickensian town and I wondered if I was living in a story-book or was really on my strange trek up to New York. But of course appearances are deceptive and in this case they are retained to attract tourists from Buenos Aires. Really things were quite up to date: I stayed in a pleasant hotel with a private bathroom. I decided not to waste money on supper since Mrs. Shaw had prepared a little hamper of delicious foods for me, but in the morning a continental type breakfast was brought up to my room at six o'clock on the dot, as I'd requested. My bill for the lot was 90 pesos, roughly 7s. 6d. Small boys came to help me out with my baggage, hoping for a penny or twopence tip, but when they saw the car forgot all about it, and unintentionally in the commotion I did also. Soon quite a crowd of people on their way to work had gathered around and began asking questions. 'De donde viene, Señor, y donde va?' 'Where have you come from and where are you going, Señor?' They seemed amazed to hear that I had come from Buenos Aires and I felt afraid to say I was going to New York, and only dared say Chile. 'But, Señor, you have to go over the Cordillera to Chile and the Andes are very high mountains. You will never do it in that little car.' 'How many cylinders has it?' 'How many forward gears?' 'What horsepower is it?' I was beginning to understand questions like these now and I knew how to answer them in Spanish. But to myself I thought as I left them, 'You may know the Andes but you don't know my little Austin Seven. If it is properly treated it can do anything or almost anything. You will have a big surprise when you learn that I am on the other side of the Andes.' And so I drove on through the rest of the arid sun-baked province of San Luis towards Mendoza. In the province of Mendoza vast irrigation schemes have been constructed to utilize the great quantities of water tumbling down from the Andes, and this has had the unfortunate subsidiary effect of draining the water of the San Luis province also. A few years ago the farmers got on satisfactorily by digging wells when the water was short, but now the wells are empty and a new desert is appearing. Dry scrub, hungry cattle and ramshackle houses, many built of adobe bricks with sun-baked tiles on the roofs, made up the scene along my route. The rain and storms of yesterday seemed as if they had been part of a dream.

A great archway covered with orange-tinted plaster stands at the entrance to the province of Mendoza, and over it is written: 'Mendoza, Land of the Sun and of Good Wine'. Police officials checked my documents, but were courteous and most interested in my journey. Many miles before reaching the capital of the province, I found myself passing through the long strings of suburbs leading into the city and I felt that the first little lap of my journey was almost successfully completed. It was about half past one and along the verges of the road children in sparkling white overalls, that would have done credit to any washing-powder, wended their way to school. Only half a day's attendance is compulsory, for the Argentines have a shortage of teachers and prefer, wisely I think, fewer lessons to overcrowding. Farther along I had to find my way to Eduardo Herrera whom I had met on the boat, and who had won a British Council scholarship to travel through Europe, a distinction awarded to only two or three of the most outstanding students in Argentine universities each year. It was when I stopped to ask a group of workmen taking their siesta by the roadside the way to Eduardo's house, that I first learnt that the Austin didn't like South American sunshine. The engine petered out and refused to start again and reluctantly I was forced to try and entice the workmen from their siesta to give me a push.

After passing through all manner of streets and bumpy unmade lanes, I eventually found myself on a piece of motorway by-passing the city. I had approached it from a dusty lane and soon realized that I was travelling on the wrong side when I nearly ran into a motor-cyclist. By an extraordinary coincidence he turned out to be a friend of Eduardo's sister and immediately volunteered to lead me to the house. We went through a veritable maze of little streets, some paved and some exceedingly rough and bumpy, before eventually arriving at the little bungalow where Eduardo and his family lived. Most of the way had been through new housing estates with rows of flat-roofed, dull red-brick bungalows pleasantly concealed behind small trees growing at the edges of the irrigation ditches that run along both sides of all the streets in Mendoza.

I soon reaped the benefit of the hospitality that English people had shown Eduardo. I was at once asked to stay at his family's house while I was in Mendoza. I really welcomed this offer because I believe that there is no better way of getting to know a country than living with its people. I was given a little bedroom facing the Andes and every morning when I woke up I could see them through my window. My irrepressible optimism had led me to suppose that the snow would soon be cleared and that I should only have to delay for a few days. In fact I had to wait three weeks, but three weeks that I shall never forget for the rest of my life.

That evening Eduardo and I went in to see Señor Alvarez Alonso, the manager of the oil company which was assisting me. He received me with immense enthusiasm, but expressed very grave doubts about my chances of making it over the Andes in the Austin Seven. 'For the time being,' he said, 'let us put that thought out of our heads and enjoy Mendoza.' He drove us both round the city and took us out to dinner. The centre with its excellent wide streets, its many trees, its first-class shops and its gay sidewalk cafés where music and dancing go on far into the night, had all the atmosphere of a gay continental town. The city is noted for its beautiful girls who, unlike girls in most cities today, are conspicuous for their rejection of cosmetics. 'Nowhere in the world', said the widely travelled Sub-Manager of the Western Telegraph Company, 'will you see such an amazing number of naturally beautiful women.' Perhaps the reason for this lies in Mendoza's history. It was there that the great national hero of Argentina lived, San Martin, the chief architect of independence of the southern republics of South America; and the 'Mujeres de Mendoza', the women of Mendoza, gave up all their rich jewellery to help finance the Wars of Independence. Perhaps that began the tradition. Nobody seemed to know for certain.

After driving through the city we went to the Cerro de la Gloria, a hill on which a mounted statue of San Martin pointing towards the Andes commemorates his great victories and marks the spot from which his army set out on foot to cross the Cordillera by almost the same route that I was about to follow. Later, when I was visiting the San Martin Museum with Eduardo, I learnt something about the great general that I thought even more impressive. The other great liberator of the northern part of South America was Simon Bolívar. When the liberation was completed the two generals held a private meeting in Guayaquil that lasted for four hours. What they discussed was never disclosed, but San Martin expressed his opinion that there wasn't room for two liberators in South America and left for France where among other things he studied Philosophy!

Owing to a visit of Sir John Ward, the British Ambassador, who was returning from leave via Chile, the social activities of the British community in Mendoza reached their peak. I was invited to dinners and receptions and two very useful practical things emerged from them. First Lady Ward gave me one of the most valuable introductions of the journey, to a Michael Westcott in Santiago who had driven down in a Land Rover from Washington. Secondly I was introduced to a charming and very brilliant Spanish teacher whose excellent tuition for the short time I was in Mendoza had an important bearing on the whole of the rest of my journey. I trundled in daily by the little colectivo to my lesson and from there went round to the garage of the British Vice-Consul, where experts on mountain driving were able to advise me on carburettor settings and other such matters, and where I supervised a further complete check of the car. Life was beginning to take on an almost homely routine, especially in the evenings in Eduardo's house, when after a fine dinner while cheeses and grapes and empty wine-glasses were still strewn over the table, we would begin with all the family assembled to read the verses of José Fernandez, the most famous of Argentine poets, which tell of the life and oppression of the gauchos and of the fight he supported to obtain a better life for such noble members of society. For they are to Argentina as the yeomen once were to England. The old trick of the estanciero had been to sell them the necessities of life at such prices as kept them permanently in his debt and virtually his slaves.

On one of those evenings Eduardo's youngest sister, who was still at school and was also a rock and roll fan, inquired if I was married and Eduardo interpreted his father's rapid reply as 'Good Lord, no! No English wife would let him wander off on a trip like this.' He knew something about the subject as he had worked for many years with the British railway company in Argentina.

One morning just before lunchtime I was leaving Alvarez Alonso's office, when an unholy row started up in the main street. People shouting and sounds like machine-gun fire made me think that a revolution had begun. Everything seemed to be thrown into complete chaos. I went back to Alvarez. 'I say,' I said, 'I think they're starting up a revolution outside.' He seemed quite unperturbed and began to explain that it was the end of the school term and that the boys made the noises I heard with wooden rattles and fireworks and marched through the streets thoroughly dislocating the life of the city. Everybody enjoyed it and there was absolutely nothing to worry about. It was strange to see this from boys who had previously seemed so calm in their trim white overalls. To add to the impression, one of the circus people had come out to drive through the streets with a puma lying across the bonnet of his car.

That same night I happened to go for a walk through the city with Eduardo, principally to see the results of the road race across Argentina at the newspaper office. We happened to notice an occasional pair of policemen patrolling the streets, otherwise everything was perfectly quiet and normal except for a little excitement over the racing results. Next morning I struggled away as usual to try to read the newspaper. 'What's this about a revolution in Mendoza?' I said, and Eduardo remarked, 'It probably refers to those extra policemen we saw out last night. There was some voting going on in parts of the province yesterday. Anyway, we usually learn about our revolutions from the newspapers; our papers get their reports from the international news agencies!' This started a discussion on newspapers and scandal. I had noticed that there was very little scandal in Argentine papers and I had heard that one or two attempts to interest the Argentine public in it had proved miserable financial failures. 'Still,' I remarked, 'some pretty sad things get into your newspapers. Look at this case of the little boy who shot himself accidentally with his father's gun. It does happen in England, but this general habit of having guns around seems a little odd to us.' 'The law is much more in the hands of the individual here,' Eduardo replied. 'In the vast open spaces it has to be, and yet, you know, although the penalty for murder is only a few years in prison, we have quite low crime figures. In fact Argentine people are sometimes horrified by murders they hear have been committed in England. I have only heard of one really horrible murder in Argentina and that was up in the hot northern part of the province. A young man living out on a farm with his mother came down to Mendoza and found himself a beautiful wife and brought her home. The mother became furiously jealous and made the girl's life hell in every possible way. But even that did not content her and she finally persuaded her son to consent to murder the girl. One day the mother and son took her out for a ride in the farm cart, carrying with them a box of venomous snakes. When they were far out in the country they lifted a cover off a small opening in the box and forced the girl to thrust her hand in. Nothing would ever have been heard of that murder if the young man had not been filled with bitter remorse and admitted the whole affair to the police.'

The chapter on Mendoza would not be complete without mention of one of the most notable personalities of the district in which Eduardo lived. A small boy of two and a half named Germán (pronounced Chermán) lived almost opposite; and distinguished himself by giving hilarious amusement to all adults with whom he came in contact. He had three principal lines of attack. First was a remarkable imitation of Peron delivering one of his harangues to the people. Secondly he had a deep understanding of how to shock adults and had learnt many obscenities in Spanish which he could use in such a disarming manner that everybody was forced to burst out laughing instead of attempting to restrain him, and thirdly he distinguished himself by being able to count up to ten in English, a performance he was often asked to put on specially for my benefit. Stories were filtering in every day of how Germán had visited some household or other and said or done something shocking. I had to be very careful of the Austin of which he was very fond, and it was not until he fully realized that it would involve parting from his mother that he decided not to join me for the rest of the trip.

One way and another the days and the weeks went by, and one morning there was news that some taxis had made their way over from Chile and that the route was open at last. I bought a big Christmas hamper for the Herreras to celebrate my crossing into Chile and as a small sign of appreciation. I then drove round for a greasing and a fill-up of petrol at Alvarez Alnoso's service station, where we discovered certain problems that were to recur all through the journey. The tiny vehicle was too narrow to fit on to the two platforms of the ramp and just a little bit too wide for one! Moreover, the greasing-points were of a kind that had never been encountered before in that part of the world. The result was that we were all down on our hands and knees, crawling under the car, with the little antique grease-gun I had brought with me. Spectators came in from the street and laughed at the idea of such a car attempting the Andes; Alvarez had tried in vain to persuade me to undertake trial runs, but I saw no point in straining the car to any degree whatsoever if it was not helping me to get nearer to my final goal. He insisted on the best grade petrol but I knew that he didn't share my confidence in the little car's climbing abilities. I returned later for dinner and found that a little farewell celebration had been prepared for me. Germán was there, and Saurez Marsal, an Argentine painter famed for his pictures of the Andes, but as the champagne corks popped, I thought only of the packing I still had to do.

III

The First Baby Austin on Top of the Andes

After only a couple of hours of anxious sleep, I rose at four-thirty to begin one of the most exciting but most frightening days of my life. My feelings made me think of accounts I had read of early mornings before great battles during the war. Everything possible had been organized down to the last detail and the onslaught on the Andes was about to begin. Thus after a hurried bite of breakfast, I loaded the car with Eduardo's help, waved good-bye and began to trundle in darkness over the rough bumpy lanes leading towards the centre of Mendoza. The city was still asleep and dimly lit as I passed through it and out on to the road towards the Andes. The shadowy scene seemed to be a reflection of the strange feelings of apprehension I felt within. There was about two hours' drive over a good concrete road before the actual climb began. The car seemed to be on top of its form and ready for the challenge that was just in front of it.

Daylight had begun to break and the first rays of the early morning sunshine were beginning to spread across the foothills ahead. The landscape was barren and stony but still fairly level with the exception of a few hills of bare rock across the plains to the right. They looked as if they had been thrown there by some powerful giant as a warning of what lay ahead. The deep red rays of the rising sun made them look even more terrible. I seemed to be able to hear two conflicting voices within. One seemed to tell me that my attempt was madness and to turn back before it was too late, and the other just said, 'You cannot, you cannot.' As these doubts and fears were passing through my mind and I was wondering exactly what I'd let myself in for, I saw a little hut by the roadside and a notice ordering drivers to stop to have their documents checked before proceeding up into the Andes. The guards couldn't believe their eyes, but were helpful and told me I was very brave. Was it, I wondered, just the polite South American way of telling me that I was attempting the impossible? For a few moments as I continued on, sad reflections at the thought of leaving Argentina where I had had such a pleasant time passed through my head. I was jerked suddenly out of these thoughts by the realization that the engine seemed to be rapidly losing power although it appeared that the road was still almost level. I was forced to change into second gear in which I continued for some way, following the road round as it veered towards the little village of Villavicencio, situated at the very foot of the main climb into the first range of the Andes. Gradually the whole panoramic view of the mountains ahead came into sight. I stopped and took out the big and very powerful ex-naval binoculars I was carrying with me. My heart sank at the sight I saw through them. Winding up in a tremendous zigzag, through countless hairpin bends, ran the track, and along precarious ledges of mountains, to a position in the sky where one would only expect to see aeroplanes. I'd seen plenty of mountains before but I'd never seen anything like that. In a flash I realized the meaning of what the geographers and the members of the vintage car club had told me, and I started talking to myself about it. 'I've already had to change down into second gear and the road still seems to be flat!' I said to myself. 'I don't stand a hope in hell of getting up there.' It was in that depressed mood that I moved on to Villavicencio. 'Well,' I thought, 'I'm here, I've come six thousand miles by sea and crossed Argentina to get here, so I may as well have a try.' The idea of going back and admitting failure without even an attempt was out of the question.

In order to reduce weight for the climb I had decided not to carry extra petrol, but instead to fill up at the single antiquated pump that I was assured existed in the village of Villavicencio. I could find no sign of people about anywhere and was forced to go on, knowing that even the little Austin Seven on such severe climbs could soon gobble up the meagre four and a half gallons that had been put into the tank on the previous afternoon. By now the paved road had long ceased and I was travelling over what are known as 'improved earth roads'. Shortly after leaving Villavicencio the track split in two, and a sign which read 'Contra Mano', meaning one-way, indicated that one track is for going up and the other for coming down. Eduardo had warned me to be careful at this point as the penalty for Argentine drivers taking the wrong lane is about £100 fine and three years' loss of driving-licence!

The zigzag and the hairpin-bends were just beginning and I was now travelling in bottom gear. The car was certainly climbing much better than I had expected. At the bends the engine laboured and throbbed like a man about to die of heart failure, but time after time it managed to get round, and although I shuddered to think what the strain might be doing to the big ends and crankshaft and connecting rods as well as the poor little pistons, I was beginning to build up confidence again. At the same time a lurking suspicion that things might not go so well in the rarefied air farther up did not disappear. Hour after hour went by, and up and up I went at very little more than walking pace. The road was dusty and bumpy but at that speed it didn't matter, and occasionally cracked edges where landslides had occurred enabled me to peep out of the side of the car straight into emptiness stretching thousands of feet below. The slightest slip might have been fatal and, had I stalled on one of the hairpin bends, the brakes would almost certainly have been insufficient to hold the car back from slipping over the edge. The braking surface of the Austin Seven was nearly doubled in 1926, which means that the brakes from that date onwards were nearly twice as good as mine, but even with the improvement the brakes were the one weak point in those early Austin Sevens. In spite of all my worries my confidence was steadily mounting with each new bend. I marvelled at the power of the little car and began to imagine myself back in England explaining to the critics just how I did it. At that moment there was a sudden who-o-sh. The bakelite top of the radiator cap blew off and went hurtling down the side of the Andes, and a considerable volume of steam shot up in front of the windscreen. The engine faltered and petered out. I was on one of the hairpin bends and it was indeed a moment for quick action. I put my foot down hard on the inadequate foot-brake pedal and at the same time pushed open the door, which I kept always unlatched in case I had to jump out quickly, grabbed one of the empty petrol-cans on the floor beside me and shoved it under the front wheel, while at the same time keeping a firm grasp on the steering-wheel, without releasing any of the pressure of my foot on the brake. Having halted the car in this way I decided I would have somehow or other to manœuvre it back off the bend to a safer position. I removed the can and reversed the car slowly downwards for ten or fifteen yards along the edge of the precipice until I had it safely against the rocky side of the track. I then let the engine cool off for a few minutes before topping up the radiator and starting up once more. Again I found I was able to continue, but only for a few hundred yards. Once more the engine petered out but this time in a safer position. When it stalled the third time I decided that a deeper investigation was necessary. Fortunately it didn't have to be very deep, for as soon as I lifted the bonnet up I noticed that the fan-belt had slipped off; and after replacing it and carrying out a slight readjustment of the tension, I was able to start off again.

The engine was back on form once more although it was necessary to add a little water to the radiator every quarter of an hour or so, and I was becoming increasingly anxious about my petrol and water supplies with every minute that passed. Furthermore mountain winds were beginning to blow up. I had been warned about them and advised to travel with the hood down, as they could easily blow a light car right off the edge at the bends. They were not, however, I felt at this stage of sufficient force to justify that, and I wanted to keep the hood up for as long as possible to shield my eyes from the glare of the intense sunshine. Just to remind you of the risks you are running in this mountain country, you will see every here and there a rough wooden cross indicating where cars have gone over the edge. These crosses are usually put up by friends or relatives to commemorate the dead but they also serve as healthy reminders to the living who happen to be passing that way.

It was at about twelve o'clock that I breasted the last sharp rise of the first range, passed between two dark mounds on either side of the track and turned on to a small patch of level land. On the far side was a notice which read 'Cruce de Paramilla' and indicated that it was exactly three thousand metres above sea level, which is almost 10,000 feet. The worst had been accomplished, but what lay in front looked terrible and breathtaking. It is beyond the power of words to describe fully what I saw in that moment. It was truly the sort of view that one might expect to see on some mysterious new planet where men have never been: an endless succession of dirt-grey peaks with glistening fingers of sparkling white snow cast on top of them, and beside them sinister streaks of blood-red earth, where the vast copper deposits of the Andes push their way up to the surface. A faint blue haze topped the amazing scene and produced a mysterious sense of stretching on into infinity, and above that a cloudless blue sky stood still and intense. In another respect also it resembled a different world: the rarity of the atmosphere, about the effects of which on both the car and myself I had heard so much beforehand. Perhaps my lungs had been strengthened by fast breathing at precarious points on the way up for I merely gasped a little and felt slightly sick as I nibbled at various packages of food that Eduardo's family had prepared for me. In spite of all that lay in front, I was happy. I was now literally on top of the world, and my Austin was certainly the first Baby Austin to stand on top of the Andes, perhaps the only Austin Seven that will ever do so in all history.

For the next twenty miles the road runs downhill to a place called Uspallata, and there I knew I would be able to replenish my supplies. I trundled along over gravel and stone and rock, turning the engine off wherever possible and keeping my fingers crossed that my petrol supply should last out. All was going well and after a short while a little green valley appeared in front. A few Indians were out working on the road and others could be seen in the fields. They had nothing of the colourful aspect of those that I was later to see in Peru and Ecuador, but were merely dressed in shabby European clothes. Only in the shortness of their stature and the Mongol appearance of their brownish faces did they resemble their northern relations. They were certainly interested and waved in a most friendly manner. Their lonely life apparently makes them anxious to welcome the infrequent passing vehicle. In the village I found a couple of petrol pumps and when I stopped I was quickly surrounded by a crowd of curious men and children. I liked meeting them, but they made it pretty difficult for me to carry out the careful systematic check of oil, water, air and so forth, that I had planned to make at every point where any supplies or assistance were available.

I was now all set for the next stage of the journey through the

48

fabulous Andean scenery to Puenta del Inca and the little Western Telegraph outpost where I was planning to spend the night. It was an up and down journey always at pretty severe heights. The water in the radiator was boiling away merrily and I was constantly adding more, so that once again the problem of water began to loom large in my mind. The annoying thing was that it was really a case of water, water everywhere and not a drop—for the car! To the right of the track there was snow on top of the rocks, but climbing up to get it was out of the question, for, although fortunately I was still suffering no serious ill effects from the height, I had certainly lost more than 30 or 40 per cent of my own horsepower. I was quite puffed out after walking only a few paces round the car. Far down on my left in a deep valley torrents of melted snow cascaded down to form the Rio Mendoza and to water the dry land I had left early that morning. How far away it seemed. A day no longer seemed to be a day but a lifetime of unforgettable experience. A little farther along there appeared the famous Cathedral of the Andes, which is a natural formation of rock and from a distance had the appearance of a cathedral with cloisters and rows of pillars.

Still farther along the road joins the railway line that crosses the Andes—and what remarkable railways they are up there, among the most fascinating ever built, especially in view of the fact that most of them were constructed by English companies many years ago, under unbelievably difficult conditions. The highest railway in the world is in the Andes in Central Peru. The builder was a man named Henry Meiggs, nicknamed Honest Henry, who was determined to build a railway to carry the vast quantities of silver that could be mined in that high part of the Andes. The engineers unanimously declared that his plans were completely impossible, but he told them he was going to build his railway even if he had to hang the lines from balloons in the sky, and he made his workmen work from baskets precariously suspended from ledges of rock, to hack out tracks in the cliff face wide enough to set rails on. It is estimated that at least ten thousand of his labourers died accomplishing the task! It was not quite so difficult to make railways in the parts of Argentina and Chile that I was then passing through, but even there many miles of tunnel had to be bored through the mountains, a central rail with cogs had to be built to engage with the engine and countless

D

miles of shed had to be constructed to keep the line free from snow during the winter and to protect it from snow-drifts.

The railway was a particular boon to me since beside it I noticed a hut where some of the Indians who maintain the line live. Like all those who inhabit the higher regions they have developed very strong lungs to withstand the heights, but I was puffed out after I had scrambled over a small pile of sleepers to get the water I needed. Then, not more than a mile farther on, I came to a small stream that ran right across the road, and had to drive through it! From there I climbed up again and continued along the track which passed across a vast level plateau, over which were scattered enormous boulders, often several times as high as a man and looking as though they had just rained in from outer space. The afternoon's climb was really going very well: some of the ascents were slow but I was building up tremendous confidence because it seemed that the worst of the dangers were over. But on a journey like mine it is always when you are least expecting it that sudden danger can spring upon you. I was just leaving the field of boulders and climbing up a little rocky pathway leading to the entrance of a small roughly blasted tunnel. I was travelling no faster than a person walking when not more than ten yards in front of me a dark animal emerged from the tunnel. I knew at once it was a puma, the mountain lion of South America. The side of the car was wide open and there was no chance of turning round without falling off the edge of a precipice. I gulped and put my foot instantly down on the accelerator, but the engine could carry me no faster. The puma walked slowly past the side of the car, peered in and moved slowly onwards. The danger passed away just as suddenly as it had come, but after that experience I felt very differently about getting out of the car to add water to the radiator or to stretch my legs, and I waited to find wide open spaces where I could view the landscape for some distance around.

From there on I passed through a series of great valleys. The sheer size of the mountain ranges at each side of me made me realize the massive scale of the Andes. I had often stood and looked at the massiveness of great hills, but here was something outside all proportions I had previously known or conceived of, bare and solitary and with nothing of beauty to interrupt the giddy impressions of size. I was now drawing close to Puenta del

The First Baby Austin on Top of the Andes

Inca, The Bridge of the Inca, for the great Empire of the Four Directions, as the Inca kingdom was called, stretched down as far as what is now Argentina. The natural rock formation which spans the river is classified as one of the seven natural wonders of the world. From the presence of this bridge I knew that it was along this very same route that General San Martin and his army had approached Chile a hundred and forty-three years earlier. After considerable searching I eventually found the little house which is the Western Telegraph outpost. I had a cold shower to wash the dust off, answered a telephone call from Mr. Drayton, the manager of the Western Telegraph in Mendoza, who promised to spread the good news of my successful climb to all my friends in the city, struggled to speak Spanish to the man and his wife who ran the station; but feeling too tired to have much success, I retired early to bed. Although absolutely dead beat I was quite unable to sleep owing to the effect of the height, which caused a dizzy, sleepless hum to continue in my head all night long.

I simply tried to relax as much as possible and get the maximum amount of rest out of merely lying down.

I got up rather late the following morning and drove on over severe and rocky roads for a further twenty miles, where the arrangement of the peaks played the most drastic optical tricks: the severest ascents when the poor car was labouring violently often looked to my eyes to be actually running downhill. At the end of that twenty miles I was at Las Cuevas where the Argentine customs are situated, and passed through them without any difficulties. Mr. Drayton had telephoned them and they remembered his occasional visits by the bottles of good Mendoza wine he always opened up on his way through. There, also, are the barracks of the frontier guards, a railway station and a large modern archway, built when Peron was dictator of Argentina. When I passed through it I felt I was truly saying good-bye to that country, although it is not the official border. From there the road sweeps round through a valley of grey gravel and stones. After a mile or so one track turns off to the left and leads up to the Uspallata Pass, while the other leads straight on to the International Tunnel. I was hoping to go over the top, but the road was blocked by a line of boulders indicating that the route was still snowbound and impassable. So I continued till I came to the

The First Baby Austin on Top of the Andes

International Tunnel. In spite of its fine-sounding name, it is a very rough tunnel crudely blasted for a couple of miles through the mountain, and containing the single line of a very narrow gauge railway. In a little hut at each end sits a man who is in communication with his opposite number by means of an extremely antiquated-looking telephone. When the first man has made sure that there is no train or car coming the other way, he opens a little gate and helps you get two wheels between the lines and in that way, jerking slowly over the sleepers, you drive through the tunnel which is in fact more like a dark, dripping cave. In the very middle, where you would expect to see stalagmites and stalactites, is the exact boundary between Argentina and Chile and so when you emerge at the other end you are really looking at Chile. Chile had always seemed a strange and distant country to me and I felt a tremendous thrill as I emerged and missed the way off the track, so that the Chilean railway official had to come running after me. 'Señor, Señor,' he called in an accent that was new to me, and he indicated that I was to start reversing back to his hut.

I had heard many stories of the bad road on the Chilean side, which is even worse than on the Argentine. The track was often covered by boulders brought down by the winter's snow. The descent, as I passed down 'Las Noventas Curvas', the famous ninety hairpin bends, was very treacherous indeed. It was all I could do to prevent the car from slithering over the edges, and I kept the door constantly open and was ready to jump out. The only good thing about it was that I had no doubt that I would reach the bottom in one way or another.

The main descent was quickly and successfully accomplished without any special problems. It had been nerve-racking but the car had remained always just under control in spite of numerous small skids at every bend, and the dangerous camber of the track, which almost tipped it over. On the straighter stretches I tried once or twice to bring the car to a halt but found it completely impossible. Thus I travelled for several miles relying entirely on the gears for control and not daring to let my eyes stray over the edges. I wasn't at all sorry when the road began to level out and I passed over a stream by means of a bridge that consisted of only a very few old planks. For once I felt sure that the lightweight Austin was the best possible vehicle to be in. The descent was now very much more gradual and wound down through a beautiful green valley filled with wild mountain flowers. After what I'd been through it seemed like fairyland. Soon little villages began to appear. The houses were rather like log cabins and very primitive, and around them strayed chickens and goats. The peasants looked out for a moment to see what strange contrivance was rattling past, and then at one point a man stepped out into the road and stopped me. 'Señor,' he said, 'you will need to know that the time is one hour different in Chile.'

Los Andes is the first proper town to be reached in Chile after crossing the Cordillera. At the outskirts of the town concrete paving appeared and it was like a good dream to drive over. A couple of long modern coaches lined up outside a large garage conveyed a strange sense of return to the so-called civilized modern world. A van was parked by the roadside and as I approached it a man stepped out and hailed me. 'I am the manager of the West Coast Cable (Western Telegraph),' he explained to me in Spanish. 'I have been waiting for many hours to meet you, now you must come with me to eat and drink.' And together we went to a pleasant restaurant in the town.

The first of the great obstacles in my journey had been conquered. That afternoon I drove across Central Chile to the port of Valparaiso, a name which means the Vale of Paradise, and was given to it by the weary Spaniards who had come with Pizarro in the sixteenth century. After crossing the Andes, the deserts in Peru and the terrible Atacama Desert, a journey of over two thousand miles during which many of them died of hunger and thirst, they at last reached the beautiful fertile valleys of central Chile. Although there are still many arid semi-desert parts even there, they immediately named it Paradise, for to sun-baked men dying of thirst its waters and sweet fruits were the water and food of heaven. There were animals here too, unlike the Atacama Desert, where for hundreds of miles nothing, absolutely nothing, not even cacti live. What a wonderful land it must have been to those wild starving adventurers!

Although I was feeling quite gratified at what I had just accomplished, the afternoon was far from heavenly. I made my first acquaintance with the regularly corrugated roads I was to see so much of later on. They were also desperately dusty, and the billowing clouds of fine powder thrown up by every passing vehicle had to be experienced to be believed. It choked my lungs and blocked my nose, and even my clothes which were wrapped up in plastic bags inside a suitcase became covered with it and had to be thoroughly shaken on the following day. Chile is a much poorer country than Argentina and during the afternoon I could see the peasants working in the fields. Towards evening they began to wend their way in little groups along the verges of the road to the hovels which were their homes. A few were riding on donkeys and every now and again a Huaso appeared on horseback. They are the cowboys of Chile and they wear the wide-brimmed flat-topped sombreros of Chile. Most people in England associate the word 'sombrero' with the famous Mexican hats, but that is really a great mistake because each Latin American country has its own traditional type of sombrero which tells a great deal about the people that wears it. The Chileans have lived in a poor infertile country, where existence on the whole has been hard, and there is a fierce warlike streak in them, in spite of their famed hospitality to visitors from other countries. I believe that all that is somehow symbolized in their stern flat sombreros.

The sun was descending steadily as I reached the hills that surround Valparaiso and the beautiful seaside resort of Viña del Mar (Wine of the Sea). I stopped once or twice to look at the engine which was firing a little unevenly. Paved road began, but occasional potholes of remarkable magnitude, which appeared every now and again, demanded a state of constant alertness if I was to avoid breaking the car in two. At last I reached the brow of the hills and suddenly in front of me I beheld a vast expanse of blue. For the first time in my life I was looking at the Pacific Ocean. I felt a wild thrill as if I were really one of the Spanish explorers of old looking at the unknown ocean for the first time. I started up again and sped along the coast road towards Valparaiso, and the sight of it was surely paradise to me after what I had been through, but a couple of minor troubles still lay ahead before I could rest. At one point I took a wrong turning which led up a very steep hill. It was even worse than the Andes and the Austin was quite unable to cope with it. I learnt later that there were iron railings at the top and that no traffic could climb it. It was only for pedestrians and actually part of a cliff! Once in Valparaiso, I found it pretty difficult to find my way through the maze of rather haphazardly arranged streets. I was looking for the house of the second good South American friend I had made during the crossing, Yolanda Pizarro, a descendant of the first Spaniard in South America, the brutal but enigmatic Francisco Pizarro whose preserved body still lies on view in the cathedral in Lima. I was faced with a new problem now. Chileans speak with a very different accent from the Argentines and the little bit of Spanish I'd managed to learn wasn't much help. Furthermore trying to telephone in a strange country in a language one hardly knows is almost as frightening as crossing the Andes. I just managed to understand that Yolanda was out but would be back in half an hour. 'Come to the house,' said her mother. But that was exactly why I was phoning—because I couldn't find the house. It was just too difficult to explain so I continued on round various turnings and up and down various streets until suddenly, as I was going over a crossroads near the centre of the city, a policeman blew his whistle and stepped out in front of me.

'Your documents please, Señor,' he said as he signalled me in to the side of the road. 'Did you not see the signals over the crossroad?' In my very best Argentine Spanish I struggled to explain that I had just crossed the Andes, that it was my first time in his beautiful city, that I was very tired and having great difficulty in finding the address I was looking for. With that he was most kind and helpful and took a great deal of trouble to give me the clearest possible directions.

It was not until early morning that I finally found a hotel and was able to lie down and snatch a few hours' sleep, and even then as I was dozing off the singing and dancing were still in full swing in the restaurant below. The tangos and cha-cha-chas seem to go on for ever in South America.

IV

New Year Festivities and
a Pirates' Tea Party

In spite of my rigid time schedule, I decided to spend three complete weeks in Central Chile before setting out on the road to the north. I hadn't intended to stay so long, but I felt I needed a rest as well as time to prepare for the thousands of miles of rough waterless trails ahead. Everything depended on attending completely to the details of preparation, trying to foresee every possible kind of difficulty that might arise. One has to rouse oneself out of the normal semi-torpor of life, the slightly stupefying reliance on the amenities of civilization that in everyday life one takes for granted. The chances are, out in the desert, that one will become not wise after the event but dead! With that thought in mind I tackled the problems of water supplies, emergency rations and additional equipment for temporary repairs. I also had to obtain a suitable syringe and needles for giving myself anti-snakebite injections, for once I reached Peru this danger would become critical. I was a little nervous on this score since a rather large needle is required for intra-muscular injections and they are quite difficult to give. Most injections are into the bloodstream and are given just under the skin. Anti-snakebite injections have to be given deep into the muscles and have a momentarily paralysing effect. What with this and all the other matters I had to attend to, I was certainly experiencing all the feelings of preparing for another critical adventure. My problems were made more difficult by the fact that it was important to avoid overburdening the little car: it was due for a battering that most people thought it couldn't possibly survive and, in fact, did only survive by a peculiar stroke of good luck. In spite of all my forethought I gravely misjudged the desert. In some respects I blamed myself, but when it came to my worst catastrophe I felt I should be excused a failure in foresight. Who on earth would expect to be almost drowned in a desert?

I must admit I was glad to stay and make my preparations, for Chile was welcoming me royally. Valparaiso is a pleasant town about which more must be said later; and Mr. Elton, the owner of the Austin Agency there and a true Chilean though of English descent, was making my tasks as easy as possible. He possessed to the full the Latin American capacity for feeling and expressing enthusiasm and almost went crazy about my having crossed the Andes in a 35-year-old Austin, and what a remarkable achievement he considered it to be. As we drove round to the newspaper office on the morning after my arrival, he called out 'Stop, stop!' every few hundred yards and signalled to some friend in the street or in another car. 'This chap's just crossed the Cordillera in this little Austin car, isn't it unbelievable?' He wisely never omitted to mention that it was an Austin and quickly a group of people would gather round and again with typical Latin American enthusiasm start exclaiming '*Que fantástico! Increible!*' Nearly always in such situations, here and everywhere else, some tough old man would step forward and lift the front of the car clean off the ground to the delight of all the onlookers. This was a practice that began to cause me real concern when, later on, I saw four such strong men walking down the street with my car in their hands! The interest was great because such a car had never before been seen in Chile. On the following day a large picture of the car and me together, with an article beneath red headlines, appeared on the front pages of the Chilean newspapers.

At the newspaper office I was asked what I thought about Valparaiso, and as my Spanish was still very inadequate, Mr. Elton stepped quickly into the breach to sing its praises with great fluency. It is indeed a very attractive and modern port with a slightly Continental air. The shopping centre and the main part of the town are situated on a small piece of level land close to the harbour. There are many shops of excellent quality and a number of attractive squares, which were then brightly decorated with Christmas trees and coloured lights. The traditional English influence on the town is shown by the name of the main square, Plaza Victoria, and by the typical English names that appear over many of the shops and business houses. This central part of the town is almost completely surrounded by a small range of extremely steep hills on which are placed a great variety of residences, ranging from mansions to what up to that time struck me as the most ghastly slums imaginable. The latter are remarkable structures of corrugated iron built against the almost vertical hillside, and some three or four stories high. A quite fantastic area of these unsightly dwellings, unkempt and with rows of shabby washing hanging from balconies, assailed the eye. Despite all this, however, Valparaiso is a very attractive port. I know few that rival it in Europe. A good road and a railway run along the coast to the neighbouring seaside resort of Viña del Mar, which is Mediterranean in style and, with its famous casino, a sort of miniature Monte Carlo of South America.

I extended my visit to Valparaiso for two reasons I haven't yet mentioned. I didn't at all fancy the idea of being stranded in the middle of the desert with the knowledge that my fellow countrymen might be devouring turkey and plum pudding while I was suffering. It seemed to me at least preferable that it should happen when they would be trudging drearily off to their daily tasks through the snow and fog. And secondly I had been firmly advised by Yolanda Pizarro not on any account to miss the fabulous New Year festivities in Valparaiso. I decided in the meantime to pay a short visit to Santiago, the capital. I remember I proposed making the journey one Monday morning, but unfortunately on the previous afternoon I had arranged to give Yolanda a drive in the car, when she had promised to show me some of the beautiful Chilean countryside she had so often spoken of on the boat. Alas the real beauty of Chile lies much farther south in a region that has since been dreadfully disfigured by a series of terrible earthquakes and volcanic eruptions; and in any case very soon after we left Valparaiso volumes of steam began to emerge from the radiator. Before the engine had time to splutter to a humiliating halt, I jumped out to investigate the cause. My pride had somehow become enormously wrapped up in the little car and I imagined that every passing Chilean was saying to himself: 'That's the fellow the papers said crossed the Andes in that machine . . .?' I contrived with difficulty to struggle back to Mr. Elton's house in Valparaiso, where I was now a guest, finding it necessary to stop every few hundred yards to beg for a fresh gallon of water to compensate for the rapid leaks in the bottom of the radiator. I related my trouble to Mr. Elton. 'Tomorrow,' he said, 'I will take you to the finest radiator expert in Valparaiso.'

On the following morning, therefore, instead of setting out for Santiago, I set to work to dismantle the radiator. It had been a very good radiator but I had kept it in store for several years and although it appeared excellent on the outside unseen corrosion had been working havoc within. We put it in Mr. Elton's car and drove off. My heart sank when he drew up at a little backyard absolutely strewn with radiators in various stages of decay or repair. After picking my way carefully through the radiators, I was soon introduced to the great expert himself who was shuffling around even more radiators inside a building. When he had examined mine he exclaimed, 'This radiator is in very bad condition, Señor,—even after it has been repaired you will have to drive with much care.' At this point Mr. Elton butted in with a lengthy explanation in Spanish that included something about crossing the Atacama Desert; and after much smiling and back-slapping we departed, returning again later the same day to collect the radiator. We were assured that it had been tested under considerable pressure and next day I was able to try it out on my delayed trip to Santiago.

In the Southern Hemisphere it was then the height of summer and the scenery as I travelled towards the capital was mostly barren and parched. In certain small valleys the peasants laboured to extract the maximum from the grudging land, but I had seen nothing of real beauty in Chile since I passed through the valleys of wild flowers in the foothills of the Andes. The road was excellent from the car's point of view but, like all main highways everywhere in the world, it had begun to attract those commercial hoardings which in my opinion are the first indication of failure in the progress of civilization. In my own small way I had fought that evil resolutely by refusing to allow advertising slogans to be stuck on the Austin.

The total distance is about ninety miles and the route includes two mountain ranges that would be regarded as big almost anywhere but in South America, where one learns to refer to hills rather than mountains. Indeed, outside Lima, where the road ascends sharply to 18,000 feet, the inhabitants speak casually of it as 'going up the hill'! Through one range I found an excellent modern tunnel had been completed, the refreshing coolness of which gave the engine an unexpected extra burst of power. At the next range a second tunnel was under construction and consequently the road over the top had been left in a pretty rough state. However much South Americans may be given to understatement when describing the massive mountain routes of their continent, I had no sooner reached the top and stepped out to stretch my legs, than I found car and lorry drivers pulling up to congratulate me on the successful climb. It was some compensation for the blow my pride had suffered a couple of days earlier, to be able to mention nonchalantly that I had just recently come over from Argentina.

Descending gradually I wound down the mountainside. Suddenly Santiago came into view. The city spreads out in a great plain encircled by snow-capped peaks of the Andes. I can think of no other great city that is so spectacularly situated. Mexico is set among high mountains certainly, but they do not present the same unearthly glistening effect of the Andes where the white peaks are thrown into peculiarly brilliant relief by the grey and shadowy substance of the mountains beneath them. The spell is somewhat broken as one draws closer to the commercial outskirts of the city; the stately and spacious squares and the wide avenues in the centre are partial recompense. The majority of the older buildings are fairly low, but others, new and shining and high, seem to be symbolic of the progressive future of Santiago and of the vitality of all the great cities of Latin America. Brazilia is said by its architects to have been produced out of an intellectual revival. This I feel is true throughout Latin America, which is awakening to its enormous potentialities in the modern world. In the universities and in the business world a new sense of seriousness mingles with a sense that whatever people are undertaking is an adventure. That is the most amazing and the most important thing about Latin America today. Tschiffely, in his day, noted a tendency in the cities to ape North America and at the same time to complain about it, small-minded jealousy in fact. Today that seemed to me to be no longer the case except in the Central American Republics. In South America and Mexico the spirit has become very different. They are indeed anxious to take full advantage of all the worthwhile things of North American civilization and are respectful towards them, but they feel, too, that they have a deep and valuable culture of their own, embodying not only Spanish traditions but also many of the insights of the great Indian civilizations, which must never be drowned in inhuman progress. One of the failures of the West is to think of Latin America as an undeveloped area. It is true that there are boundless resources still to be developed and certain types of economic assistance are called for to achieve that development. But what is much more important is to realize that Latin America has so much to contribute to the world in the cause of a better understanding of what civilization really means. I returned to England in the company of the director of a theatre in New York who had recently visited Russia. Being somewhat surprised to find English and Spanish the principal languages taught in schools, he questioned some university students on the matter. 'Why Spanish?' he asked, and was met with the reply, 'English for North America and Spanish for South.'

The history of the Wars of Independence in South America is a complicated subject of which many aspects are still shrouded in mystery. I do not propose to dwell on them here, except to stress the strong European influences that lay behind them, especially English. Many mysterious characters from the British Isles were mixed up with the revolutionary plottings of San Martín and Simón Bolívar, for it was in their interests to clear the way for British trade and to assist in casting off the Spanish yoke. Chile is probably more truly international than any of the other South American countries. On the one hand, her Indian population was not exterminated but actually joined the patriots. Few families are without some strain of Indian blood in them. On the other hand, the influence of the British, Germans and Yugoslavs is also particularly pronounced. The great national hero of Chile is Bernado O'Higgins, after whom the chief avenue of Santiago is named. I was not surprised, therefore, to be told by one Chilean: 'Not until you reach Peru will you feel that you have both feet out of Europe.' I found that so true that by the time I reached Ecuador I wondered if I'd left South America!

It is not my intention to launch into a description of cities or to moralize over Latin America's part in world affairs, but rather to stick to a simple narrative of a journey in a vintage car, a subject I was rudely brought back to on my first evening in Santiago. When I was in Argentina I had heard about a group of Cambridge graduates whose homes were in South America and who had driven in a Land Rover down from Washington after leaving Cambridge the previous summer. Michael Westcott who lived in Santiago was among them and I was sure that he was just the man for me to meet. It should not be difficult to imagine, therefore, how pleased I was when I phoned him up and received an invitation to dinner the same evening, and the promise of a viewing of some of the films of the difficult parts of his journey. I doubt if either of us was aware at the time of quite what I was about to be subjected to. The Devil himself couldn't have invented a more exquisite or subtle form of torture to add to his repertoire, than to show those films to a person dedicated to the idea of travelling from Buenos Aires to New York in an ancient Austin Seven. One film of Central America was particularly effective in bringing me to the verge of a temporary nervous breakdown. It covered the journey over one of the four great gaps in the Pan-American Highway between Costa Rica and Panama, and showed Michael and his party winching their way from tree to tree through jungle swamps, crossing rivers with logs tied to their wheels and slithering through veritable seas of mud. I had something to think about that night when I went to bed. I was absolutely sure it would be impossible to get through such country in an Austin Seven on my own. There was only one ray of hope. For two or three weeks a year during March that part of the route dries up considerably and the rivers—there are nearly forty of them to cross without bridges—mostly change from raging torrents twenty or thirty feet deep into little streams. It was imperative to keep on schedule and reach Panama at the end of February. Meantime I put that film resolutely out of my mind and returned to Valparaiso.

The time soon came for the New Year festivities which were truly terrific. Parties lasted for twenty-four hours solidly, but the most spectacular thing of all was the firework display out on the bay. At midnight exactly, guns fired and every ship illuminated its outline by a blaze of little lights. A tremendous barrage of fireworks shot up off the sea high into the air and searchlights flashed over the waters and across the skies. Magnificent as it all was, I was told that it was a poor year since the Navy which foots the bill for the display happened to be short of money. It was thus that my New Year began on a beautiful still summer night with the great display spread far over the calm reflecting waters of the

New Year Festivities and a Pirates' Tea Party

Pacific. I had little chance to think what fate the year might hold in store for me as everyone rushed about kissing and hugging everybody else in sight. After wiping off the various brands of cosmetics that Chilean women indulge in fairly liberally, we returned indoors to continue the feasting and drinking. After that dancing began, including a great variety of the old traditional dances of Chile. This continued all through the night and was continued on and off during the next day. I was so tired at one point that I actually fell asleep with my head hanging over the side of a sofa in a position that caused me to snore loudly, a performance which, so I learned later, gave great amusement to the revellers.

For me, however, all these festivities were the signal that the time had arrived to be setting out again. I noted in my diary that after a little sleep I set out early in the morning of the 2nd January, aiming to reach Coquimbo where I had contacts and would have a last chance to make a few adjustments before heading right into the desert. I noted also that I drove out through a string of small towns and villages along a narrow but quite good tarred road. As soon as it grew light I could see the peasants, or peons as they are called in Chile, just leaving their adobe houses and setting out for the fields. Some were walking, some were on ox carts or on donkeys, but a good many I saw were being conveyed in lorries, the owners of the estates evidently being keen that they should start work in good time—I couldn't recall seeing many returning from work in that way on the evening I first drove into Valparaiso. The villages were mostly primitive and poor and many of the adobe houses, which are simply made of mud bricks dried in the sun, were tumbling down and crumbling away. In the centre a church, a few stores and sometimes a petrol pump formed the core of the little labouring community. After a couple of hours' driving I left the villages behind and arrived at a newly constructed part of the Pan-American Highway. The road was excellent to drive over, passing through delightful pastoral scenery. Cows grazed leisurely in the warm meadows, and orchards were filled with the luscious fruits which are one of the many delights of Chile. I felt I had only one small trouble in the world: I had forgotten the picnic lunch the Eltons had prepared for me the previous evening. The new road wound gently over a fair-sized range of hills which the little Austin climbed with the utmost ease and grace. It was such an absolute contrast with the rugged fierceness of the Andes and with the dusty road across central Chile, that I felt able to indulge in the luxury of irritation over a few hard-boiled eggs. This gradually vanished, however, as the pleasant farmlands faded away and the landscape started to grow dry and harsh. Not only was the car beginning to get thirsty because of the intensifying heat, but only one lane of the highway was completed and that, I knew from the maps, was due to vanish at any moment. I marvelled at the endurance of the Chilean workmen struggling to complete the rest of the road in the sweltering sun, for despite the arduous job they were engaged on they summoned up the energy to give me a rough hilarious cheer as I passed. Shortly after passing the end of the road works, I drew up at the Chilean equivalent of the lorry drivers' café. It was set some way back from the road and as I started to step out of the car an extremely suspicious-looking character with an old suitcase in one hand came running towards me. 'Señor,' he said, 'I wish to join you on your journey wherever you are going.' I explained that there was just no room in the car and that I couldn't possibly fit him in. 'It is not possible to take another man and his luggage in this little car,' I said and sincerely believed. That he could cook and was a wonderful mechanic, was the gist of what I understood his flow of Spanish to mean. A slightly menacing look on his face made me feel that it was best to get away from him as quickly as possible and avoid a dispute. The Chilean peasant has a reputation for fast knife work and I had no wish to experience it in practice. 'Does this engine sound good?' I said, starting it up, and as he was listening I drove away as fast as I could.

Over two-thirds of the route between Valparaiso and Coquimbo is paved. The remaining sixty-odd miles suffered in a freak storm a few years earlier and was a mixture of dust and chunks of broken concrete. It is no exaggeration to compare it with the sort of thing that can be seen after a row of buildings has been demolished and roughly levelled out. It was my violent initiation as a driver in the Atacama Desert, where one witty American had christened the main road 'The Washboard International Highway'. I had not long been on this stretch of the route when a modern car of a rather sporty variety overtook me. I was struck by the fact that although it was fairly new its bumpers and other parts were held together with wire and string. Having gone a

1a. Buenos Aires—where I was told that the city traffic was the cradle of Argentina's fame in the motor-racing world

1b. Gauchos at an estancia out on the plains of Argentina

2a. Rodeo in progress with Chilean huasos about to pin a steer to the stockade

2b. Santiago de Chile. The capital is encircled by the glistening, snow-capped peaks of the Cordillera

little way past, the driver waved to me to stop and began to relate
the whole story of the road, which had been built by a former
president, a native of La Serena, to add to the glory and pros-
perity of his home town, and had been destroyed by a storm that
had suddenly burst in that area where not a drop of rain had been
seen for the previous thirteen years. A great cloud movement,
that moves regularly in from the South Pacific and hits the Andes
in the south of Chile, suddenly and inexplicably changed its
course and brought torrential storms raging down on this sandy
approach to the Atacama Desert. The very foundations of the
road were washed away from underneath and the President's
cherished project collapsed into an irregular heap of concrete,
worse than the earth or gravel tracks it was supposed to supersede.
That was why it was almost impossible to keep nuts and bolts
tight and people resorted to wire and string. That didn't worry
me too much as I had already had plenty of experience of cars
that were only kept going in that way and I was carrying a large
roll of iron wire with me. After all wire won't shake loose, and out
there what do a few extra rattles matter?

I started up and once again the Austin rattled and banged and
bumped and jerked in a way I'd never before known a car to do.
It was something that had to be experienced to be believed. I
knew that metal becomes brittle and liable to break suddenly
after some years of rough wear and tear—as the metallurgists
say, it becomes tired or fatigued—even those inanimate lumps of
iron have more qualities in common with us than we imagine! I
couldn't help recalling some words of advice I'd received before
leaving. When I'd phoned up Peter Riviere of the *Autocar* to ask
him what the Chilean roads were like, he had said rather casually
that they were full of holes and bumps in the best places and
non-existent in the worst. 'Couldn't I ride round the potholes?' I
suggested. 'Oh, yes,' was the reply, 'if you don't mind going into
bigger ones.' He doubted if it was really good sense to attempt it
in a machine that had already suffered many years of hard wear.
Another motor manufacturer had told me that they thought the
idea was wonderful, but that, even if it was geographically possible, they considered I would be straining an aged piece of
machinery too far beyond its limits.

When I was living on a farm in Norfolk, I had once tried
breaking up an old Austin Seven chassis with a sledge-hammer

and had given it up after a long and exhausting struggle. I had gained enormous confidence from the memory of that episode. It had fortified me against all words of advice; but now that I felt the poor car being ripped and pulled and torn in every direction at once, I began to doubt. I crept along that sixty murderous miles of road—or should I say no road! I knew it was a mere foretaste of what was to come. Half-way across I stopped for petrol at the only place where petrol is available between the villages outside Valparaiso and Coquimbo—a total distance of about two hundred and fifty miles. A car pulled up soon after me, and out jumped two pretty Chilean girls. They put their arms round me while their father took photographs; and after congratulating me on my journey with a liberal array of Spanish superlatives, permitted me to proceed.

Towards late afternoon I finally came to the end of what I then thought must be an unparalleled sixty miles of bone-shaking highway. It would be difficult to imagine the delight and relief I experienced as I started to speed along a newly paved road that ran straight for many miles across a vast plain. On either side of me vines and other forms of vegetation were growing, the land being irrigated by waters led down from the Andes whose mighty ranges were still visible in the distance. My whole journey, however, was a supreme example of 'one damn thing after another' as if it were meant to dispel any inclination to complacency that might beset me. A powerful wind that cut straight across the plains proved a dangerous menace to a light car and I was quickly forced to reduce speed. In addition a nasty knocking noise rose high above that melody of bangs and rattles which I was prepared to regard as normal in a car that had just been over such a shattering route. I knew that in such out-of-the-way places it was essential to check every sign of trouble before it grew into anything serious, and whilst I wasn't very particular about my clothes during the journey, I made the old proverb, a stitch in time saves nine, my motto for looking after the car. Fortunately the trouble proved to have a simple explanation. In Valparaiso I had rigged up a rubber cover to put over the universal joint in an endeavour to protect it from the all-penetrating desert dust. With the excessive movement and scraping over pieces of rock the cover had got torn to pieces, and loose ends flying around at high speed were hitting the floor of the car. I ripped them off and from then on simply relied on a smearing of heavy grease to do its job.

As I passed over the plain a car suddenly shot past me; waving hands came out of every window to cheer me on my way, and I recognized the two girls I had met at the petrol station. I was now drawing close to Coquimbo. The Information Officer at the British Embassy in Santiago had told me that half the town was owned by the Macauliffs, an Irish family who had been established there for many years. I was to ask anyone in the streets for Barry Macauliff's house and he was sure that I would be made welcome there as long as I remained in Coquimbo. Apart from the pleasure of staying with people instead of putting up in hotels, a lurking suspicion that I might run out of cash and get myself hopelessly stranded in some wild part of South America evoked a mean anxiety to get everything I could for nothing. Much as I disliked having these feelings, I preferred admitting them frankly to people who I felt would understand.

After leaving the plains I passed over a small range of dry stony hills that skirted the little bay of Guayaquan. The bay was once a favourite haunt of pirates, from which they could set out to attack ships carrying gold from the mines near Copiapo, a strange town a hundred miles or so inside the desert about which I shall have a lot more to tell further on.

There was still an hour or so to spare before nightfall when I finally arrived at Barry Macauliff's house. I was quickly made welcome, especially by Barry Macauliff's son, who was a keen motorist and was, at the time, in the middle of trying to construct a small car for himself out of a collection of bits and pieces. An Austin Seven, he told me, would have fulfilled his wildest dreams. Life is pretty tough for British people living out in those parts and they have to be prepared for all kinds of emergencies. That night at dinner both Mr. Macauliff and his son were suddenly called away. A dam had burst in the irrigation system and they had to spend the night and most of the next day repairing it.

On the following morning I went to see Lito Macauliff, who owns an agency for British cars, and can often be heard travelling round the town in a battered old Ford from which the silencer long ago dropped off. I was beginning to suffer from slight stomach trouble—what English and American people visiting Chile call Chile-itis—and so when Lito invited me to dinner, telling me that one of the local doctors would be there, I was doubly pleased to accept; I felt quite sure that since a good deal of the conversation would hover round my journey there would be every likelihood of picking up some good advice. In this supposition I was absolutely correct. I wasn't on any account to eat butter. I wasn't to drink milk. I wasn't to touch fruit of any kind except bananas, oranges and lemons. Eggs were dangerous and sea food, which forms the main part of the diet of people in the towns along the coast, should also be scrupulously avoided. Everything except bread and well-cooked meat was struck off my list, and as meat is exceedingly scarce in the desert towns I couldn't avoid feeling a little anxious about what I was supposed to live on. The half-dozen tins of bully beef from Buenos Aires wouldn't go far; they were only intended for emergencies. The evening, however, in all other respects was lively and pleasant. I was told yet once more that I was mad to travel without a gun, as in some of the valleys in the north I might be attacked by a particularly vicious variety of wild goat, or possibly even by condors or vultures if I happened to stop and be in a slightly faint condition from the heat, not to mention by human beings, of course. There had been a hold-up outside the town hall that very morning, and Lito mentioned how he had taken some pot shots at a suspicious character hanging round his house a few nights earlier. As usual I agreed with everybody but regretted that at that stage I felt it was too late to do much about it. Amongst other things I felt very unwilling to spend money on firearms.

Life seemed easy for me in Coquimbo, but a little piece of excitement was in store for that very night. Lito and his wife came out to see me off as I was about to drive back to his brother's house. The air was still and a little intense. 'I predict an earthquake tonight,' said Mrs. Macauliff, and just to reassure me Lito added that she was nearly always right in her predictions. It was with a slightly uneasy mind that I settled down in bed that night. Only that day I had met a survivor of one of the terrible earthquakes in Concepción in the south of Chile. He had saved himself by standing under a doorway instead of rushing panic-stricken out into the streets. I lay awake for quite a long time thinking about earthquakes before gradually dozing off into a light sleep, feeling that perhaps it had been a false alarm after all. Suddenly in the middle of the night I woke up. The whole house was shaking with a strange kind of shudder from underneath. Like a shot from a gun I was under the bed for that would at least save me if the ceiling fell in. The shaking lasted for several seconds and produced an odd sensation in me, the kind of feeling that I imagine would be felt by someone lying on top of a huge jelly that had been given a sharp jolt from underneath. I climbed back into bed again and lay on the edge, tensed up and rather like a runner waiting for the starting-signal. But as time went on and nothing happened, I gradually subsided into sleep once again, and if any further earthquakes occurred that night I certainly knew nothing at all about them.

The following morning I went with Lito to the newspaper office. He was very pleased with the reporters at the time because they'd hushed up a little aeroplane crash he'd had and saved him from getting a black mark on his pilot's licence. The practice of awarding such marks Lito seemed to regard as a sign of the growth of officiousness in the Chilean Government. He was glad in the circumstances, however, to be bringing the sympathetic reporters what he thought they would consider a good story to make up for what they missed. After that we kept an appointment to meet Francisco Soto Figueroa, one of the greatest characters I met in Chile or anywhere else in the world for that matter. He was the man that knew the cure for my stomach trouble. At lunchtime the three of us went to a casino by the beach where an enormous meal had been prepared. That, he reckoned, with plenty of whisky would put anybody's stomach right. Lunch was merely the prelude to the afternoon's merriment which proceeded in true Chilean style. I always loved the way South Americans were ready to drop work whenever a bit of festivity was in the air, but I think it is a mistake to jump too readily to the conclusion that, therefore, they are lazy and shiftless. Indeed I have heard that many South Americans visiting England get that impression of us when they find the shops and work closing every day at about five-thirty. At first Lito acted as interpreter and I had very little direct conversation with Francisco for he appeared in every way a mighty man, huge and sturdy in build and wild in temperament; not at all, I thought, likely to treat my clumsy Spanish with patience.

When we returned to his house after a protracted lunch he looked at me and said, 'Father, Grandfather, piratas,' and by a sharp movement of his hand across his throat indicated the manner of their deaths. This man was a true descendant of one of the wildest bands of pirates that have ever existed on earth and whose booty was the fabulous gold of South America. The first thing I had to be shown was a remarkable collection of pirates' gear stored in an eerie cellar under the house. Clothes, pistols, cutlasses and implements of torture that had belonged to his forefathers for many generations were carefully preserved. Francisco began to act the part of a pirate so realistically as we climbed down the stone steps and entered the cellar lit only by an old ship's lamp, that I felt myself giving several irrepressible shudders of fear. My shaken nerves, however, were quickly soothed when we returned to daylight once more to be greeted with a beautiful recital of traditional Chilean songs and music by Francisco's numerous sons and daughters who varied in age between about two and twenty. Whisky and Pisco, the traditional liquor of Chile, began to flow most liberally and were passed round in drinking-horns carved by Indians, and the party began singing various English songs for my benefit. One of the climaxes of the afternoon was reached, however, when Lito began to improvise a song about my journey set to the tune of 'Tipperary', which began: 'It's a long way to Vallenar' (next town on my route) and ended each verse with the refrain: 'In an old Austin car.' It mentioned incidentally a double range of mountains that had to be crossed on the way to Vallenar.

Around five o'clock we all retired into another room where a fine tea, prepared by the womenfolk, was spread on a table of tremendous length. It was a simple and delightful attempt to be English for my sake, but I couldn't help wondering how many times a gang of wild pirates had sat at that very table feasting and celebrating some successful expedition and raising their glasses with frequent 'saluds' as they thought of their glittering plunder. Even now it took very little imagination to see Francisco as the 'Pirate Chief'. It was even easier after tea when the whole family dressed up in pirates' clothes for me to photograph them. Alas, the picture of that ferocious spectacle has been lost. Something perhaps even more precious, however, survived the rigours of the journey, a striking water-colour of the car standing outside the house painted by one of Francisco's talented sons.

The photographs really fired something off. In various machines, with the Austin at the head of the procession, we made our way to the local slaughter-house. The purpose of this visit was to photograph the car with an enormous Chilean condor that was kept there and fed on scraps. The boy who looked after it contrived with great skill to make it stretch its wings so that they spread along the whole length of the car. An instant later a couple of Huasos (Chilean cowboys) appeared and Lito at once set to work to bring them into a further picture. It was a delicate manœuvre, he explained afterwards, and required that they should be rewarded, so that the last I ever saw of Lito was as he was galloping off wildly with those two Huasos to one of the bars in town. The feats they performed on the way were hair-raising. He is one of the finest men in Chile, remarked Francisco.

Next morning I was ready to set out to Vallenar. The purpose of going to see Francisco was to get a letter of introduction to certain truck drivers who venture out into the desert, but this had been forgotten amidst the whirlwind of entertainments of the previous day. I delayed my start a little and called round in the morning. A letter was quickly composed, which said that Francisco Soto Figueroa recommended very specially his 'amigo' Mr. John Coleman who was making a valiant journey through the American continent, to all the drivers of vehicles in Chile. Even this great 'Pirate Chief' who looked as if nothing could daunt him told me that the very thought of my journey made him shudder a little. Was it, I wondered, a case of fools rush in where angels fear to tread?

The road to Vallenar was marked on the map as having an earth surface, not having even a foundation of rough stones and gravel. I expected hard going and I got it. But now I was growing gradually more used to my painfully slow travel over tracks and trails and was beginning to put my theories about patience into practice. The route wound once more along by the shores of the Pacific. It was a beautiful blue and the idea of plunging into it to escape the burning rays of the sun, by now well up in the sky, was almost irresistible. Sometimes the sea was no more than a quarter of a mile away over a beach of soft and enticing sands and I longed to throw off my clothes and run towards it as fast as I could. Yet I knew there were two good reasons for not doing so. To be more than a few minutes out in that sun uncovered is disastrous; and the sea, in spite of the great heat and its enchanting appearance, is icy cold, for a stream of freezing water, known as the Humboldt current, flows from the South Pole up the three thousand mile coastline of Chile and right on to the very north of Peru.

Leaving the coast once more, the road wound inland. Many more experiences were to happen to me before I was to see the Pacific again, when it would herald the approach to safety from a position of near personal disaster. Every trace of vegetation had disappeared from the landscape. Not even the rough desert scrub or cacti could survive in this area, nor the little dust-covered desert foxes that scuttled about in parts where animal life appeared impossible. It was with some surprise, therefore, that when I came to a concrete bridge spanning a bone dry creek, I noticed some boys holding up sea urchins for sale. I wondered where or how they could possibly live. A little farther on I found the answer to this puzzle. I hardly know what to call the pitiful constructions in which, in some of the desert regions of Chile and Peru, human beings appear to live. Four or five rough posts, thrown up by the sea in all probability, support a loose weaving of seaweed. I looked into the lone house in the sands. No one was at home. A few old rags lay on the floor. Outside another covering was set over a few blackened stones; the boys' kitchen utensils consisted only of a few sticks and some old smoke-blackened oil-cans that had been cut open to serve as saucepans. Their only food must have come out of the sea and anything that a passing traveller might give them in return for cooked crabs or sea urchins. The most surprising and for me the most ominous sight of all was the remains of an old truck. Things like that start up trains of thought when you are travelling alone in the desert!

Twenty or thirty miles farther on I came to a fairly large light structure set back from the road. Several trucks stood in front and a notice bore the welcome word 'restaurante' for I knew there was a good chance of getting a bottled drink. Most of the drivers who were lodged there waiting for assistance were busily devouring their lunch when I arrived. I swallowed down a couple of bottles of soda water and chatted to the proprietor about my journey. He was interested to hear about England and about my trip across Argentina. 'Los Argentinos are very . . .' and he stuck his nose up in the air to show that he shared the prevailing Chilean view of them. Such rivalries are strong between the Latin American countries and they bear all the signs of intimate family tension so

I felt it was always wiser to smooth over the controversy rather than agreeing firmly either way. I told him quite truly that I liked both. His conversation ranged intelligently over many topics and he showed the utmost patience with my language difficulties. As I was leaving and drew out my wallet to pay, he wouldn't hear of it. The idea of a visitor from another country paying obviously seemed preposterous to him.

The afternoon was drawing on and all had really gone very satisfactorily. I had noticed one or two points outside Coquimbo where ambushes had been prepared for vehicles by placing rocks across the tracks, but I was easily able to pass them by. I was not terribly worried by them because in the first place I felt my car would not attract the bandits particularly (at least not from the point of view of plunder) and secondly the Chilean bandits are reputed to be relatively merciful. They merely tie up their victims in their own vehicle so that they can be released by the next passer-by, a very different custom from what is practised in some parts of Central America, where the chief fun in banditry is derived from chopping off the hands and legs of the victims with jungle knives. In Chile I was keeping up a slow but steady pace. My worst worry was that I might break the car in two over the terrible roads. But another plague was soon to emerge unexpectedly and to prove even more frightening, in a quite different way, than bandits or wild animals or mountains. Just at present, however, I was approaching the double range of mountains that John had mentioned in his song. For some distance the climbing was severe and the engine struggled as it had in the main ranges of the Andes. On the final bend it was unable to make it. I went back and tried rushing it again but failed twice and finally resorted to tackling it in reverse, taking advantage of the lower ratio of the reverse gear. Slowly, slowly the car crept up. This time my own heart was throbbing with anxiety like someone waiting to hear the result of an important examination. Every moment seemed like an hour as the car crept gradually, very gradually round the last bend. It had really been touch and go and might have meant the end of my journey, but after what was in fact only a short time the car was standing on top. A little distance ahead a lorry was parked and appeared to be in trouble. They also had had difficulty in climbing and were letting their weary engine cool off before adding fresh water. After a brief chat they insisted on loading me with some of their cargo of huge and delicious-looking melons. I looked at them, thought of the doctor's advice and looked at them again. 'No,' I murmured to myself, 'I won't eat them. I'm taking quite enough risks already and I've had one taste of stomach trouble which is absolute hell.'

Once again as I approached the second range of mountains I detected the old trouble of uneven firing, and once again I put it down to the extraordinary conditions in which I was travelling: intense heat and severe climbing. Finally the engine refused to run any further. After half an hour's tinkering I still had no success, and when I heard a lorry in the distance I prepared to stop him and show him Francisco's letter. I was in a pretty wild and lonely part, but I was not yet in the absolute isolation of the true desert farther north where it was actually much safer to spend the night out alone. The car had almost started once or twice and with the help of the truck driver I managed to face it downhill and get going again. I was glad to hear the engine running once more, but felt a little apprehensive as I noticed the truck driver hurrying off on his way to Vallenar without waiting to see how I got on when I turned upwards again. The engine kept running but the climb was becoming increasingly steep and once more I was forced to tackle it in reverse, only this time the situation was much more drastic. It was not just a single hairpin bend as before, but a long climb along a narrow ledge cut round the peak of the mountain. The track veered round to the right so that I was only able to see it for a very short distance, and travelling in reverse with a disastrous drop just at the edge of the car was unnerving. I didn't at all mind tackling sharp hairpin bends when the sensation was quickly over, but this was really terrifying. Furthermore had anything happened to have been descending, I would simply have been swept over the edge without even time to jump out. That however was only a very slight chance and I gave it no thought. My whole mind was concentrated on steering the car backwards along the very narrow track without slipping off. I cannot quite describe how horrible was the sensation as I strained my neck as far as possible out of the side of the car and twisted it round to be barely able to see the edge of the cliff that I had to keep on at all costs. On top of everything was the fact that the whole time the engine was giving signs of being on the verge of packing up. Without any exception I considered this the worst piece of mountain climbing of the whole journey, and the worst experience of mountain driving that I believe it would be possible for anyone to have anywhere in the world. However I reached the top after what seemed an eternal nightmare and from there on I knew the road wound steadily downhill to Vallenar. On one occasion I had to guess which track to follow, but fortunately made the right choice, and towards sundown I saw what I thought must be a mirage in front of me: a small cluster of trees in the distance. As I drew closer I was able to make out that a group of boys were playing football beside the trees and I knew that I was almost in Vallenar. For about a mile downhill into the town the road was paved. Here also I was expected at the petrol station although my precise day or time of arrival was for obvious reasons unknown. I presented the attendants with the melons I had been longing to eat, while the manager phoned a representative of the local radio station who appeared with amazing rapidity. He helped me to find a hotel and although I was dead tired insisted on recording an interview with me in Spanish, my first broadcast in that language and I think it must have made good entertainment for the listeners when they heard it on the following Sunday afternoon. It had been a strange day. At one moment I had seemed to be on the verge of death and at the next I felt myself playing in a local comic turn.

I shall leave Vallenar and the hotel undescribed because they were similar to though much less interesting than Copiapo, the first town inside the Atacama Desert itself. A dinner of a local trade guild was going on in the courtyard on to which my room opened and sounds of masculine hilarity accompanied, and somewhat retarded, my gradual descent into the unconscious world of sleep.

V

Troubles Begin Early in the Desert

I woke up on the following morning feeling far from well and failed to make my usual early start. In spite of the miserable feelings in my stomach as I sat in the open courtyard of the hotel sipping lemon tea, the only part of my breakfast I felt able to touch, I experienced a sense of being at the beginning of a thrilling day, at the very threshold of another great landmark in my journey. I merely had to climb out of the little valley in which Vallenar is situated and almost immediately I would be at the official boundary of the Atacama Desert. That great desert stretches for nearly a thousand miles up the Chilean coast between the Andes mountains and the Pacific Ocean. Its average width is only about a hundred and fifty miles and several small valleys carrying the melting snows from the mountains sustain oases and enable little pockets of life to exist in one of the world's most barren regions. Before leaving England I had seen television films of the Oxford and Cambridge expedition making the crossing in Land Rovers and it had appeared a pretty formidable task even when undertaken by a group of people setting out in the latest type of overland vehicle. I wondered once more if I was a complete fool to be attempting it alone in a thirty-five year old car.

With feelings of an unknown sickness coming on it was anything but a joke to be starting out into such a formidable desert. Still I felt, incorrectly perhaps, that I'd never find a doctor in Vallenar and even if I did I could not be sure that he'd be much better than an African witch-doctor, and so I saw no point in delaying. I considered that I had every chance of reaching the town of Copiapo well before nightfall. It was under a hundred miles away, the track was reputed to be much better than that of the previous day and there were no mountains to cross. To the cheers of little groups of inhabitants who evidently thought my venture was a great joke, I drove out past the rows of houses in the centre of the town and began to climb the hill on the far side towards the sandy rocky regions once more. As I did so I was struck by two things. First the increasing intensity of the heat, which I sensed was likely to be one of my greatest problems, and secondly the way the houses of the poor people became more and more primitive as I ascended, just concoctions of sticks and stones with a few rags and old tins thrown in.

At the top of the hill a long desert vista spread out ahead as far as the eye could see. On my right were the bare hills of sand and rock that eventually merge into the foothills of the Andes whose mighty shadow seemed never far away during the whole of the South American part of my journey. On my left was the famous solitary eucalyptus tree of the Atacama Desert. How it grew there appeared a mystery. Its roots must have stretched deep down to some underground source of water in the rocks, for not another sign of plant life of any description was visible during the whole day's travelling. I had already seen many pictures of that famous tree in travel books but now seeing it in reality almost made me begin to wonder if life itself were real. Could I really be at this strange point in my crazy journey or was it all a dream? I often experienced that sense of unreality at times when circumstances were not too harsh. That tree, however, was not the only interesting sight. Beneath it sat an aged woman with an enormous basket of assorted goods. She was dressed in dusty black clothes and looked much as an old gypsy might anywhere in the world. I was unable to fathom from her conversation why she was there but was delighted that she readily consented to pose for a photograph which was intended to include her, the tree and, of course, my inevitable car.

A little farther along on the opposite side of the road was a battered old tin notice. Looking carefully I was able to decipher the words 'Desierto de Atacama'. For a moment I forgot my sickness, I forgot everything. Really the Atacama Desert! I had been constantly asking people exactly where it began, and now this was it. My feelings of excitement didn't last long, however, for as I walked back to the car I found myself beginning to stagger. I had made the mistake of getting out of the car without wearing the fine Australian bush hat I had brought with me, and three or four minutes in that sun is enough to knock out anybody not long accustomed to it. It is not just a matter of the heat alone. As there is no water in the desert it follows that there is no moisture in the atmosphere, which in all other types of climate serves to filter the harmful rays from the sun. It is quite a different kind of heat from anything known in this country or even in tropical climates, although I believe that similar effects are sometimes experienced on high mountains. In addition the dry scorching air causes the mouth to become parched and furry and an almost agonizing thirst sets in. To combat this I had borne in mind some comments of Tschiffely's when making my preparations. In his *Ride* he has pointed out that in desert regions he found it better to carry lemons rather than water as a mere taste of sour lemon is sufficient to take the edge off the violent thirsts experienced. I always made a point of having a partly cut lemon wedged in the side of the passenger seat, which I licked every now and again, and in that way contrived to keep my thirsty feelings more or less in control.

The road surface for the first part of that morning was really quite fair by the standards of the Chilean desert and I jogged along at a gratifying fifteen to twenty miles per hour. While doing this I began to reflect on that battered notice that announced the official beginning of the desert. It suddenly occurred to me that the numerous holes pierced in it were obviously caused by bullets. Every traveller in those parts carries a gun, and the very occasional notices that the government takes it into its head to erect are regarded as a splendid opportunity for a bit of target practice. What better way of keeping your eye in and yourself ready for all emergencies during a journey? As I was thinking about this subject, my attention was suddenly arrested by a sight that brought my thoughts immediately back to Tschiffely. By the wayside lay a dead horse, a mere skeleton encased by skin and dehydrated in the sun. I could not help wondering how near Mancha and Gato had been to that fate on occasions, nor recalling the stories of other desert travellers who had seen human beings in a similar condition, a sight which I was glad the good fortune of my journey spared me. I little realized then how near I was to come to that fate myself before the nightmare of crossing that desert was accomplished.

My attention was later turned to the car once more as a violent and unexpected deterioration in the track made it lurch and plunge like a rowing-boat in a storm at sea, again giving the impression of being torn in about twenty directions at once. The corrugated gravel surface changed into a trail that had been formed by dumping large stones and lumps of rock on it. I had covered perhaps ten kilometres of this murderous stuff when I observed a restaurant similar to the one that had made me so welcome on the previous day. Again there were broken-down trucks outside and I myself must have given the impression of arriving in a dilapidated wreck. My front number plate was hanging on by one loose bolt and all the nuts and bolts holding the radiator had disappeared completely leaving it connected to the engine solely by the rubber hose pipes. Already, after traversing only the first few miles of desert, the car was being shaken to pieces as some people had predicted . . .

'How much more of this hellish road is there?' I asked the driver of one of the broken-down trucks. Rather amused at my rawness, he gave a sympathetic laugh. 'Oh, it's similar all the way to Copiapo and much worse up in the north of the desert,' he replied. 'Es terrible,' I said. He agreed and explained that that was exactly why they were all stuck there. The scorching heat made repairs out in the sun impossible. Here at least I was able to pull in under a rough shelter at the side of the restaurant. First, however, I quickly disposed of a couple of bottles of beer and began to gaze round at the decoration of the primitive establishment. The walls were plastered with pictures of pin-up girls and film stars in the midst of which was one poster of Alessandri, who is now President of Chile. It had remained up since the election and the claim it made was interesting: 'Vote for Alessandri who stands for the benefit of all the people.' It certainly appears now as if that claim is being borne out. Not only is industry developing rapidly and road-building forging ahead under the most difficult conditions, but vast slum clearance schemes, long overdue it must be admitted, can be seen in nearly every town. Rich and poor alike seem to be pinning high hopes on the new President. I am sure that those who go to Chile in five or ten years' time will have a very different story to tell from mine.

Troubles Begin Early in the Desert

The establishment was run by a woman and her daughter. The slightly Mongolian appearance of their faces indicated their Indian descent and although they were very obliging the Spanish hospitality was absent from their nature and this time I had to pay the full price for my drinks before leaving. Far away in the distance I could see the road stretching across a great dry plain and then winding round the side of a hill before finally disappearing. From afar the track appeared as if it might have been an excellent road—almost like the mirage of a beautiful lake that appears to a man dying of thirst. The scenery, however, was not dull, as I had expected, for, although the whole landscape was composed solely of shades of brown, the lack of vegetation made the contours of the land stand out and resemble certain works of modern art, reflecting shapes that appeared to have some dim meaning for the subconscious mind. I was beginning to understand that strange fascination that is reputed always to bring the children of the desert back to their home, and many and enticing as were the attractions of the strangely varied regions through which I passed, none left me with a more compelling need to return than the Atacama Desert.

Occasionally the heat caused slight prevapourization of the petrol and brought me to a temporary halt for several anxious moments, but I was blessed on two accounts: first by a gentle breeze that blew from the north and kept the radiator functioning, and which only died out for a short period on one hill where I used up a gallon of water in less than half an hour, and secondly by a quite unexpected improvement in the road. Once again I was able to speed ahead at a full fifteen miles an hour. Only those who have been reduced to walking pace for considerable distances over piles of rock can realize the wonderful sensation of even a small relative increase in speed. I learnt that the sense of speed is much more important than the actual speed for it is that that relieves any feelings of boredom.

The sun was still a fair way up in the sky as I started rolling down the last hill into Copiapo. Down in the valley the road begins to widen out to the ambitious size of a four-lane highway. Although still unpaved and covered with rough stones it is surely a sign of Chile's future. Poplar trees lined both verges and as I descended I could see the town spread out in front of me. Rows of houses ran out in various directions from the inevitable central

3a. Typical track across the Atacama Desert with the welcome view of an oasis ahead

3b. Memories of previous travellers

.4. Andes towering over the town of Pisco near Cuzco in the very heart of Inca
country

plaza at one side of which stood the typical Spanish colonial church with its attractive twin towers. It could have been some foreign town in the Middle Ages but for three high posts that stuck up incongruously above the buildings and bore the names of three oil companies, two being extremely familiar and one that of the Chilean National company. I had learnt of the remarkable history of this town at the British Embassy in Santiago. It was once famous all over the world for its gold mines and its opera house. In the last century this strange town in the Atacama Desert was visited regularly by opera companies of international fame and was then the most fashionable place on earth to see a performance of the great classical operas; an indication of the curious homage that rich men pay to the 'Yellow God'! In 1851 the first railway in South America was opened between the little port of La Calera and Copiapo, to carry those wealthy visitors and that precious metal. Today, however, the town is very different, now that only copper is mined and the opera house has been burnt down. Poor miners shuffle along the streets. Lurid posters advertise the cinema programmes.

At the bottom of the hill I had to cross a small river by means of a bridge that I guessed was originally designed to carry tanks. It was not difficult to deduce from this and many other signs that Latin America has been a good customer for the ex-Army equipment sold off by the United States Government. From the bridge I could see the first rows of crudely constructed wooden houses. Little attention has been paid to the roofs. Board and sheets of metal, probably once old oil-drums, have been nailed on to uprights of uneven lengths. Children whose feet were bare and whose tan matched the desert looked out of the doors of these wretched shacks or played in the dusty street.

It was still only mid-afternoon when I arrived at the Chilean company that operates on behalf of a well-known brand of English petrol. As I sat down and began to relax I realized that the pains I was suffering from were more than the effects of travelling under uncomfortable conditions. My first need was to find a hotel. I always made a point of asking for one that was inexpensive but clean, and judging from results I appear to have done far better than the various travellers whose books contain vivid accounts of the filthy holes that asking for the best hotel led them into. The Chileans are a witty people and probably thought they meant the best for writing a book about. All that I stayed in in Chile had clean sheets, a clean towel and a bowl of water for washing. Perhaps things are improving for I noticed an occasional office of the Ministry of Public Health in several towns. Nevertheless the shortage of water causes great problems in the lavatories which, although usually of the water-closet type, are frequently smelly and almost unbearable to use. Used toilet paper is put in boxes in order not to block the drains, with the result that on entering a lavatory one is immediately assailed by flight after flight of flies that emerge from these stinking containers.

The imprint of old-fashioned English life is everywhere evident in Argentina and Chile, so I was not unduly surprised to find myself guided to the Hotel Inglés. In spite of its name it was built on the typical Latin American pattern described by Tschiffely, although distinctly cleaner than the one he described in the north of Argentina. The rooms all opened on to a *patio* or open courtyard at one end of which was situated a large and moderately pleasant dining-room. Behind that was another, smaller, earth courtyard and then came the kitchen, a large rough shack also with an earth floor. In the centre was a huge primitive range which was kept constantly burning and on it and around it stood many large old-fashioned pots and pans, black with soot and age. My own condition was deteriorating very rapidly and I felt unable so much as even to look at the heavy greasy food provided. Instead I slipped out and made my way to a small bar in town where I was able to obtain some brandy mixed with sugar and water to take the place of a meal. When the kindly old barmaid heard that I was a traveller I had quite a job inducing her to accept any money. At the time I didn't know the risk I was running when I drank at one of these small town bars. I learnt later that fake concoctions are often sold in the place of normal spirits and are highly dangerous to the stomach.

In the night my sickness began to grow really violent. I became even more certain that I was suffering from something much more serious than ordinary stomach trouble. On the following day, however, I felt slightly better and Carlos, the representative from the oil company, came round to see me and insisted on taking me to his house where his wife attempted to prepare suitable nourishment for me. Terrible language difficulties arose. While I was asking for such simple things as bread or meat I was all right, but when it came to explaining the complexities of my condition or the kind of non-greasy food I wanted I was absolutely stumped. I would have liked to have gone into the kitchen myself and picked out the things I wanted, but I knew it would be a very un-Latin American thing for a visitor to do. I finally settled for 'sopa' which means soup and left it at that. Meanwhile I struggled to sit in the drawing-room and make polite conversation in Spanish with Carlos's mother and other relations. The ordeal became too much for me and I asked to be allowed to lie down. I was taken into a little bedroom and shortly afterwards a bowl of soup arrived. Great globules of grease floated around on top of it and I felt I should die if I touched even a spoonful. I picked out a few small pieces of chicken and not long after became violently sick. Eventually I returned to the hotel in a horse-drawn cab and prepared to face the night. I could have looked for a doctor but once again I considered it not worth while and feared that it might merely cause me to waste too much of my dwindling cash.

It may perhaps seem that I have made a lot out of just a bout of sickness but the seriousness of it became fully evident in the night when I began to vomit up blood and what looked like portions of intestine. There are in those parts forms of dysentery in which the bacteria attack the tissues of the gut itself and bits of the intestines come away and can be spewed up. I had heard about this and guessed that that was precisely my trouble. It was a horrifying thought in such circumstances where my best hope, slender though it seemed, was that nature would somehow effect a cure.

Another sign of former English influence even in the most out-of-the-way parts of Chile was the presence of a British Vice Consul. John Davidson who held this office was born in Chile and had spent his whole life out there. His father was among those attracted out to Copiapo in the days of its wealth. Today John Davidson works in the mines. I had tried to contact him several times but he was working night and day on rescue work after a disaster had occurred in one of his mines. The next day I felt it was imperative to eat something in order to live and yet it was absolutely impossible to get anything to suit the condition of my stomach. I would warn anyone undertaking any expedition which might involve that risk to be sure and carry at least a small

quantity of light food for such emergencies. At last John Davidson arrived. He told me about an American hospital on the coast
at a place called Barquito. It was the headquarters of an American
firm that exported copper from Chile, and was about 120 miles
away over the roughest of trails. Davidson advised me to make my
way there as soon as possible, as it was the only place where I
would be able to get the food and medical attention I needed, but
he warned me that there was a climb of sixty miles leading out of
Copiapo and that it was essential to get it behind me in the very
early morning, as only then is there a slight downhill breeze.
Meantime he provided me with some soup and jelly and with a
letter to the Englishman in charge of stores at Barquito, Ken
Woodruff. I began to feel that I might possibly survive the ordeal
after all and decided to follow his advice on the very next morning.

At four o'clock I walked round to the oil company's half-built
plant and workshops where the car was garaged and drove it
round to the hotel to collect my baggage. Carrying it out and
packing it exhausted me and I simply fell into the driver's seat,
pressed the starter which had so far been working with wonderful
regularity and headed towards the coast. After a few miles of
paving I found myself approaching the trails once more and
wondering how I was going to stand up to the banging and
bashing I knew they would give me. I no longer thought of the
poor car now, but thought chiefly about myself. Only the hope
that I should reach that hospital before nightfall and receive
treatment that would relieve my pains and worries spurred me
on. The landscape was grey and rocky, the sky was of a similar
hue and the gentle breeze that John Davidson had predicted was
there to bestow its blessings on the Austin's ridiculously inadequate radiator. Later the sun began to rise and send its powerful rays across the grey rocks. It was still early morning and there
seemed to be a new hope in the air so I relaxed and let the car
carry me steadily uphill. Alas, how wrong our feelings can be at
times. I was a little more than half-way up the hill when the
engine began to repeat its old habit of misfiring. The morning air
was still cool and the breeze was blowing mildly so the trouble
this time could not be ascribed to the blazing desert heat or to the
rarefied atmosphere of the mountains. The broad beams of the
sun merely hinted at the heat that was in store, an hour or two
away.

Troubles Begin Early in the Desert

For a few moments the engine seemed as if it were going to pick up again. The vain hope crossed my mind that perhaps it was just a little dirt in the petrol or that there might be some simple explanation of that sort. It was a shortlived burst of optimism that died out as the engine spluttered to a decisive halt. The ignition was completely dead. I tried a couple of bursts on the starter motor but there was not a sign of life in the engine. I cursed the car with every kind of blasphemy at my command for failing me at the time when I felt least able to cope with it. I could expect no help from the lifeless desert, however, and I knew underneath that I must resign myself to a systematic check of the electrical system. It soon became plain that the trouble was inside the magneto, which is the electrical gadget on old-fashioned cars that produces the sparks to explode the petrol. I removed the cover. My consternation at the sight I saw would be difficult to imagine. There before my eyes was a mass of brass and fibre filings. I was miles out in the desert and the piece of mechanism that produced the vital spark to keep the car going was absolutely chewed to pieces. My case, however, was still not absolutely hopeless since I had an alternative form of ignition system with me, which I immediately proceeded to try and fit. It had been obtained for me at the very last moment by Mr. Warne, the engineer of the Montagu Motor Museum. There had been no time to check it but he assured me that it was correct. On discovering that it had completely unsuitable fittings for my engine I almost dropped dead on the spot. I was past swearing now, past even slinging a hammer through the engine and setting out on foot for Copiapo. I merely sat down in the road in complete despair.

The only possible hope was to be found by examining the ruins of the magneto and, as I couldn't sit for ever, I started to do that, muttering that it was just my luck to have trouble with the one part of the car with which I was not well acquainted. It soon became clear that the two main troubles were a broken rotar arm and a disintegrated brass bearing. Mr. Warne had advocated carrying a whole collection of spares which for obvious reasons I had rejected; I had not, however, refused a small assortment of old magneto parts because they were almost no weight and took up a negligible amount of room. I remembered that among them was another rotar arm. That at least was one problem solved. I solved the other by making up a crude bearing out of a strip of the

85

old tobacco tin in which I was carrying these precious spares. It was a tricky job and the growing heat was beginning to have a powerful effect on my already weakened condition. After some while I had the magneto together once more. I tested it before replacing it and it sparked as well as ever. Once again I felt hope but determined that at the next town I would try and send a cable to Austins asking for a new magneto—or rather a reconditioned one because new ones are obviously not obtainable. Through no fault of the company it reached me finally in Mexico City—7,000 miles farther on!

Just as I was about to put it back on the engine again I heard the sound of a vehicle in the distance. Soon a small truck came in sight. Like all good Chilean drivers he stopped to see if I was in trouble—I was told that their motto is 'It's you today but it'll be me tomorrow.' I explained what my problem had been, but as he leant over from the opposite side to have a look at the engine he suddenly exclaimed, 'Look, Señor, *el fondo* (the chassis) is broken.' I think he must have seen the look of despair on my face. I could have confronted all these difficulties in good health, but truly I felt half dead. He tried to comfort me by telling me that he had a garage in Antofagasta and that he would be happy to do any repairs for nothing, but Antofagasta was still between three and four hundred miles away. Meanwhile we decided to tow the car to a railway siding not terribly far away where he thought it might be possible to get the car carried back to Copiapo either by train or truck.

It is supposed to be an ill wind that blows nobody any good and it must be admitted that there was a certain degree of amazing luck in all my misfortune. It was the small front member of the chassis, technically known as the goose neck, that had split in two, and had I gone on travelling with it in that condition with the engine bolted down I might well have split the aluminium lower section of the engine in two, which would almost certainly have meant the end of my trip. We turned off the so-called main road and proceeded for some distance until we reached a railway line. A little way along the line a small group of shacks were visible. It was indeed the sort of place I should have avoided like the plague had I been travelling alone, fearing it to be a most likely sort of spot for a bandits' hide-out.

On arrival we were told that a truck standing by the railway would probably be leaving at about two o'clock, and when its driver, who was also the owner, returned, he readily agreed to carry my car back into Copiapo, but warned me that he had to go via one of the copper mines up in the hills. My wariness about the place I was in had caused me to insist on staying with the car. Several children came round as I sat in it, filled with curiosity and asking me all sorts of questions about my journey, about my car and about England and Europe. At times they became a little impatient of my bad Spanish, finding it especially difficult to comprehend why anyone couldn't understand them when they had repeated some phrase clearly several times. A look came on to their faces which simply said 'We give up'. I certainly understood enough to be amazed by their good general knowledge. One of the little dark and dusty bare-footed boys seemed to take a particular fancy to the rather attractive sweet tin in which I carried my needles and cotton. '*Es muy linda* (it's very pretty),' he said and was surprised and overjoyed when a spontaneous urge prompted me to tip its contents into another box and hand him the pretty tin.

My conversation with the children caused me to feel reassured that I was in a safe place and when the driver of the truck came out again and asked me to come into one of the houses I agreed. I refused food but was very grateful for a cup of lemon tea, a drink that had won my highest favour in the desert. In spite of its rough exterior, the house was surprisingly clean and neat inside and indeed very comfortable. I was attended by a young girl whose slightly oriental appearance indicated her Indian descent. Both she and her mother were extremely kind, refusing to consider any kind of payment for the tea. That was only the beginning of the kindness that made such a day of misfortune bearable. When I went outside again the car was gone. For a moment I was worried, but when I looked round the side of the house where it had been standing, there it was already up on the truck, with several men around it nailing blocks of wood to the floor to keep it secure for the journey back to Copiapo. It appeared that they had purposely brought me inside to save bothering me with the task of loading it on to the truck! Once we were ready to go I was asked to sit in the car and several Indian workmen climbed on to the back of the truck. They were not of the colourful sort to be seen in Peru, Ecuador, Mexico or Guatemala. Their clothes were the shabby remains of a more or less European type, but they themselves were friendly enough. The truck had also, it appeared, had a pretty long and tough life; it was battered and dusty and looked as though it had not seen paint for many years. In one corner an enormous galvanized iron barrel holding about fifty gallons of water was firmly secured. We set off up into the hills away from the road. The road was rough but in the direction we were going there was no road or track at all. We weaved our way through lumps of rock and over sandy earth surfaces, occasionally crossing the wheel marks of another vehicle.

The afternoon was wearing on and I began to wonder when we were likely to return to Copiapo. The route seemed so strange that I even wondered if they might be taking me to some bandits' hideout in the desert. Eventually we came to the top of an eminence from which it was plainly impossible to travel any further. The driver and his companion jumped out and began looking round and pointing in various directions, but a look of bewilderment in their eyes showed clearly that they were lost. Down below was a vast rocky valley with not a sign of a living thing in it. After much discussion and what I concluded was a vain search for landmarks, they decided to turn back and follow their own tracks. This was done until we came to where another set of wheel marks crossed ours. With a great deal of hesitation they decided to follow the direction in which that former truck had passed heaven knows how many weeks or months before. At last we reached the mine, which bore little resemblance to what we in England think of as a mine. There were no buildings and no mine shafts, only a few dejected-looking Indians of a similar colour to the rocks and sand and with rather sad resigned faces, squatted chipping the ore away from lumps of stone. People say that factory work in England is soul-destroying, and I agree with them, but here was proof that soul-destroying work is not the result of mechanization alone.

'How long do these men spend here?' I asked the driver. 'They spend several days or even weeks at a time,' he explained, and I thought of them squatting on the sand and chipping away at the seemingly valueless stones from dawn till dusk. 'Those shelters (a sort of reed thatching perched on four poles) are where they spend their nights and do their cooking.' I knew that they resigned themselves to this consummation of drudgery through the need to return with a few pence in the pockets of their shabby clothes to sustain their struggling families.

Troubles Begin Early in the Desert

Back in Copiapo I asked the driver if he would be good enough to drop my car off at the workshops of the oil company that was helping me. When we arrived the workmen were in the process of packing up for the day and came out shouting and laughing. They were indeed as rough a bunch of mechanics as one could possibly meet anywhere, and without any word from anyone they set about unloading the car in a manner that to put it mildly might be described as boisterous. A couple of planks of uneven length were placed up against the back of the lorry and about twenty men, all with varying ideas about how the operation should be carried out, amidst much shouting and arguing began to lower the poor dusty Austin on to a piece of ground that was obviously reserved for scrap metal. There was little I could do to stop or control them. I jumped around nervously trying to offer words of caution in Spanish as twice the car came perilously near to toppling over into the heap of junk. I suspected that some of the men might even have thought that that was where it was meant to go.

When it was safely down I began to thank the driver and asked him how much money I owed him for his good service. Twice he refused and then said a handshake was his price and wished me good luck on the rest of my journey. He will perhaps never know how grateful I felt and I should not have begrudged him a few pounds of my dwindling supply of cash. Shortly after he drove off the chief mechanic or foreman of the workshops came out. The car was pushed inside the main workshop which, although rough, was equipped with a few inspiring pieces of fine modern machinery. The doors were locked and I was asked to be back at eight o'clock on the following morning. Grabbing a few pieces of indispensable luggage I returned to the same hotel, tired and weary and more than a little apprehensive at what the car might have to suffer at the hands of that rough band of workmen on the following day. Still, everything considered, I was really remarkably lucky.

In spite of all my hardships and lack of medical attention, or perhaps because of them, I was feeling rather better next morning, and John Davidson who had heard about my plight arrived at the workshops to help interpret the nature of my problems to the chief engineer, who I soon learnt was a man of remarkable capacities. Not only was he clearly a very fine engineer, but he seemed also to be possessed of an almost uncanny ability to get good work out of men who would have made any lesser foreman throw up his hands in despair. He walked round the twenty or so workmen and seemed to arrive at each one just in the nick of time to prevent him from committing some ghastly error. After a brief conference we quickly agreed on a plan for welding and reinforcing the chassis. He was emphatic that nothing could be done to adapt the device for an alternative ignition system to suit the engine. I later gave it to him as a souvenir of my strange visit to his workshops and I daresay it still stands on the window ledge where he decided to keep it. He insisted that I should tackle the repair of the magneto while he saw to the making of the new parts I needed. I must admit I felt a little uncertain of my abilities in this direction, but by lunchtime both jobs were completed. The magneto was working better than at any time since crossing the Andes and the chassis, far from being weaker, was actually much stronger than before, having a cunningly shaped metal bracket fitted under the welded cross member! At a press of the button the car was ready to run once more, and indeed it was actually a blessing in disguise, pretty heavy disguise taking into account my own condition, that the trouble should have occurred at this first stage of the desert crossing.

I can hardly say that after a further attack of sickness during the night I was ready to set out at 4.30 on the following morning. I had it firmly riveted in my mind, however, that that was what I was going to do, come what might short of falling down unconscious. I managed to get up and dress myself but carrying out the baggage exhausted me and brought me to the verge of fainting as I fell into the driver's seat. It was some minutes before I was able to press the starter and begin rolling towards what was now my only hope, the hospital at Barquito. I kept wondering every moment what fate the day would have in store for me as I crawled steadily up that long sixty-mile drag, past the point where I had broken down a couple of days earlier (how I hated every kilometre I had to cross twice! Fate it seemed had cheated me, but if I reached the hospital that night, I thought to myself, I would be very pleased to call it quits). I went on past the track leading down to the railway siding. The sun rose once more and began to produce the overpowering heat of another desert day. The kilometres were slipping by, and just as the morning breeze was beginning to vanish I arrived at the point where the road finally started to level out. Ahead lay nothing but desert and more desert, complete lifeless desolation. I avoided a certain amount of the bumping by keeping one wheel on a narrow strip at the verge which hadn't been so badly affected by corrugation. In addition I kept the tyres down to less than half the recommended pressure for England. It was tough work for them but they stood up to it amazingly throughout the whole journey.

The sickness of the previous night and the constant jerking were having their effect on me. My throat was desperately parched, I felt extremely weak and every now and again I was forced to stop by fits of giddiness. The car had had its turn. Today it was mine again. Lest the details of my sickness should seem to drag out too long I shall only say that eventually, when I was almost at the end of my tether, I reached the little mining village of Inca de Oro where I obtained some brandy and hot water from which I derived a sufficient renewal of energy to reach Barquito.

The ports of Chañaral and Barquito are more or less adjacent, being joined together by two or three miles of tarred road. Miners and dock workers were doing various jobs all along the route. They let out loud, wild shouts, half jeering and half welcoming. At any rate I was not sorry that I didn't have to stop among them or I should probably have been carried the rest of the way with even more jerking and bumping than the rocky roads could provide. It was late afternoon when I finally drove into Barquito and saw before my eyes a modern American settlement. Covered in dust, I barged round various offices. The notoriously scruffy tramps of South America had nothing on me. It was no wonder therefore that I was not greeted with a round of applause but merely told rather curtly that Mr. Woodruff was on holiday. Somehow or other the word had got round that I had arrived in a most peculiar contraption, which caused one or two of the managers of the firm to go out and look for themselves. As usual the car did the trick. It was arranged for a Chilean boy to show me to comfortable quarters, take me to the hospital and order a meal if I wished it. Life was taking on a new aspect. No doctor was there that night but the Chilean Sister-in-charge made me take some tablets that provided most welcome relief from the pains I'd been suffering. I was not allowed to stay in the hospital but went to see the doctor on the following day. A Chilean nurse insisted that I queued up with the Indian employees of the company and it was some time before I was examined by a kind and apparently very good Chilean doctor. After a careful examination he handed me over to a partly qualified doctor of the kind to be found in many of the Latin American countries. These men, known as 'enfermeros' hold a position half-way between a doctor and a nurse and are qualified to give injections and to carry out much of the routine work of the doctor. The idea is to relieve the acute shortage of well-trained doctors.

I received various strange injections and one rather large tube of stuff that looked like blood was pumped into me. In addition to this I took certain types of tablets sent from the United States to deal with various acute forms of dysentery. The result was amazing and within a few days I was eating the excellent American fare shipped down directly from North America. My story up to date was printed with various photographs in the company's newspaper. Although I felt I would have been very happy to pay all the money I had, I was treated as a guest and even my hospital treatment brought about no reduction in my slender purse.

By the following Saturday night I was ready to join in a party at Ken Woodruff's house. The party was amazing in one respect. Although held in a remote little port in the Atacama Desert, it was truly international. There were Ken who was English, several Chileans, some Argentines, an Austrian with a beautiful Swedish wife and several other nationalities. We counted ten in all at the stage at which our mathematical abilities were still unimpaired. The only strange thing was that there was not a single person actually born in the United States in spite of several decidedly Yankee accents.

With a new stock of suitable food, and feeling like a new man, I was ready to set out early on the Monday morning. I had always made a point of going easy on the drink and behaving rather like an athlete in training: an absolutely clear head was needed to deal with the expected and never-failing succession of emergencies. But in any case it was an amply sobering thought to consider how much trouble I had already experienced crossing the mere perimeter of the Atacama. The bulk of the crossing still remained in front of me.

VI

Too Much Water in the Desert

It was early morning once more. I was on the road again. I was well enough to experience the *pleasant* sensations of adventure and I could not help recalling all the summer mornings in England when I had woken up with the call of the open road surging up from within and reluctantly I had had to make my way to work. Now it was all happening. I was on one of the distant mysterious routes of my dreams and it felt almost too good to be true. Glancing at my diary now I see that I was aiming that day to reach Taltal, another small port on the coast similar to Barquito; that I had a letter from my 'Pirate Chief' in Coquimbo to the mayor of the town, whom I was to find by looking for a shop with a petrol pump outside, the only one in Taltal; and that it was a normal day of desert travel with no special obstacles, but only the amorphous monster of insecurity, who seemed to regard it as a good game to manifest himself in the various rattles that kept coming and going on the Austin, and whom for want of better company I had now almost come to regard as a human companion.

There had only been one real hazard. During the early part of the day I had been rash enough to attempt a short cut between two parts of the road, with the enticing prospect of cutting a mile and a half off the total eleven thousand odd! Thinking that the narrow track could scarcely be worse than the road, I turned on to it with full confidence. I soon discovered that it was absolutely full of sand holes and I could only get through them by rushing and steering a series of quick minute zigzags with the front wheels. The drastic experience was soon over, but while it lasted I knew that with the least wavering of intention I would certainly be stuck and asked myself—for how long? Afterwards I could only wonder how much damage it might have done to the Austin.

93

Too Much Water in the Desert

It was one of innumerable small occasions on which something made me suddenly depart from my normal routine of extreme patience and caution and fly to the opposite extreme. Car and everything had to be risked then, otherwise there was no hope of getting through at all.

Another glance at my diary tells me that at precisely 2.35 I pulled up beside a rather dusty blue petrol pump outside a large old-fashioned general stores. I found the mayor inside with his shirt-sleeves rolled up and busily at work. He spoke good English. He was proud of his town and began by relating how a year earlier Peter Townsend had suddenly rolled up in his Land Rover and, being surprised to find fluent English spoken, asked if he had arrived at an English colony. The question, indeed, was not so very wide of the mark. Until twenty or thirty years ago there had been in Taltal a flourishing community of English people, who operated a group of now almost extinct nitrate mines. While we were talking, the mayor's son who was the English teacher in the local school arrived, and undertook to show us the town including the rows of empty houses where English and Welsh people had formerly lived.

The mayor had another surprise for me. Taking me round to a backyard he introduced me to two Chilean bus drivers from Santiago, who were attempting to drive a 1930 Pontiac up to the United States. They were in trouble with a broken half shaft. I was to see a good deal more of them at various points in the journey, but I felt that it was unfortunate that I happened to be doing a similar journey in a car five years older, alone and without a wireless transmitter; and I later heard that it prompted them to put round various stories that I hadn't done the journey by car at all but mostly by boat. Perhaps in reality I should congratulate them on their restraint. It would not have been difficult for them to have murdered me in some out-of-the-way spot.

When the time came to close the shop, the mayor gathered together his various sons and daughters and all their families and invited me to join them for a picnic on the beach a few miles north of the town. We all piled into a truck to drive to the shore, paddled along the beach for a while, turned up bits of rock to discover various shellfish and had a picnic of beer, sandwiches and cakes. If he had wanted to impress upon me that he understood all the basic principles of an English family outing to

Too Much Water in the Desert

Brighton, he could hardly have done it better. The impression was blurred somewhat by the absence of crowds, except in so far as the mayor's own family constituted a crowd, and by a small but very Latin American incident at the end of the outing. The mayor had a building project in hand, for which he wanted some of the fine sand to be found on that beach. Four or five sacks were duly filled but as we lifted each one in turn the bottom fell out! Only with great difficulty and struggling to hold the bottoms together did we eventually manage to load a reasonable quantity of sand, on top of which the women and children hurriedly clambered to return to town before dark.

The main purpose of my visit to the mayor had been to seek advice about the next section of the road. It was a very hazardous part of the journey, an extremely narrow road winding between gorges of rock and along the edges of cliffs. Earlier the mayor had said in true Latin American style 'My house is your house while you are in Taltal,' but now he looked at me and said: 'If you are going to take that route you must set out not later than three o'clock in the morning and cover the first fifty kilometres to the little fishing village of Paposo before daylight. It is essential for you to do that for then your headlights will warn any trucks coming in the other direction, otherwise they will just knock you into the sea. It is a very dangerous journey. It would be best for you to stay in a room at the restaurant opposite my shop and leave your car beside my petrol pump where my watchman will guard it.' This plan was settled upon. It was the advice of a sensible practical man and there was no disputing it.

Of all the rooms in Chile where I passed a night, the room in the restaurant was the dirtiest. I felt sure I would come out with more than I took in, and after a few hours' sleep I wasn't at all sorry to drag myself out to the car, at about a quarter to three in the morning. I found the watchman lying sound asleep on the pavement beside the car and gave him a dig to wake him up and let him know I was leaving. 'Esta bien, Señor,' he murmured, and turned round on to the other side apparently finding the cobble-stones a little uncomfortable. I rattled out of town and along the bumpy track, past the point where we had had the picnic on the previous day. Sometimes I knew by the roaring of the sea far below that I was running along a cliff edge; sometimes great shadowy forms on either side of the winding track indicated that I was passing through the rocky gorges that the mayor had spoken about. Once I thought I saw a light in the distance, but as nothing materialized on the road I assumed it to have come from a ship out at sea.

Gradually the forms around me became clearer and clearer and at about quarter to six I could see the sea in front of me and two little cottages built of sturdy rock. Along a narrow strip of land by the sea a little vegetation survived and goats and a few domestic animals appeared around the cottages. Together with a couple of fishing-boats this made up Paposo, a village marked on the map as having less than five hundred inhabitants. Not a soul stirred and the peace of another morning was broken only by the whispers of the now tranquil sea and the crowing of a cock, which seemed to herald my arrival over another treacherous obstacle in my journey. As always, however, when one difficulty had been overcome a new and worse one came into sight. On this occasion it came into sight before the existing one was completely over, for as I was driving down into Paposo I looked over to my right and saw in the distance a thin zigzagging line up the side of a cliff. This was the second and last severe range of mountains I had to cope with in the Atacama Desert. The track when I came to face it was narrow and very difficult, being set right into ledges in the cliff. The engine was on its best form, fortunately—there would not have been the slightest chance of turning the car round. My worst fear was that something would come down in the opposite direction; and so sharp and steep were the bends in places that I almost doubted if even the little Austin would scrape round. I had three things in my favour, however. First I started from sea level and so there was none of the effects of height to reduce the power of the engine. Secondly there was some slight moisture in the air which had a remarkable effect on combustion, a fact which many motorists who have experienced their cars running exceptionally well on a slightly moist summer's evening will appreciate. And thirdly the magneto was now giving excellent results.

In a little less than an hour I came on to a wide, straight but still steep road proceeding steadily on upwards. The only way I dared to stop was by backing off the road itself in such a way that I could come on to it again at right angles and so build up a little power before turning into the climb once more. I had been on

Too Much Water in the Desert

that part of the road for no more than ten minutes or a quarter of an hour when a convoy of four lorries came clattering down. The drivers shouted, 'Bravo, Señor!' as I passed, and other exclamations in Spanish. They were not noisy shouts, but full of encouragement and appreciation, and meant a great deal to me in that lonely and arduous climb. I climbed steadily for another two and a half hours before the road finally levelled out to reveal one of the most magnificent desert views of the whole journey: beautiful fine yellow sand spread out in gentle undulations as far as the eye could see, and a long straight track ran over it and also disappeared in the remote distance towards the port of Antofogasta, the biggest and most important port in northern Chile and the half-way mark in my journey over the desert.

I thought it had been quite a severe climb, but I was surprised when I read on one of the usual battered notices that I was three thousand metres above the level of the sea. Ten thousand feet is quite a climb when you start from the edge of the sea! To realize that I had that as well as the piece of coastal road from Taltal behind me by half past nine in the morning was to say the least of it stimulating, and revived my old sense that with an Austin Seven all things are possible! With that thought in mind I permitted myself the luxury of half an hour for breakfast during which the engine got a well-deserved rest and an opportunity to cool off, for there was still another hundred miles of blazing hot desert to cover and the day was giving every sign of becoming a scorcher.

From there on to Antofogasta it was just another day of normal desert travel. Despite the heat, the miraculous breeze from the north continued to keep the radiator slightly below boiling-point. I didn't dare to think what would happen if the breeze suddenly died away and left me to the mercy of the direct sun. I could no longer see the Pacific Ocean but I was conscious always that it was not far away, and as I travelled through that lonely sea of sand I found myself comparing my position with that of the Kon Tiki Expedition out in the middle of the ocean a few years earlier, moving patiently across its vast waters. For some reason or other the very lifelessness of the desert made me think of the teeming life of the sea. I wished that there had been a little pilot fish swimming underneath the car. I would even have welcomed a friendly smile from a shark! But as I jogged on towards Antofogasta sand and rock were my destiny for the time being, to-

G

gether with an occasional acceleration of my heart-beat as pre-vaporization of the petrol brought the car to a few temporary halts.

The road surface improved somewhat as I drew nearer to Antofogasta and in the middle of the afternoon I met a road-surfacing machine thirty or forty miles outside the town. The driver, poor devil, had to travel even more slowly than myself, pushing a great weight of gravel and sand in front of him. This, of course, was an opportunity to stop and chat that we were both eager to snatch. When I asked about the rest of the route, 'Ah, Señor,' he said, 'I have flattened the road out for you and you will have a good ride, and the last twenty kilometres is pavimento.' With that I waved good-bye and scuttled along at twenty to twenty-five miles an hour, humming some tune or other to the glories of speed. Antofogasta, I wanted to say, with a sort of childish glee, here I come. As usual my papers were checked by the Carabineros at the entrance to the town. My array of four christian names before reaching the surname caused confusion among the officials, who hadn't room for them all in their books and usually flung their pencils down before reaching Coleman.

Antofogasta is quite a large sprawling town with nearly a hundred thousand inhabitants, an inadequate water supply that is brought nearly two hundred miles across the desert from the Andes and a conglomeration of docks that make it the main copper-exporting port of Chile. A short piece of dual carriageway leads into the town, with palm trees lining both sides. After driving down this elegant avenue, I had to wind my way through the alleys in the dock area to find the service station I was seeking. To my great surprise I found that it was owned and run by an English couple who had emigrated from Peckham just after the war. They had not received notification of my arrival and were dumbfounded at the sight of an Austin Seven in Antofogasta. Once again British influence was in evidence, but more that of yesterday than of today. Yet another of Queen Victoria's tiled clocks had been presented to the town to impress upon the lazy Latin Americans the importance of the 'hora inglesa' by means of a structure where surface of dreary-coloured tiles made it re-semble a nineteenth-century public convenience turned inside out.

Two bits of bad news reached me while I was in Antofogasta.

Too Much Water in the Desert

First there had been flooding in the Camarones Valley in the north of the desert, caused by late and rather sudden melting of the snow up in the Andes. My chances of crossing that valley for several weeks or even a month, I heard, were very slender. Then, too, severe earthquakes had been reported in Peru. Arequipa, the second city of Peru, had been almost wiped out and an international relief fund for the victims had been set up. It was said that violent tremors had spread far around and what had happened to the roads in the south of that country was unknown. There was no point in waiting, however. It is always best to view such disasters on the spot; they often become exaggerated in the course of reporting.

A fine new paved road has been built from Antofogasta to the mines at Chuquicamata, in the foothills of the Andes. I was able to benefit from a hundred miles or so of this road running beside a far from new railway line. The smoothness of the road gave me the opportunity of an exhilarating race with what looked like a vintage railway engine. We were neck and neck for some considerable distance, before road and railroad divided and went their separate ways, and the engine driver and I exchanged parting waves of admiration and recognition of each other's potentialities. At the speeds at which I was travelling in the pleasant coolness of the early morning it didn't take long to 'knock off' a hundred miles of nearly level new road. Four hundred miles of the most desolate and rough track lay ahead. Only one moderate-sized mining camp, Humberstone, lay between there and Arica, the end of the Atacama Desert and also of Chile itself.

From the motoring point of view I was now about to face the toughest proposition so far. It was here that a great question-mark hung over both petrol and water supplies. It was here that I was told to expect long sections of road out of use. There was one point, I had been warned by the Information Officer at the British Embassy in Santiago, where the road appeared to go on but actually wound round the edge of a sheer drop. 'Be sure you watch out for it,' he said. 'Many an adventurous motorist has realized the need to turn only when it was too late.' According to my diary, however, the day was marked by nothing but the excellent running of the car. One day in the desert had come to be much the same as another and I lived and drove to be able to reach the next distinguishable mark on the map. In my mind's eye I saw an enormous egg-timer through which the sands were slowly running. On the track itself I saw not one but several points at which cars might easily have gone flying over the edge. But the low speeds at which I was forced to travel hardly made me regard them as serious hazards. In the late afternoon I descended into a small valley. A little red circle on the map indicated that a tiny village existed in the middle of this remote part of the Atacama Desert. There below me as I descended I could see a small patch of green less than half a mile long and not more than a few hundred yards wide, irregularly shaped and with a little stream running through it. One big house and several shacks in a row contained its isolated population. A few squares had been superimposed on the green, one or two for cattle to graze in and others for barley and beans.

After so many days of weary travelling in the sand, the sight of this little blob of greenery provided a welcome feast for my weary eyes, but not until they had blinked a few times to accustom themselves to the almost forgotten colour. At such moments one sees not just the patch of green before the eyes but the whole world of green things comes flooding into the memory—cool, beautiful and soothing after the blinding, intense yet impellingly attractive desert. I believe it to hold for human beings something of the same irresistible attraction that causes moths and other little winged insects to hurl themselves to their death against artificial lights, the attraction of light for all living things.

My list of people to contact for advice and assistance ended in Antofogasta and from there to the end of the desert I had to rely completely on my own resources. Occasional mining communities, I had been warned, were more likely to be hostile than helpful. My best bet was to contact the local Carabineros where they existed, and I looked for the green signs with crossed rifles on them. One of the police check points in the desert for tracking escaping bandits and criminals was situated in Quillagua. The two guards came out of the hut as I approached. 'What have we here, Señor?' came the friendly greeting as I pulled up, and I launched into one of my longer accounts of my journey up to that date, for often I had resorted to Tschiffely's time-saving formula 'I have come from the South and I am going to the North,' which avoided complicated explanations of where and what New York is, as well as the interrogation that might follow the explanation.

Too Much Water in the Desert

'You hope to get through to Arica, Señor, isn't that so? I'm afraid you will be disappointed.' 'Why?' I asked. 'First because nearly a hundred miles of the road has been destroyed and you will not have such good roads as you have had up to now to travel over. And secondly if you do get over that you will come to a flooded valley where no vehicle will be able to pass for at least a month.' 'I am used to difficulties,' I said, 'and I have made it my policy to proceed to the point where I can go no further and then to find some way of continuing. Right now I just want somewhere to stay the night.' He explained that there was one house in the village where travellers could stay but that it was very dirty and full of insects, and as he did so he pulled a face that said more than words. Not wishing to pick up any extra passengers, I suggested camping. All the land was owned by an Italian farmer who lived in the big house, and together one of the policemen and I went to see him. We knocked at the door of the old Spanish-looking farm-house and in a moment it was opened by a tall, dark man with kindly and dignified features. He came out, spoke rapidly to the policeman for a few seconds and looked at my car. He smiled and quickly agreed that I could camp in one of the fields on the farther side of the stream, whose presence alone brought life into this little valley. Over on the other side a track ran towards a gate that led into a small cluster of farm buildings. Behind them lay the fields to which he was referring. As we watched a boy with a couple of mules was opening the gate and the farmer shouted at him and pointed to me.

I drove away over towards the boy, who waited for me and then led me past several ferocious-looking dogs and into a yard where a number of hogs were busily rooting around. After passing through several more gates he showed me into a small meadow surrounded by willow trees. He seemed to understand nothing I said and the only indication I had that he wasn't dumb was a slurred 'Muchas Gracias', when I gave him a few pesos for his trouble. I felt very safe and cosy as I set up my camp kitchen and bathroom on the trunk of a large tree that lay beside the car. The dogs were there to guard me and the noises I heard reminded me of childhood holidays on farms. I prepared the car for spending the night in and after a fine meal I settled down to sleep. As I gazed at the bright southern stars the desert seemed far, far away. A breeze rustled through the trees and the stream murmured quietly in the distance as my journey became more and more unreal and with the whole panorama of life died gradually out of my weary mind.

Next morning I had trouble with the primus stove and was eating a cold breakfast out of tins when the farmer arrived. Did I want anything? Perhaps I needed breakfast? I thanked him and said I would be very glad of some tea to take with me in a flask as I wasn't able to make it myself. I tried to question this interesting hermit who lived with just his few servants on this strangely isolated farm, but was able to discover little except that he was contented. It was with regret that I collected my vacuum flask of tea and waved him good-bye.

One of the scavenging habits I had picked up was about to stand me in good stead. As I climbed slowly up the stony track on the north side of the valley the radiator began belching out volumes of steam. I thought it was a strange thing to happen so early in the cool of the morning and guessed that it couldn't be due to normal overheating. For that reason I investigated straight away. Once more the fan-belt had come off owing to the slightly uneven pulley drive which had never really been quite true since the beginning of the journey, and which was growing gradually more and more wobbly. Several attempts to replace the leather belt failed. It was then that I had the idea of cutting a band off a piece of burst inner tube that I had picked up in the desert. The rubber clung on much better than the leather, its only snag being that it couldn't stand the strain for more than two or three hundred kilometres and had to be continually replaced. In that way I travelled for over two thousand kilometres to Lima where I finally had a new pulley wheel made. What with the boards I was carrying either to sleep on or for getting the car out of trouble, and the rest of the bits and pieces I was collecting, I was rapidly assuming the appearance of a mobile junk shop. Far from trying to eradicate this impression, however, I studied what I could do to add to it; and I believe it did a great deal to save me from attacks by impoverished people who were able to regard me as one of themselves. Inwardly also the illusion often became strangely real, and I could never look at the local inhabitants with the detached superiority of the ordinary traveller.

Once I had climbed the hill the road seemed relatively good and little travelled over. Mile after mile of it continued so and I began to wonder about the warning of the police. They must be entirely mistaken, I thought, since they seemed to suggest that my problems would start as soon as I had climbed up the side of the valley. After that pleasant surprise of twenty miles of passable track, a notice by the side of the route read 'Provincia de Tarapaca': the last province of Chile but the most bleakly desolate and undeveloped. At this point the road began to deteriorate pretty rapidly and within another few kilometres another notice appeared. 'Carretera Destruida', it read, and road destroyed was what it meant. Sand holes began to appear, small at first but later getting gradually larger until they were as much as a hundred yards long and the full width of the road. To begin with I drove through them. The fine white sand billowed up in great clouds in spite of my slow speed and seeped through every imaginable crack in the floor. Unpleasant as the experience was I was even more worried about what this penetrating powder might be doing to the bearings and various parts of the motor. After changing the oil a little farther on, I looked in amazement at the sludge that came out and realized that I was running on a mixture of——oil and the Atacama Desert!

I soon noticed from wheel marks that other traffic had simply left the road and made its own way as best it could over the desert surfaces and between lumps of rock, weaving its way through and keeping the destroyed road in sight as a guide. I followed suit. Sometimes the wheel marks would lead to a dead end and it was necessary to return and guess at a better alternative. After some hours of this I happened to put my hand under the dashboard and found to my surprise that it was wet. A sniff, and I knew instantly what it was. The smell of petrol began to increase as it vaporized rapidly in the hot atmosphere. Tiny and innocent as the car looked, one little spark would have made it as dangerous as a block of dynamite. All the soldered seams of the petrol tank, which is situated just behind the dashboard and almost directly over the engine, were cracking with the constant vibration. I was carrying some material for stopping petrol leaks but the awkward position of the tank made it impossible to stop much of the leakage with it, and I resorted instead to chewing-gum which I had carried with me to chew in the mountains where it helps to prevent the onset of mountain sickness. The seepage was reduced and I disconnected the battery and ran on the magneto to reduce the chance of any accidental sparks behind the dash panel.

Too Much Water in the Desert

The day was wearing steadily on and progress registered itself in my mind not in kilometres but in stretches of a hundred yards or so. I would look at a piece of rock ahead, for instance, and for the moment make it my destination. For that moment it would seem like the end of my journey: everything beyond it simply disappeared from my thoughts. It was by a series of illusions of this sort that I saved myself from going mad. In the late afternoon I heard a high-pitched engine noise ahead and wondered what on earth could be approaching. Soon a couple of scooters came in sight. I learnt that the two Chilean boys driving them had come from the port of Iquique over to the west and were on their way to Antofogasta. It was easier to pick out a less bumpy course for two wheels than it was for four, but they also had trouble with leaking petrol tanks. We exchanged information about the respective parts of the roadless section that we had each covered and it appeared that we were roughly in the centre.

I covered a few more kilometres that day, slept the night in the wild, lonely desert and continued on the following morning. My petrol supply was dwindling rapidly. A couple of gallon cans in the back was all I had left when I came to the point where I could start travelling on the road again. The car seemed in a sorrier mess than it had ever been in before. It is pointless to list all the bits and pieces that had to be wired up to keep it together at all. The day went by with no special incidents and I made my gradual way towards Humberstone. The sun was getting low and preparing for the sudden change to darkness. Occasional patches of scrub appeared, which indicated that water lay somewhere beneath the parched surface. The little dust-coloured desert foxes, the size of a cat, once more darted across the road and every now and then a group of vultures could be seen busily devouring one of them. I was approaching another mining district. A track ran off to the east leading to Pica, a famous oasis in the desert noted for its orange and lemon groves and its old Spanish-style houses. I had heard that it was very picturesque and longed to visit it, but as I had only managed to cadge a couple of gallons of petrol off a truck during the day, I didn't dare risk it. Another police control point was set up at the road junction and a piece of amazing news awaited me. The floods were almost over. Only a few inches of water remained to impede traffic. I was to have no difficulty— 'Está bien ahora, Señor.' I could obtain no more petrol, but I proceeded with a lighter heart feeling that the news was a wonderful reward for my two days' struggle over the gap in the highway. Two little girls had been with the policeman. They had a large basket full of delicious oranges and the tiny lemons from Pica which are so strong that they make your face screw up as you lick them.

Night was impending and I would either have to find somewhere to stay or reconnect the battery to give me lights. When I saw a village half a mile or so off the main road, I decided to turn in towards it and try my luck. At the approach to nearly all the outlying villages in Chile the Carabineros have a little wooden office and beside it is set a pole that can be raised or lowered to block the road. In this instance the office had been broken up and the pole had been wrenched out of its socket and thrown to one side. There's no smoke without fire, I thought to myself, and proceeded rather hesitatingly. As I drove towards the houses I could see a building rather larger than the rest, probably the Almacén or village stores. One or two stray persons glared menacingly at me and a sudden impulse prompted me to think that the chance of the petrol blowing up would be a much better risk to take. I saw no point in heading into an unnecessary danger and swerved the car round just as someone had pointed towards me from the crowd; then I headed for the road wondering what the fate of the poor guards had been in this godforsaken village. The map showed some paved road for a few miles in the Humberstone district and I was soon rolling along once more at a reasonable speed with my headlamps lighting up the new black surface of the highway. Lights appeared in the distance and grew steadily closer and closer until I finally reached the entrance to Humberstone itself. The guards were not at their post but the barrier was up and both were completely intact, so I drove confidently on towards the rows of long low huts that looked more like an army camp than a town.

If policemen were in short supply, children were certainly not and appeared to me in all respects equally capable of performing their tasks. If a bandit had been entering they would have set up such a hue and cry that he would never have been able to silence them except perhaps with a machine-gun. I stopped and asked an intelligent boy of nine or ten if any English people lived there, thinking that the name of the place made it a reasonable chance.

'No English people,' he said, 'but there is a German engineer and I think he speaks English.' Within a few minutes and with an ever-increasing train of children joining on behind, we reached the engineer's house. He spoke about as much English as I spoke Spanish. Still I explained my presence and my problems to him and he quickly suggested that he would find me a garage where I could spend the night safely with my car. The only condition was that I was not to use fire of any kind. There was electric light and so, after securing the door as best I could from the inside, I prepared myself a meal and laid my bed out on the dirty floor. Feeling very much of a traveller of fortune I settled down to the last night's sleep in security and relative comfort I was to get for several days. No bright stars or rural sounds this time gave their poetical touches to my descent into unconsciousness; only a profound sense of thankfulness, with the image of the wrecked office of the Carabineros vividly in my mind.

Next morning I decided to check the car before refuelling and attending to supplies. The rear spring that had been repaired in Copiapo was broken again though in a slightly different position. I was starting to make a temporary repair with clamps and a wooden block when the German engineer arrived. It must be repaired properly, he insisted. I was to wait till eight o'clock and then bring the car round to his workshops. It was certainly a kind offer and it would have been stupid to reject it, but I felt impatient and that a delay in setting out might have serious consequences. The workshops were just another object lesson in the deceptiveness of appearances. They were several hundred yards away and I reached them by a bumpy path running through heaps of junk, which even included the last remains of a steam engine that had seen heaven knows how many years of valiant service in the blazing desert and had now found its final ignoble resting-place. We backed the car up a narrow passageway and four men came out to tackle the job.

I wanted to take the spring off myself, but they wouldn't hear of it. Two of them set to work, quickly sizing up the job and foreseeing the snags that I feared they might not realize. Unlike the Chilean engineer in Copiapo, the German had succeeded in instilling attitudes of caution and precision into his mechanics. When the spring was off he supervised the job of repair himself and had the spring reinforced with several steel bands. An excellent and careful job had been accomplished, but time, precious time, had been slipping away. It was well on towards midday when, with kind and enthusiastic farewells from the German engineer and the mechanics, I finally left Humberstone.

Several miles of paved road runs both south and north of the mining settlement. At the end of the paved road was another police check point. A further report that the trouble from floods was over was the good news I received there. Nevertheless it was not exactly with a light heart that I set out on the last wild section of the Atacama Desert. I passed through several ghost towns during the early part of the afternoon. Santa Catalina stands out most in my mind. Only the shells of rows of adobe houses still remain, crumbling away into gradual dust. The heavy roofs had fallen in. There were one or two shops and a bar also. The counter of the latter still remained intact and pictures still clung on the wall behind. A little carefully marked-off square of crosses at one side of the town indicated that fate had suddenly struck it and brought life to a sudden shaking halt, leaving an atmosphere almost reminiscent of ancient Pompeii.

As I jogged steadily away from the ruins a savage dog suddenly came hurtling out of them towards me. I shook a spare axle shaft at him and increased speed to avoid an unpleasant engagement. I was glad he hadn't discovered me during the few moments I stopped to glance at the ruins. I found it hard to make out what he must have lived on—there could have been neither food nor water for him. Possibly he had wandered out from Humberstone and was already half mad with hunger and thirst. I was never too keen on meeting dogs on account of rabies, which is reputed to be very common among them in the outlying parts of South America.

For the rest of the afternoon I went steadily onwards, feeling quite pleased with the progress I was making. My world consisted simply of desert and a road with increasingly deep corrugations. Still after my experience during the previous couple of days I was thankful for anything to which the word road or track could be applied even in the loosest sense. The sun was moving well over to the west when I reached the first of the great valleys in this northern section of Chile. I had hoped to reach the Rio Camarones before dark and wait there until a truck came along; a truck that could carry me across the floods pick-a-back if they turned out to be too deep for me to ford in the little Austin. My mind was set on getting there—too set, unfortunately. The valley that I was just coming to was called Tana. Half-way down, away over on a ledge which commanded a view of the whole valley, I could see a man sitting upright on horseback and wearing the broad-brimmed hat of the Chilean Huaso. I wondered why he should have stationed himself at that point, surveying all that might or might not be going on in the valley below. I had a suspicious feeling about him as I noticed that he had heard the noise of my engine and was glancing over towards me. I had no reason at all for such suspicion, except the possible presence of bandits, living by highway robbery, in these valleys. As I descended to the bottom of the valley I could see that he was following me down with his eyes, till I came to a point where a fast-moving stream, about fifteen or twenty yards wide, had burst its way across the road. A couple of large dogs were sniffing around the water's edge.

I had clear information that the water was only a few inches deep. I had been through numerous streams previously during the crossing of the Andes, and I decided it would be better to move slowly and cautiously into the water rather than getting out to test the depth. So, throwing to the dogs the remains of a tin of corned beef I'd opened for lunch, I moved into the water, hoping to get through and carry on quickly up the far side of the valley. It looked as though the reports about the depth of the muddy water were correct until, near the centre, the front wheels suddenly plunged downwards. Nothing I could do would hold the car back and within moments water was rippling about my waist inside the car. The fast-moving water had torn away the base of the road and left a deep treacherous gully. Cursing and swearing at the swine on top of the hill who hadn't warned me, I walked through the rest of the stream to test its depth. I looked back from the far side and there were the windscreen, hood and radiator cap rising out of the rippling water. I felt sick. Even that miserable hundred miles of roadless desert was infinitely better than this. Although a certain latitude has now been established for previously unprintable words, the most liberal censor, unless confronted with the situation himself, would take exception to my soliloquy during those few sickening minutes.

After the brief period of madness came the realization that the situation must be faced and some attempt must be made to get out of it. Though coping with the very reverse of fire and ashes (which might well have been my fate with the leaking petrol tank) the image of the phoenix came to mind. I waded back to the car and tried to push it through the rest of the stream. My temper began to deteriorate once more when I found myself quite unable to make it move up the steep side of the gully. I gave a vigorous wave to the Huaso above to come down and help me and was glad to see that he responded by descending slowly towards me. I didn't like him any better at close quarters but he waded in without too much hesitation and together we contrived, though not without great difficulty, to get the Austin into shallow water once more and then right out of the stream. My first concern was not really the car but to strike up some sympathy in my new companion. We talked about Chile and I said and meant many of the good things I told him. 'I don't like the Argentines,' he said when I mentioned that I had come through Argentina, 'they are boastful men,' and he screwed up his face to show his deep disapproval.

Evening was now drawing on and it was beginning to get uncomfortably cool, so I turned my attention to dry clothes and to the car. Fortunately most of my luggage was piled up on the back seat and was above the water level, and the bedding was in a waterproof plastic bag. I managed to find a pair of dry shorts to put on and then examined the car. Practically every working part had been under water. I took the sump plug out of the engine and several pints of water, followed by a little oil, gushed out. The rest of the engine oil had gone floating down the river. The same happened with the back axle. I poured water out of the carburettor and then tackled the worst problem of all, the magneto. Electrical equipment least of all can stand the presence of water and I was bitterly to regret that I hadn't managed to seal the magneto effectively. There were signs to show that the magneto might spark again but they were few and far between and it was getting too late to start drying it out.

The Huaso was taking a keen interest in the dismantling of the various parts of the car; and I had to struggle to describe each operation as I did it and explain the principles of the internal combustion engine in general and the function of the magneto in particular. One of the worst minor hazards was the presence of insects like large horse flies, which were prone to make a sudden attack every now and again and tear off a piece of skin in the shape of a letter H. Finally the Huaso said he must go, but that if I needed anything I could come to his house. I had no idea where his house was and I didn't trouble to ask. I felt it far too important to remain with my car and equipment. I merely laid groundsheets on the floor and back seat and prepared to spend the night sitting up in my sleeping-bag.

Darkness descended and all was still and quiet except for the movement of the water. I remained nervously awake as the hours went by. I looked at my watch just after eight o'clock and again at a quarter to nine. As I was about to look at it a third time, I suddenly heard shouts and noises coming from a gang of men on the farther bank. Two came wading through with their trousers off and sticks in their hands, prodding at the bed of the stream to find the best way across. Meantime I learned from them that their companions and their womenfolk were repairing a burst tyre before crossing. They were rough but friendly enough and I was glad to feel fairly assured that they were not a gang of thieves. At last they came splashing into the water and had no better fortune than I had had earlier, despite the height of their van. Although it was only a fairly small vehicle of its type and there were four men to push it as well as several hefty women and girls, it obviously required great exertion to haul it up the bank of the gully in which it was stuck. Realizing I could do little to help, I settled down in the back of the Austin once more and, to the accompaniment of yells and shouts and splashing of water, began to doze off from sheer fatigue. Suddenly I was woken by blinding lights glaring straight in through the windscreen. I wondered for a moment whether I was dreaming or if what I saw could be real. Dozens of people were milling round the car and the lights came from an old bus parked almost immediately in front of me. Plans were in progress to pull the truck out. People seemed to be everywhere. Several leant against my car but I sat still inside, disinclined to take the trouble to explain my position and problems in Spanish and feeling fairly confident that during the warmth of the next day I would be able to get moving once more. One old woman leant against the car puffing cigarettes and spitting every now and then. She was so fat that she made the car jerk violently every time she leant back and I wondered that she didn't succeed in pushing it right over.

Too Much Water in the Desert

At all events I was glad to have honest human company round me. I learned later that the reason for the presence of so much traffic at one time was that for a couple of weeks the water had been several feet high and only on that day had it become possible for any vehicle to pass. For that reason there had been a bit of a build-up of traffic. The bus pulled the truck out and towed it a few yards up the valley and round a bend, and then itself plunged through the water successfully. I was alone once more. The stars glistened in the dark night, but this time I felt neither safe nor comfortable. I felt like a sentry on guard as the long hours went by until finally I could keep awake no longer. At the crack of dawn there was a stirring outside and the noise of someone tampering with the sidescreens of the car. I sat bolt upright and saw two men trying to open the car door. With a sigh of relief I recognized them as the two I had met wading in the stream on the previous night. They had come to borrow a spanner to repair their petrol pump. I sorted out one or two that I thought might be correct. The men had spent the night only a couple of hundred yards away. Within minutes their problem was solved and I was left alone with mine.

I didn't bother with anything except setting immediately to work on the magneto. The water had permeated it more deeply during the night and it was as dead as a doornail. Within half an hour I heard the sound of heavy engines in the distance once more. Shortly two large heavily laden lorries came plunging through the water and pulled up beside me. There was a family in each and they were travelling in convoy. Furthermore they had read all about my journey in the newspapers and had been hoping that they might meet me. One of the men was a trained mechanic and insisted on taking over the magneto from me, while the women prepared a fine hefty breakfast: thick slices of ham, hunks of bread and large enamel mugs full of steaming hot coffee. I was as hungry as a horse but by the time I had finished I felt fortified to face anything.

For five hours my new band of companions remained with me making every attempt to get the Austin running. We fixed a biscuit tin up as an oven and set it on top of my primus stove, and baked the magneto in it. But all our efforts were of no avail. There was no room on their trucks for the Austin and I refused to leave it, so it was decided that they should go on and inform the British

Vice-Consul in Arica of my position and the nature of my distress. Meantime I dismantled the magneto once more and left it out in the sun with all my other clothes and belongings that had been soaked on the previous evening. Reassembling the magneto again later in the afternoon I put it back on to the engine and turned the handle. A miracle occurred. After a couple of spits the engine began to race away in perfect style. I grabbed all the things that were lying on the ground and threw them into the back of the car in one lightning operation, jumped in and started to put my foot on the throttle. At that very second it stopped again, but the mere fact of having heard it running for a couple of minutes was like an inspiration from the gods. My hopes ran high indeed. To cut a long story short, I managed to continue for only a few miles breaking down afresh every few minutes. Night came and morning once again. Hour upon hour went by but no further sign of human life appeared. I began to be worried that I should be forced to abandon the car and take what transport might come within the next few days.

Late in the afternoon a Jeep arrived. In it were two young men and a very pretty girl. They were students on vacation returning to the University of Santiago and spoke quite fluent English. It was an immense relief to be able to discuss my problems with someone in my own language. We made further attempts with the magneto which had once again become absolutely obstinate. As we worked away and talked an empty truck arrived. Reluctantly I decided to ask the driver to take me, car and baggage and all, into Arica. My adventurous student friends were getting a little concerned about themselves and said to me, 'Now we must say good-bye and leave you in the hands of this driver. The Chileans are very clever at arranging problems like this. We are sure you will be quite safe.'

We towed the Austin along until we came to a convenient mound of rocks, from which the driver, his companion and I were able to load it on the truck and secure it firmly with rope. We hammered along until we reached the Camerones Valley where the Chilean customs are situated. In the rest of Chile free importing is allowed. The sight of the Austin on top of a truck must have seemed a little strange to the officials but the formalities were completed with the utmost dispatch and good will. The three of us then repaired to a nearby truck drivers' restaurant. The meal

5a. Spanish Colonial architecture in Lima, Peru

5b. Mountain Indians with llamas 14,000 ft. up in the Andes

6a. Machu Picchu, the Lost City of the Incas

6b. Indian fiesta in the Altiplano

was a heavy fried concoction consisting mainly of rice, so I satisfied myself with some drinks and the memory of my breakfast on the previous morning—I had of course had various snacks from tins meanwhile. I learnt that the driver's companion was in fact a paying passenger, that he was studying English and had read translations of many English books and that he lived in Arica.

Before setting out again we picked up an Indian miner, who joined me in the back of the truck. He talked incessantly in spite of the constant banging and battering that was going on and I could only make out small snatches of his conversation. He was a communist and hated all governments which made him and his kind live in dejection and poverty. His mine was once owned by a British firm but had been bought by the Chilean Government. They were both bad but one was worse than the other but I couldn't make out which. I wondered once or twice whether the car would cause him to regard me as a bloated capitalist eligible for his liquidation list. Though I couldn't hear much of what he said I could see the fierce hatred that blazed in his eyes. Later when I saw where he lived I found it not difficult to understand. As this conversation was going on, the lorry jerked to a sudden and violent halt and the driver's companion jumped out, rushed back along the road and picked something up. It was an old chipped enamel mug, and the driver seemed delighted with the find. A little farther on the same thing was repeated and another mug was hauled in. At another point they found a plank of wood and at yet another an old oil-can.

The driver was remarkably good and careful, especially on the dangerous descents into the valleys. His every manœuvre seemed to correspond to the impulses that had become conditioned in me through my experiences with the Austin. I was surprised therefore when I saw him turn off the main route on to a track where a notice had been very recently erected, which read 'Motor vehicles strictly forbidden. Very dangerous'. A mile farther on we stopped at the bottom of a very steep hill. We all jumped out to survey the prospect. 'This is a short cut to Arica,' the driver explained; 'there are seven ascents and then a straight road downhill.' We all looked aghast at the sight in front of us. In numerous places the side of the track had crumbled away and in others heaps of rock had fallen over it. The driver made the decision and I was in no position to object. The climbs were fierce and the bends so sharp that the driver sometimes had to make half a dozen manœuvres before he was able to get round. That was the most terrifying part of all. The young man would jump out each time and shout 'Come on, come on,' to the cautious driver. He was getting on in years and his reactions were considerably slower than the young man allowed for. Several times the rear wheels were perched right on the edge, the back part of the tyre and wheel actually protruding over it. While the wheels were perched there I was perched on one side of the truck and the Indian was perched on the other, both of us ready to jump for our lives.

It grew dark and cold as we drove on towards Arica. At twenty past one distant lights appeared and a little later we were met by a ghastly smell that the wind brought from the direction of the port. I felt sick, doubly sick. Sick because of the filthy smell and sick because of the ignominious manner of my arrival. I had dreamed of approaching Arica in triumph, with a stirring sense of having conquered the Atacama. I had conquered nearly all of it, I knew, but I felt as though I had accomplished nothing. We drove around alleys between miserably stinking erections. Poles and sticks upheld every imaginable kind of material from cardboard and newspaper to rusty corrugated iron. Such were the slums of Arica. I was surprised beyond measure when we stopped outside one of these and the intelligent and well-read young man stepped down, to be welcomed by a woman and a dog who emerged through a piece of sacking in one of these dwellings. The contrast between the place where the young man lived and his conversation on the journey brought home to me the Chilean policy of educating the poor out of their slums before providing new homes for them. It is perhaps not such a bad idea when one remembers the coal-in-the-bath type stories which invariably arise around slum clearance schemes in our own country.

At about two o'clock, after dropping the Indian miner at another squalid hovel, the driver took me round to the service station where the staff had been informed of my venture. An Indian sat on a chair beside a row of petrol pumps. Everything else was locked up and he was there merely to serve petrol through the night and knew nothing at all about my arrival. 'Come back at eight o'clock in the morning.' The driver left his truck outside the garage and I spent the remaining few hours of the night sitting in the car.

Too Much Water in the Desert

The manner of my arrival could hardly have been better cal-
culated to avoid inspiring confidence in me or respect for the car
among the gang of dark-faced mestizos that staffed the service
station. What I suffered on behalf of the poor car as it was being
lowered from the truck defies expression. After that I seemed to
spend most of my time stuck down in the slum area trying to find
an electrician who could tackle the magneto. Several days went by
without any success, and I had to spend a considerable sum of
money on three abortive attempts at repair. Finally through the
Vice-Consul, who had not himself received my message although
it had been left at his office, I was recommended to try an old man
who saved bits of cars and was reputed to be quite a knowledge-
able electrician although not actually in the business. I visited
him with the Vice-Consul and we were invited into his drawing-
room, where he at once laid the magneto on the table and proceeded to dismantle it. After a few comments he announced that
he would have it in order on the following morning.

I could breathe again, and instead of looking at the dirty old
trucks and carriages of the State Railways of Bolivia, which ran
down the centre of the street where the service station was situated, I could now think about Arica itself. It was a free port and
attracted, I thought, the worst type of Chilean. Cheap goods
which the world had flooded in gave its small shops the appearance of a Petticoat Lane behind glass, and seemed to have in-
fluenced the minds of the business people. I was in no mood to
like the place, of course, but I doubt if I should have liked it
under better conditions. Although the port actually belongs to
Chile its main function is to give landbound Bolivia access to the
seas of the world. There is a more attractive side to Arica round
which I wandered on my last afternoon in Chile. The Plaza with
its few palm trees and Spanish architecture reminds one that this
cheapened port has seen better days. Farther round the sea front
stands the Hotel Pacifico, an important hotel in the days when big
air liners travelling from the United States and other South
American republics stopped at Arica airport on their way to
Santiago. Not far away is the Morro, a hill on which a famous and
bloody battle was fought between Chile and combined forces of
Bolivia and Peru towards the end of the last century. The Chilean
Government, realizing its need to own the Atacama Desert because of the vital importance of the mineral deposits for its

national economy, had summoned a group of lawyers and put into their hands the task of fabricating a justification for attacking the republics of Bolivia and Peru. A great army struggled over the Atacama Desert, attacked the Peruvian Army defending Arica from the almost impregnable Morro and drove far on up into Peru. It was thus that Arica became part of Chile and I could only reflect that I was glad that I didn't have to storm a fortress after my desert crossing.

On the following morning I collected the magneto, repaired and in excellent working order. I couldn't persuade the old man to tell me exactly how he did it, but he refused to take a single peso for the job and wished me Chilean good fortune for the rest of my journey. It seemed as though with the repair of the magneto my luck was repaired also. The sight of the little car running seemed to strike a certain awe into the attendants of the service station, a condition which was substantially reinforced when the mayor's son who had just heard of my venture came to visit me and offered to accompany me over the border into Peru. While I was getting ready to leave there occurred an incident which I've already mentioned. The foreman of the garage took me to the emigration office to have my documents stamped. I was a little unhappy about leaving the car in the street and glanced round as we were entering the door of the office. Four men were carrying the car bodily along the street. 'Look!' I said, and was about to bolt when the foreman grabbed me by the collar. 'Don't worry, Señor, they are only admirers.' And I had to grit my teeth and remember that I was in Latin America where people just don't worry.

VII

Earthquakes in Peru

'El Péru'—the land of the Incas, and of the historical romance that made it the heart of all that had attracted me to South America since boyhood; a land where Spaniards and Indians exist in more or less equal numbers, five million of each; and land of the Kon-Tiki Expedition; and of the great Lake Titicaca, so high above the level of the sea that the reduced air pressure allows the fishes in it to reach world record sizes, and along whose shores I would join up with the trails of Tschiffely once again to remain more or less with his memory for the rest of the journey.

At about three o'clock I was speeding over the new black road across the sandy wastes between Arica and Tacna, the first town in Peru. Adolfo was leading me on his motor-scooter as I left Chile, a country to which the length and variety of my experiences, both good and bad, had welded my feelings for ever. I had developed a sense that in moments of desperate need Chileans would not let a fellow human being down. Without their aid I should never have come through, so it was not without strong emotions that I saw their flag fluttering for the last time over the small customs house in the desert.

After passing through a kind of no-man's-land of sand for about twenty miles, we reached the Peruvian customs. The whole gang of officials there came out in full force. They were obviously a far less disciplined crowd than the well-trained and intelligent Carabineros of Chile, in spite of the fact that they wore uniforms of a much more fascist style, presumably a hangover from the recent dictatorship of Odria. Nevertheless they were interested and pleasantly disposed and once more I wasn't even troubled to lift my baggage out of the car. A few miles farther on we came to

118

fields in which peasants were at work tending the various crops which included the vines from which the rather second-rate Peruvian wine is made. There was little that was remarkable about the scene, and the peasants looked much the same as the peons in Chile. What was strange was that the scene itself should exist at all. It was not in a valley where a river would bring down water from the mountains and I thought myself to be in a region where rain fell not more than once in the course of ten years. But I learnt that, owing to the configuration of the Andes in the background, there is a small area around Tacna with a regular rainfall and moderate fertility.

Tacna is a much more solid and much more up-to-date town than any of those in northern Chile. There is a luxurious tourist hotel, there is a big agency for American cars, where the latest models were on view and where twenty to thirty mechanics were employed, and these together with rows of neatly painted and whitewashed houses and good quality shops gave quite an air of civilization, for some of the advantages of which I felt quite ready. After getting papers signed and stamped in four different offices to regularize my presence in Peru, Adolfo and I went to see the owner of the American car agency as I had a letter to him from his nephew in Arica, who was with the oil company that had helped me. He was a gruff old man and about to turn us both out of his office until Adolfo explained that I wasn't seeking economic assistance from him and I pulled out the letter from his nephew at the same time. 'You can keep your car in my garage,' he said, 'and my mechanics will be at your disposal and it will cost you nothing.' He gave Adolfo directions to his workshops and arranged to meet us there after I'd taken my luggage to one of the hotels. When we arrived at the big workshops, which looked more like a factory than a garage, with iron railings running along one side and a machine for the men to clock in at one end, the fierce old man summoned all his employees together around my car, and with a menacing glare literally roared 'No tocar!' (Don't touch!) 'Now,' he said, 'your car is safe, absolutely.' I thanked him and I felt quite sure he was right; indeed, I even detected a slight tremor in myself when I took one or two small things out of it before leaving to ride down to the hotel on the back of Adolfo's scooter. Adolfo was going to spend the night with his aunt and I was going to what I was told was the next-best hotel after the

Hotel Turistica. Although it lacked a private bathroom and one or two luxuries of that sort, it was furnished with modern furniture, had spotlessly clean tiled bathrooms, excellent food and excellent service at a cost of only ten shillings a night. An odd tremor during the night reminded me that Peru was a land that had just been shattered by a series of devastating earthquakes, from the worst of which, I realized later, my apparent misfortunes and delay in Chile had probably saved me. However, there was still much doubt about whether the road to Lima would be re-opened for some time. I recalled a phrase in the American Automobile Association handbook of South America: 'A road that exists today may be gone tomorrow.' They do add that new ones are constantly appearing!

I had no contacts for the rest of Peru until I reached Lima. The route lay across nearly a thousand miles of desert and a big question mark hung over the highway which until a few weeks earlier, I was told, 'was like glass'. I spent much of the next day with the mechanics checking over the car. Among other things, we took the petrol tank off and soldered all the seams very heavily, a precaution from which I derived a considerable sense of relief. I nevertheless found time to have lunch with Adolfo's aunt and to visit the Indian market with Adolfo, where I bought stores for the rest of the journey at very low prices. I shall always remember the incomparably delicious jams and toffees of Peru.

Early the next day, which was Friday, Adolfo led me to the outskirts of the town and put me on the road to Lima. If he hadn't had to return to the university in Santiago he would have accompanied me the whole way to Lima, and it was with much mutual regret that we had to say good-bye to each other. A signpost, new and shining, with the name of an American tyre company on it indicated that the distance to the capital was precisely 1,394 kilometres. Unlike Chile which has railways running the full length of the country, Peru has to rely on roads for communications north and south of Lima. The railways run only into the interior. As a result, the roads are good, although there is a miserable lack of signposts and a complete absence of safety precautions on steep and dangerous bends, and the Peruvian drivers are notoriously reckless. On that Friday morning, however, I had little to worry about. The car purred away at a fair pace over an excellent road. The scenery was similar to Chile, sand and rock. An artist might have noticed a certain dramatic immediacy about the configuration of the landscape, but perhaps it was just me for something was all the time saying, 'This is Peru!' The sandhills and rocks through which the road twisted all seemed to say it. I had been warned to fill up with petrol at every possible point because there were very few supplies available on the way to Lima, so when I saw a roughly painted notice that read 'Gasolina' outside a primitive village stores, I stopped at once and hurried in. The floor was made of earth and at one side a girl was cooking some excellent-smelling but dirty-looking concoction over a fire. Beans and bread and the basic necessities of life were on sale, and at one side of the shop stood a big rusty old oil-drum of about 100 gallons' capacity. The proprietor, who looked more Indian than Spanish, picked up a jug, a funnel and an old piece of filthy black rag. He filled the jug a couple of times and filtered the liquid through the dirty rag into my tank. 'Dos galones,' he said, for which I had to pay either a penny or two more or a penny or two less than two shillings. I was delighted with the price of everything in Peru. In Peru I was a rich man!

A small wing of the Andes sweeps down to the sea, and the main road which crosses it has been left unpaved for approximately fifty miles on account of the frequent landslides to which it is subject. As I bumped once more over the stones and corrugation the sensation of being in Peru became a little blurred and I kept thinking it was horribly like Chile. The benevolent wind which had kept my radiator from boiling in the Atacama Desert no longer blew, and my water supplies diminished rapidly. Fortunately there was a certain amount of traffic about. The first truck driver I met told me that he had just used up the last of his water supply and that he was hoping to get down to the village where I had bought the petrol before needing any more himself. The next vehicle I stopped was a colectivo, and while the interested passengers looked on, the driver poured some of the filthiest water imaginable into my radiator. Flakes of rust and bits of dirt flowed steadily in while I tried in vain to suggest filtering it. I was in no position to argue when the driver said something in Spanish that I thought probably meant, 'For God's sake don't fuss.' After reaching the top and travelling down a long rocky slope for some hours, I came to black tarmac once more and followed the road as it wound down into a fertile valley and to the

Indian village through which the River Tambo runs. Children
ran out of the houses and huts to look, for they were only used to
new cars and trucks! As I started climbing up the other side of
the valley I came to a petrol station. Three modern but dusty
pumps stood outside the half-finished structure of an up-to-date
garage. There was a restaurant also connected with the establishment. It was set under a flimsy shelter of reed matting. At one
side were several half-built rooms which were one day to be
bedrooms for travellers. The tables and benches in the restaurant
were of the type seen in an army cookhouse. When I went in a
group of people who had been watching my car with evident
interest beckoned me to their table and immediately ordered
coffee for me.

I had to tell the full story of my journey and, as I did so to those
attentive listeners, I knew that I was with men who could give me
first-hand information about the state of the road ahead. 'At the
moment it is closed,' one of them told me, 'but very shortly an old
trail over the mountains is going to be opened up as a diversion.'
He told me many sad tales of the destruction caused by the
earthquakes. In one place two hills had fallen down on a bus, and
along part of the coastal road the traffic had been completely cut
off, at one end by a tunnel which had caved in, and at the other
through part of the road along the edge of a cliff falling into the
sea. Lifeboats were coming in from the sea to rescue people
stranded on dry land! It all seemed a little topsy-turvy. When we
had finished talking my companions left me and hurtled off in
their American car, hoping to reach Tacna late that night, and I
was left alone. I glanced at the kitchen to see tin cans and vegetables strewn about the floor and a couple of rather dirty women
squatting on it and peeling potatoes. I decided that whatever I ate
there it would have to be well cooked, so I began by ordering
soup. I could gain no idea of what variety it was supposed to be,
but I named it ant soup because of the number of those insects
floating around on its greasy surface. I followed that with a tough
piece of steak and a bottle of beer. I asked the proprietor if I could
camp by the side of the restaurant, and after a cursory wash found
myself almost stretched out in the car and falling asleep to the
sounds of the generator which illuminated the establishment.

Next morning I filled up with petrol and made a very early
start, wondering what the day held in store. The first thing I

quickly discovered was a nasty tail wind. The radiator looked like a steam engine releasing the steam valve after a long journey. Little by little, I crept up the side of the valley avoiding a certain amount of overheating by stopping for breakfast half-way up. Some time later I came to a great sandy plain, level for many miles around. In the far distance a great bank of cloud had built up and above it were some enormous forms reaching a great way up into the sky. For some while, I couldn't decide whether they were clouds or mountains, but as the great forms remained still and the cloudbanks moved, I realized that I was looking towards the central range of the Andes. Never up to that time had I received such an impression of height. I had certainly not seen the equal of it in Chile or Argentina, although I had passed close to Aconcagua, the highest peak in the Americas. Later I arrived at the road junction near Vitor, where one road runs down to the coast and on to Lima and the other climbs up over a mountain to Arequipa, Peru's second-largest city, which was reported to be 70 per cent destroyed during the earthquakes and where the movement had centred and spread outward like the ripples on a pool when fish come to the surface. The prospect along the Lima road was extremely dubious and Arequipa, I guessed, would hardly be in the mood for celebrating the arrival of a vintage car. It almost seemed a little indecent to trouble them with my presence at such a time. Still, I learnt that there was only a fourteen-kilometre climb; the other twenty-six kilometres into the city was downhill. Furthermore some of the local people around the junction assured me that there were English people in Arequipa.

The climb was straight but exceedingly steep and I did it in conjunction with a lorry which was carrying a big wooden barrel of water. We both had to stop every few hundred yards. At the top I passed through a short tunnel blasted through the mountain, and far over in the distance I could see the great volcano Misti, at the foot of which lay the sad city of Arequipa. I had already noticed many signs of the earthquakes. Bulldozers had been driven through heaps of rocks to clear just enough space for a single line of traffic, rocks were still coming tumbling down on the road every now and again as I drove along and at one or two points landslides had claimed half the width of the road or left dangerous yawning cracks. As I came in close to the city I noticed several damaged buildings and great cracks running down the fronts or sides of others. I also noticed groups of people living in tents by the roadside, but it seemed to me that reports had grossly exaggerated the real situation; and it was not until later that I discovered that the heavy ceilings of many of the old colonial buildings had fallen in, killing the occupants and destroying the houses, but leaving little outward sign of the disaster. I pulled up at a garage well on in towards the centre of the city. It was Saturday afternoon and the place was closed, but two men were there working on their own cars. One of them volunteered to take me to an office where I could use a phone directory and try to contact the English people in the city, but most of them, he feared, would be down at the coast for the week-end. I tried the British Consul first, but I learnt from his maid that he wouldn't be back till Monday. I tried half a dozen other people before eventually ringing Vernon Foulkes, one of the senior executives of the Southern Railway of Peru, an English company. 'Come straight round to the house, it's the large wooden one by the railway station known as Casa Grande.' I pulled up outside the house and rang the bell and Vernon answered. 'You'd better bring your things in; everybody on crazy expeditions to Peru stops with us!' It was the sort of welcome I liked.

I had a shower, changed my clothes and brought myself broadly within the framework of respectability. The rapidity with which I dispatched each fresh plate of teacakes the maid brought in quickly destroyed that temporary impression, however, but the Foulkeses seemed to have complete understanding of my situation. The first voracious drives of my appetite were subsiding and I'd got to the stage where I could find time to talk between the mouthfuls, when suddenly a violent vibration set up throughout the house—the floor moved inches, backwards and forwards. 'Just one of the few daily tremors we're still getting. Fortunately they don't have much effect on our house, it always springs back to its proper position,' I was told. 'I must say that while I'm in Arequipa I'd just as soon be in a house that sprang back to its proper position!' I replied. I thought so even more when I examined the ruins in the centre of the city on the following day. The rows of fine old Spanish colonial houses are magnificent to look at both inside and out—some of the finest in South America —but the ceilings with all their beautiful gilded ornamentation are deadly in the hour of earthquakes. It was in one of these gems, preserved through several earthquakes, that I met John Harriman, the British Council representative in Peru. He was flying back to Lima on the following day and promised personally to alert the appropriate people of my arrival.

I wondered if I should climb up farther into the Andes by car and descend on Lima via Cuzco, the Inca capital. The idea was thrilling but, I soon learnt, absolutely out of the question. The rainy season in the mountains had started and I met a friend of the Foulkeses who had just attempted it in a Land Rover and had been forced to turn back. The road was under as much as three feet of water in places and I had learnt in Chile the Austin's limitations in that respect. There was only one practicable way of getting to the heart of ancient Peru and that was by train. The total excursion would reduce my purse by about twenty pounds but Vernon Foulkes promised to get me all possible reductions. We then launched into a more general conversation about railways in which I heard of his interesting experiences in Bolivia, a land which seems to deserve to bear 90 per cent of South America's reputation for revolutions. A charming and educated young Bolivian who was travelling down to Chile for the sailing regatta, had been telling me how they indulged in such habits as stringing their presidents up on lamp-posts. It was like the real Texas of the old days, he told me with an air of young and enthusiastic pride. Vernon had different feelings about it. He had only just escaped with his life. An army colonel of the revolutionary party in charge of the area where his railway headquarters were situated bore a somewhat murderous grudge against the company. Fortunately he had heard in advance of a plan to ambush the train and murder him, and was able to avoid it by starting the train off an hour early. The two managers who succeeded him disappeared mysteriously. The body of one was found at the bottom of a lake. It is a mistake, however, to imagine the Latin Americans as a race of wild and fearless people. They are just as afraid of death as we are. Vernon showed me a photograph of himself driving an engine back on to the line after it had been derailed at the edge of a precarious bridge. None of his Indian or Spanish engine drivers would risk his neck. Vernon had been a pilot in the Battle of Britain!

Early on Monday morning I found myself among the crowds thronging around the train for Cuzco. It appeared that every imaginable type of humanity was there. Indian women with loads of baggage like old gypsies forced their way competitively into the second-class carriages which with their open sides were little more than improved cattle trucks. I travelled first-class with the semi-respectables, and the wealthy business people and the occasional American tourist climbed into the luxurious Pullman coaches.

The whistle blew and the train puffed out of the typically English station of Arequipa. I had an odd carefree sensation. I didn't care two hoots if the train broke down. Someone else was responsible and had to see that I got to my destination. It was an incredible change and I gloried in the irresponsibility of it as we passed through the pleasant green lands around Arequipa. The trees were laden with fruit: oranges, lemons, peaches, figs and all kinds of familiar fruits. The homes along the railway line were ramshackle and slummy in the extreme as we passed close to the foot of the great Misti and on towards the interior ranges of the Andes. Although it is possible to appreciate the fantastic engineering feats which must have been accomplished to enable the line to climb slowly up the wide zigzags to the railway junction at Juliaca on top of the central Cordillera, this approach to the mystery-enshrouded kingdom of the Incas was anything but impressive. Brownish rocks, damp coarse grass and a grey clouded sky were more or less the total composition of the miserable scenery. Only at the little stations where we stopped on the way up was life really exciting. In this region the sullen Aymara Indians from around Lake Titicaca are found. And just as in the days when the Incas precariously succeeded in ruling them, they eat their lunch between ten and eleven o'clock in the morning. Thus all along the platforms and far beyond them the local Indians catered for the hungry passengers as well as for themselves. Pickled hearts were being roasted over charcoal fires by women in bowler hats of various shades of brown and black. Corn on the cob and pieces of roast crackling were being munched by passengers wandering around among the Indians. It was a sad, weary sight, in fact, although the strangeness of it made it novel and exciting enough for me. The filth alone would have appalled most people. After my illness in Chile, I was in no mood to experiment with Indian food; and the short stops gave me no opportunity to scratch beneath the steady exterior of these first sure descendants of the Inca's people I had met on my journey. The men lounged around and it fell to the women to do almost all the work. They cooked the food, they carried the small children in blankets on their backs and kept the bigger ones by their side, they laboured in the fields, they looked after the flocks of llamas and vicuñas and they spun the yarn while they did so. Not only were they not idle but they always seemed to contrive to be doing several jobs at once, with mechanical inevitability. The men seemed only to lounge and cadge bits of food from the women cooking over their fires. Only when they got involved in episodes of rather crude sex play with the women over their charcoal braziers, could one realize that these people had normal human feelings. The women seemed to treat their responses as an extra job to be added to the four or five they were already doing.

It was late afternoon when we reached Juliaca, a dirty Latin American town of a fair size but with nothing I could discover of interest, and deriving its importance mainly from the fact of being a railway junction connecting lines coming in from Bolivia, Chile and the southern lowlands of Peru. The small English community there had known about my journey even before the Foulkeses had contacted them and warned them of my arrival. A young man with a pronounced public-school accent and an umbrella made his way through the bustling crowds of Indians and their baggage to meet me as I got off the train. He had read about my trip in one of the motoring journals and now he was here to meet me and to take me to the scruffy little hotel at which he himself was staying in the main plaza of Juliaca. After supper we walked in the rain through the dirty wet streets of the town, across a conglomeration of railway lines and over a muddy field to a group of new houses. We were going to meet another member of the Southern Railway staff and his glamorous young Anglo-Burmese wife. The door was opened by a girl with jet-black hair and black eyes and wearing a brilliant red blouse and very tight black slacks. I had been told that they were a fantastic couple. After a few drinks and a severe attack on the whole idea of undertaking such a ridiculous journey in an old car like mine, they turned the conversation to social conditions in Peru. They were both vociferous socialists, a little too vociferous to gain my complete confidence. Nevertheless I was sure that most of what they said about social conditions in Peru was perfectly true: the iron class distinction of the aristocracy, the rough treatment of the mestizos or half-castes and the utterly deplorable conditions under which the unfortunate descendants of the fairly enlightened Inca Empire lived. Until recently, they told me, it had been customary for the wealthy families to disport themselves hunting an Indian exactly as a fox is hunted in England! The Inca descendants are now depraved and subjected to regular famines against which the Peruvian government makes little or no provision. When the Incas ruled all these matters were taken care of. Today the United States sends relief during famines; but such a deep distrust of white people has been engendered since the Spanish conquest that the Indians have come to believe that the aim behind the American aid is to fatten them up in order to boil down their bodies later to produce fats and oil for road building! Some have tried to escape the hardships of life in the mountains by saving enough money to travel by train down to Lima, where a few of them are fortunate enough to get jobs sweeping the streets of what struck me as the cleanest and tidiest city in the world. Most of the poor devils end up on the corporation rubbish dump where they make a living by salvaging and selling any useful articles which the refuse trucks bring in. They live on the dump under any sort of rough shelter they can construct. Some were even born on it.

Early in the morning on the following day I found myself boarding the train to take me to Cuzco, the very heart of the old Empire of the Four Directions. It was a thrilling journey to be starting in spite of the blow which meeting real Indians had inflicted on the Incas of my youthful imagination. To begin with the scenery was very dull once more: dreary stone villages, flat coarse grasslands as far as the eye could see and the drizzle from the same grey sky. It was impossible to believe oneself to be on top of the mighty Andes; not a hill, not a peak was in sight. I sat in the train reading *La Prensa*, the main newspaper of Peru, which I had bought on the previous day. Only at the stations did the commotion of life start up once more. Boys and women rushed along the carriages selling fruit and chewing-gum and sweets and papers and magazines. One man was also buying papers and magazines and I was surprised later on in the day when I was asked to sell mine. I handed it over expecting a mere trifle and was amazed to receive considerably more than I had paid for it.

7a. Part of the Pan-American Highway in Ecuador

7b. A typical village in the Ecuadorian jungle

8a. A stark view across the Andes in Ecuador, where farming is carried on at heights of over 10,000 ft.

8b. From a high precipice I suddenly gained a breathtaking aerial view of the jungle I had to cross between the bottom of the Andes and Guayaquil

Earthquakes in Peru

Honesty was one of the noted characteristics of the old Quichua Indians and of all the Inca's peoples. Their normal greeting was, 'Be not untruthful, be not a thief, be not idle,' and the response was, 'Be this the same for you as for myself.' I wondered how time and tribulation had dealt with this trait in their character and a little unintended experiment forced itself upon me later when we were passing through one of the silver-mining regions of the Andes. A boy of sixteen or seventeen came into the train selling silver ornaments and brooches at very reasonable prices. I selected two small and inexpensive brooches: one of an Indian woman in typical dress and one of the great condor of the Andes with his silver wings impressively expanded. I had only a Peruvian banknote worth considerably more than I needed to pay the boy and I handed it to him expecting to receive immediate change, instead of which he rushed off saying that he would get it. He disappeared so quickly that I assumed he intended to make off with the money, and when the train began puffing out of the station I was sure that my impression was correct when I suddenly saw a figure flash past the window and jump on the running-board of the train. Gasping for breath, he handed over my change correct to the 'sol' and jumped off the train which by then had gathered considerable speed. The natural sense of honesty of the Indian was certainly not dead.

Two incidents delayed the train's schedule and made us very late arriving into Cuzco. For about a mile we splashed through a foot or more of water. The sleepers were set up on a bank of rocks well above the surrounding countryside. The gravel road in Cuzco ran through the flooded fields beneath at least three feet of water in places. I saw exactly why I had been warned not to attempt the journey in the Austin and I was somehow pleased that I had the opportunity of reassuring myself with my own eyes. The flat scenery of the altiplano did not last all day. In the afternoon we came to a formidable climb. Several attempts were made to persuade the engine to pull its full complement of carriages up in one go, but each time the puff puff of the struggling engine became slower and slower until with a kind of final gulp it died out and we stopped. The driver eventually decided to leave half the carriages behind and to go back and fetch them later. This shuttle service wasted a great deal of time and meant that we didn't reach Cuzco until well after dark. It was a very great disappointment and only a little compensated for by the sun appearing for a couple of hours before darkness, to illuminate the attractive villages on the way into the great city where its rays had long been worshipped. The houses were like many others I had seen before in the sunny lands of Europe, and even more like those I was later to see in Mexico. Their orange tiled roofs glittered in the descending sunlight and once more the great rocky masses of the Andes created an awesome background for them, more suited really to the Inca architecture and reminding one of the incongruous work of the fifteenth-century Spanish adventurers. I saw none of the Inca ruins from the train, but I did see many signs of the amazing terracing and cultivation of the mountainsides, in which the Incas were so remarkably skilled. Land which one would have thought entirely useless on account of its sheer steepness was being made to yield rich fruits.

There was excitement in Cuzco. The railway station was all bustle and commotion. The Indians were wearing their cleanest brightest costumes. The variety of the feminine apparel was amazing. Hats varied from the bowlers I have already mentioned to tall hats of many colours, similar in shape to the traditional hats of Wales. The short Indian women bustled about proudly. I had arrived at the tail-end of a great display. The President of Mexico was visiting Peru and had just spent three days in Cuzco where fabulous displays of Indian dancing and tradition were held in his honour and to commemorate the common Indian background of the two countries.

I was in a city with a history that could run into many thousands of pages and still be drastically incomplete. It was here that the Temple of the Sun once stood, its walls lined with sheets of gold; it was here that Pizarro dealt treacherously with the valiant Inca, Atahualpa; here that the Friar Valverde had tried to offer Christianity to the proud Emperor and failing had run to Pizarro saying: 'You have seen the action of this haughty heathen dog? At him—I absolve you!' Tschiffely described the downfall of the Inca Empire in his book *Coricancha*, as follows: 'Pizarro—who like his men was a sincere though, according to today's standards, fanatical believer—crossed himself and bowed. Then stepping outside the door, he raised his sword—the fateful signal. Almost at the same instant the cannons in the fortress thundered, muskets and arquebuses responded, trumpets blared, and out of the many doors which faced the plaza, sprang soldiers yelling the old Spanish battle-cry: "Santiago y cierra España!" . . . In wild commotion, thousands of Indians, blind with fear, swirled round like so many harassed sheep.

'Spanish chroniclers who took part in this onslaught, maintain that although Atahualpa had sent his word that he would come unarmed, his warriors carried weapons concealed under their clothes . . . Some eyewitnesses contradict these statements, declaring that the Indians were entirely unarmed . . . The tightly serried mass of panic-stricken Indians swayed to and fro . . . Three hundred were trampled underfoot, and the onrush was so violent that in a matter of seconds, a heap was formed against the wall, causing it to collapse.

'Seeing their monarch fall, immediately to be hustled into a house as a prisoner, the horrified Indians scattered in every direction. By this time it was getting dark, and when the massacre came to an end, as suddenly as it had started, a heavy, cold rain began to fall, drowning the moans of the wounded and dying Indians who lay thickly strewn about the plaza. The sun had set for the last time on the Inca's Empire, and the icy blasts from the mountains sang its threnody.'

Such, as it might be seen in the briefest newspaper headlines, was the end of the great Inca Empire with its odd combination of Imperialism and Communism. I had three days in which to see all that remained of it and I had to act like an American tourist. In fact Vernon had very kindly arranged with one of the tourist agencies for me to 'do' Cuzco and its surroundings at special cheap rates. The first afternoon I set off in a taxi to visit some ruins outside Cuzco with two American tourists and a portly young Canadian who owned a textile factory in his own country. It was raining slightly and the Americans were anxious to get back to their hotel. The Canadian expressed indignant feelings about slavery in the Inca Empire. I suspected his heart really went out much more to the poor Inca slaves who had to lift the heavy stones of the buildings we were looking at, than to his own employees. I tried to argue that the stones were really not very big and contrasted most strikingly with the great monolithic structures of many ancient civilizations. I tried to argue that the Inca civilization was a highly organized working society but not a slave society in the whip and tyranny sense, and that in any case they had much more real freedom under the benevolent dictatorship of the Incas than they have ever had since. Argument was fruitless against a great burly fifteen-stone Canadian who could almost see the Inca's poor subjects dying under the cruel lashes of the whip, as he looked at the very modest little temple of the waters. I wondered as a matter of interest how he treated his own employees.

It is craftsmanship rather than art that has struck all those who have examined the Inca ruins. One marvels at the manner in which blocks of stone of varying shapes are made to fit together so closely that they need no cement and so that it is scarcely possible to push a cigarette paper between them. What art there is lies in the marvellous variety of shapes, the constant surprises that the eye gets as it runs over the simple and solid blocks of stone which still remain as the foundation of many of the Spanish colonial buildings in Cuzco. My greatest determination was to see Machu Picchu, the Lost City of the Incas as it has come to be called, but now thought to have been one of a series of city fortresses to protect the empire against invasion and raids by the savage Indians of the jungle. It will be plain that tourism is pretty highly organized in this area and that it lacks a great deal of the natural grace of the Indian towns in Ecuador, for instance, which are too cut off for ordinary curiosity to make the effort to reach them. A small diesel train left from one of the stations in Cuzco early in the morning to climb over the mountains and run through the Urubamba Valley to the little collection of shacks at the foot of the peak on which Machu Picchu is situated. It was a highly international party that was setting out that morning and very different from the two Americans of the previous day. There were middle-aged as well as young Peruvians, there were Chileans, Bolivians and a number of Americans including a student with a large bushy beard like my own, of whom I shall have a good deal more to recount later. Everybody struggled to converse with everybody and, to start things up, songs of all the countries represented were sung. That was followed by some very interesting discussion on international affairs in which the Chileans took a prominent part. Once again I was struck by the intelligent, thoughtful and sober outlook of the young university people of the Latin American countries and I noticed here, as in almost all the other parts of Latin America I travelled through, that nobody seemed to be in any kind of fear of expressing what he thought.

Earthquakes in Peru

They explained with precision exactly what they admired about the United States and also expressed plainly and without resentment what they considered to be wrong with relations between the United States and Latin America. They believed that both Russia and America must learn to recognize the real and full meaning of individual and national liberties, but they affirmed distinctly that the Latin American countries wish whole-heartedly to maintain the friendliest possible relations with the United States.

I was struck by two examples of almost unconscious American bigotry. We stopped at one village right beside some Indian dwellings. The family in the hut just outside the window was obviously desperately poor and one small baby was crawling round with an enormously swollen stomach. I was sitting next to an elderly American doctor. 'If my wife was here,' he said, 'she'd be in tears over that, but I believe that the good Lord is wiser than we are and he means it to be like that.' And so saying he passed a bag of sandwiches which the hotel had prepared for him, but which he couldn't eat in case the butter in them was contaminated, to one of the Indian children who came up to the side of the carriage. It is remarkable how these children will touch nothing that is given to them, but take it straight back to be put in a common family pool. The second piece of bigotry was political. A respectable type of middle-aged American woman became involved in some political argument which turned on the problem in Cuba. She came out quite unconsciously with a statement that shocked me: 'What right has Castro got to say what he wants? We could blow him to pieces in five minutes.' What an anomalous question for the citizen of a country 'Conceived in Liberty and Dedicated to the Proposition', etc.!

After stormy and fundamental debates, we arrived at the little station of Machu Picchu in a village which Woodcock has aptly described as looking like a row of unpainted chicken houses straggling for a hundred yards or so. We were now in the Urubamba Valley, deep in the jungle and standing beside one of the primary tributaries of the mighty Amazon. High on a vast peak above the station stood the Lost City. Along those very parts, in the days just prior to the First World War in Europe, the American archaeologist, Hiram Bingham, was wandering dejectedly. He had read of a lost city of the Incas in the old Spanish chroniclers and he had searched for it at terrible peril through these dangerous jungle regions where the venomous fer-de-lance and the most deadly of jungle animals and insects abound. His search had been in vain and he was returning having given up hope when by chance he started to talk to an Indian who told him he was growing maize on the hillside among the ruins of ancient buildings. It was little wonder that Bingham was prone to exaggerate the importance of his city. He wanted to make it the most important city of the Inca Empire, but for many reasons it is plain that this is not the case and present archaeological evidence seems to point to the theory that it was one of a string of great fortresses defending the empire against a jungle which the Incas must have thought stretched to the edge of the world. Our guide was to have many colourful variations to add to the themes of the archaeologists and it will be best if we return to the trucks that were waiting to carry us up the mountainside.

Until very recently the tourist had to make the hard ascent up to Machu Picchu on muleback, but today he can do it in one of the trucks or microbuses which run up the steep zigzagging track to the new tourist hotel situated right beside the ancient city. It's a little hair-raising, or at least I found it so, on account of the fact that one is at the mercy of some unknown foreign driver. At last, just as you reach the top, the tiers of grey buildings which once contained the mysterious life of the Incas come into sight. You have some refreshment while you are waiting for your guide. You can go either with a Spanish or an English speaking guide. I naturally chose the latter. I noticed the American with the fine bushy beard drifting in towards our party. I wondered why he didn't join us boldly. Woodcock's remarkably accurate description of Machu Picchu was in my mind: 'Eventually we reached the highest point of the town, where the sacred dial stone called the Hitching Post of the Sun cast its sharp noon shadows among the temples. From the watch platforms we looked down over the grey contours of the city and the green cliffs of the mountains plunging into the valleys ... The view was dominated by Machu Picchu's sister mountain, Huayna Picchu; along the knife-edge ridge that joined the two peaks a path ran as precariously as a tightrope to a nest of Inca terraces on the very tip of Huayna Picchu, where a watch post had been built that could only have been reached by climbers of skill and nerve.

'The most immediately impressive aspect of Machu Picchu was undoubtedly its setting, and this tended to divert one's attention at first from the city's interest as a kind of Inca Pompeii, preserved by the jungle instead of by lava. It was in fact a carefully arranged community, protected by ramparts and ditches guarding the gentler slopes and by watchtowers hanging like swallows' nests on the more precipitous sides. Within this protecting circle life could be self-sufficient; there were terraces large enough to feed several hundred people, an elaborate water system which was still functioning when Bingham discovered the city, and a residential area arranged according to industries.'

Through all this our guide took us and he gave us detailed and lucid information. He was a man with a university education, had been educated partly in America and had obviously delved deeply into the whole subject. He told us of the long treks he had made along the old Inca road, now jungle covered, leading over the mountains into Machu Picchu, but I noticed that he was anxious to shake off the ladies of the party, who were in any case wearied by the exhausting atmosphere of the montaña. When he had the men alone, he told us that he agreed that the city was almost certainly primarily a fortress; it was obviously not a city in the normal sense of the word for its water system alone made it impossible that more than about six hundred people should have lived there. But if it were just a fortress against the jungle Indians why should that elaborate temple to the sun be there? Why should there be such extensive quarters for the virgins of the sun? Therein, he thought, lay the very natural and human clue to the purpose of Machu Picchu, over which the archaeologists argued their colder theories with such slender threads of evidence. He proceeded to tell us a most fantastic series of tales, which he claimed to have found in the old Spanish chronicles, of the Inca testing the integrity of certain Spanish priests with the assistance of the virgins of the sun in a remote city in the jungle. He thought that there was sufficient in these accounts to identify the city in the jungle with Machu Picchu. But he was not satisfied with this; and he took us to the sacred dial and asked us if we did not think that the mysterious stones on this terrace looked like phallic symbols. 'Here,' he declared, 'the Incas and their aristocracy held their orgies with the "virgins". How, Señores, could pure ladies have known how to tantalize the Spanish priests?' Machu Picchu was the 'week-end' holiday resort of the top people of the Empire! If there is any truth in that theory, it should be pointed out in fairness to the rulers that in spite of their work-laws and organization of the movements of their people they did not impose a severe sexual morality on *them*.

Beards and the confiding atmosphere in which the guide's information was imparted finally brought the American student, Clayton, and myself into direct conversation. I learned that Clayton had not joined the tour but simply bought a train ticket and come up on his own. I was to learn later that he had carried the methods of tramping around the world on next to nothing to an absolutely fine art, which made my fumbling attempts at being economical look like reckless extravagance. Clayton was unable to get into the booked diesel carriage taking back the party on the tour, so we travelled down together in a separate carriage. I told him briefly about my journey and then I listened with interest to his story. He had covered much of the ground that I was about to cover by diverse local means and usually at a negligible cost. Most startling of all he had to say was his account of a three days' walk through part of the Darién Jungle. He carried nothing with him except a canvas bag of the type people often carry tennis rackets in. It looked half empty and it was. The only things I saw in it, apart from a toothbrush and one or two small necessities, were a plastic mack and an alarm clock. It had a kind of empty droop about it as if suggesting that the idea of carrying any equipment at all was really rather absurd. 'What about wild animals when you were in the jungle?' I asked him. 'Oh, I never managed to catch them. They could all run faster than I could . . . I was going along by the east coast. At night I slept on the sands and I frightened all the animals away during the daytime by hitting the undergrowth with this bag. I made 'em think a very big animal was coming after them.' It is very true that loud noises constitute one of the best means of protection against wild animals.

Back in Cuzco I decided to go with Clayton to his 'hotel' for dinner. He paid ten soles a night for his room, which is about half a crown, and for the same sum you could buy the most sumptuous meal that the establishment could provide. I was curious to see his room so he took me there first. A badly lit and badly ventilated hall was partitioned off into small cubicles, the walls of each going up to about five feet. In each there were two beds, but up to then,

Clayton told me, he hadn't had to share. While we were talking, however, a man walked in and, after some 'Perdone Señor-ing', put down a bundle of luggage on the empty bed and walked out again. We also went out to have our dinner which consisted principally of a slightly tough but perfectly edible piece of steak. We spent the rest of the evening drifting about the back alleys of Cuzco getting the atmosphere. It was quite odd how little groups of Indian girls would burst into fits of hysterical giggles at the sight of our beards, and begin prodding each other to intensify their amusement. We were obviously tourist attractions come into their very homes! Nothing much really seemed to be going on. Once it became dark we saw nothing more than the occasional Indian come out of one door, scamper along the narrow street and disappear into another. Perhaps they'd all worn themselves out during the President's visit or perhaps it was just the provincial rut they'd got into since their town had ceased to be the capital city of a great empire. I said good-bye to Clayton. I had to leave on the following morning and he wasn't sure when he was going to leave, but there was a slight chance that we might meet again at Puno on Lake Titicaca.

Early the following morning the train steamed out of Cuzco to follow the same route I'd covered in reverse three days earlier. There were many more Indians travelling in the train that morning. I was glad I was not in the second-class carriages which were like cattle trucks and must have been desperately cold. I had no objection to the Indians but I did take exception to the old man who came and sat beside me. He was suffering from a chronic cough and constantly spat on the floor so that it would have been difficult to walk past his seat without treading in the green saliva which he was so constantly ejecting. I eventually managed to find a seat beside a fat old Indian woman. It was hard to realize that there was a spare seat because she and her bundle of baggage filled much more space than would normally be covered by three or four people. She readily moved the baggage, however, when I asked. In the afternoon she got out at one of the villages on the line and I was left with a free seat to myself. It was desperately cold in the train. A party of four priests were playing cards at a table a little way down the carriage. Nobody seemed to dare to request the godly men to close their window which was as wide open as it was possible to have it. How they stood it themselves I hardly knew, but perhaps they like heaven to look directly down upon their innocent pastime. Whatever their reason, I decided I would have to do something about it, but when I got up to walk down the carriage I was suddenly surprised by the sight of Clayton's beard and his old canvas bag. He'd been in one of the open carriages and could stand it no longer. He sat beside me and I omitted to say anything to the priests. Clayton, however, was not slow to feel the draught and quickly jumped up to deal successfully with the priests.

How was it that Clayton always seemed to go one better than I did economically and still get much the same results? When the ticket collector came round he contrived not to notice that Clayton's ticket was the wrong colour. It cost approximately half the price of mine. It was dark as we passed through Juliaca. The poor illumination of the town stretched for a considerable distance each side of the station and made me realize the size of this important railway junction. I was fed up. We were hours behind schedule and the ticket collector made me pay an extra fee when we alighted at Puno because it wasn't marked on my ticket although I was sure that I'd paid for it. Clayton's yellow ticket he accepted without a murmur, not noticing that he'd just stepped out of a first-class compartment!

As one leaves the station at Puno one is almost knocked over by boys fighting to carry one's baggage. I had to find the station hotel so I let one of them carry mine and paid him a good deal less than the rather preposterous sum he asked for when he'd done it. The hotel was being rebuilt and I got an old room opening out directly on the street at the side of the building more or less at Clayton's sort of figure. He'd already drifted off because the look of the new front of the Station Hotel had frightened him, and we had arranged to meet early on the following morning to try and get into some kind of boat on the lake. I felt quite positive that I wouldn't be running myself into any kind of undue expense by agreeing to this plan. I had a meal at the hotel and set out to see the little Peruvian official who was in charge of the two steamers which ply the hundred-odd miles across the lake. The Foulkeses had recommended me to see him, assuring me that he was a delightful character. When I knocked on the door of his house he was busily drinking whisky with a stout and affable Spanish friend. He spoke no English but my Spanish rapidly improved as he insisted that I should join the party. Indeed I had never been so highly complimented on my Spanish. He presented me before leaving with a wonderful miniature model of the Indian balsas which are still used on Lake Titicaca. It was made by Indians and constructed out of the very same reeds that the real ones are made of. I was exceedingly sorry when I found I had lost it later in the journey after being mobbed by a gang of robbers. I should have felt it more had I not been so relieved to realize that I myself with all my essential equipment had escaped intact.

Whatever kind of whisky it was it certainly did me no good and I felt I had to ascribe to it the sickness I suffered in the night. I didn't get to sleep till almost daylight and I was woken in the very early morning by artillery fire, the tramp of soldiers and rifle shots. The soldiers were in the street immediately outside my door. 'O my God,' I thought as I sat bolt upright in bed, 'there must be a revolution going on outside. I'm in Latin America and I can't expect to escape it any longer.' I forgot all about my tiredness and sickness. In due time I got dressed and when the commotion immediately outside died down I slipped out of my door, ran hastily along the street and dived in at the main door of the hotel. In the dining-room everything was proceeding with such an air of commonplace unconcern that I was completely taken aback and felt unable to put the question which had been burning in my mind until a few moments earlier. I now felt I had to say something like: 'It just occurred to me to wonder if the noise that was going on outside might possibly signify any sort of slight disturbance in your town?' But to render the correct nuances in Spanish was beyond me in the cold light of morning, and I had to content myself with simply asking what the noise was. The waiter explained that there was an army barracks opposite the hotel, which had a small rifle range behind it, and that one of the biggest artillery ranges of the Peruvian army was situated only a couple of miles outside town. That, of course, explained it all.

Clayton arrived. We went off to the shipping office together to inquire about boats. Clayton was interested in a short trip on the lake but he was also interested in travelling in one of the steamers to the other side. He was intending to travel to La Paz and then to cross Brazil in one of the trains running from the Bolivian capital to Rio de Janeiro. He was hoping to arrive there in time for the celebrated Easter Festival. There were no small boats for short trips and Clayton refused to book a passage on one of the steamers, partly because it was too expensive for him and partly because they only sailed at night and the chief point in doing it by boat was to see the lake.

We were now within walking distance of the highest navigable body of water in the world, a veritable sea in the sky, 12,000 feet above the earth's other seas! It is a great expanse of water enshrouded in ancient mystery that goes back for many thousands of years. According to one of the Inca legends the first Inca rose mysteriously out of its vast waters. But as we looked at it it was not impressive. It was a grey morning and our view out on to its distant waters was obscured by the general paraphernalia of the shabby docks. We wandered around looking for boats, without success. Clayton thought we ought to have some lunch and then set out on a serious wander. We went to the market-place where he wanted to buy an enormous trout. His mouth fairly watered for it and I felt very regretfully forced to tell him that my stomach was quite unready for more than a small portion of it. I knew I could only cope with a very light lunch and I felt more like trying the new tourist hotel. Oddly enough the idea did not appal him; the sudden longing for that trout had loosened his purse strings in quite a miraculous fashion.

After lunch we started walking along the stony track which leads round the shores of the great lake towards the Bolivian border. We didn't quite know what we were intending to do. Clayton even thought of trying to get an Indian to ferry him across on a balsa. That was certainly a romantic idea, for it was improbable that any Indian would risk going right the way across and back again in his feeble reed craft; it was a hundred miles each way. At any rate we had no success with the one or two we tried. Bad storms can sweep up out on the lake almost without warning and I think the Indians take care not to be too far from the shore in their small craft constructed solely of bunches of reeds tied together. The other idea that Clayton had was to hitch a lift on a truck going into Bolivia. As we walked along talking and thinking together, I suddenly recalled that we were on the very track which brought Tschiffely and his horses, whose trails I had departed from just outside Buenos Aires, back on to the route I was to follow for most of the rest of my journey to New York. At one point we walked across a patch of cultivated land which was being tended by an Indian, and went right down to the muddy edge of the lake where we discovered an old abandoned balsa. Clayton was seriously thinking of trying to use it for his journey. I knew that it was abandoned because it had become waterlogged, for those balsas normally have to be abandoned after only a few months of life. He was not to be put off, however, until the Indian assured us that we wouldn't travel more than a few metres in it before it went to the bottom.

The sun shone brightly on the lake as we trudged along, hardly able to realize that we were really in such a mysterious part of the earth. A lorry came towards us and Clayton put up his hand to stop it. I instantly felt that the moment had come to say good-bye to a fellow adventurer whose path had suddenly and out of the blue crossed mine and had filled in bits of the blank mystery of the rest of my journey with tales which added to my feelings of what lay ahead. Even now I always think of him as sitting in an old-fashioned train puffing slowly across the jungles of Brazil, probably in greater comfort than his inexpensive ticket should merit. He jumped on the lorry and I started to retrace my steps alone. My immediate future was secure. I had a sleeping-berth booked on the train back to Arequipa from where my motorized adventures through the earthquake-shaken country of southern Peru were due to begin again on the following morning. While I was thinking black clouds were forming rapidly in the sky. I feared I should be almost drowned in one of the torrential storms of the Andes when a little truck of the Puno town corporation came rattling along over the track. Although the front cabin was full they somehow made room for me and seemed to enjoy listening to my story as we returned speedily to Puno. I passed down the Andes during the night oblivious of the steep descent from the great altiplano of Peru, after what were really only a few fleeting glimpses of that strange land where some of the most curious scenes of mankind's history have been enacted. They had been brief and inadequate days.

As daylight began to stream through the compartment window, I could see that we were passing the foot of the volcano Misti and puffing rapidly into Arequipa once again. Back at their house I said a hasty good-bye to the Foulkeses, drove out through the centre of Arequipa where I hurriedly took a few snaps and almost before I knew what was happening I was suddenly dealing with mountains again myself. Only a few hours earlier I had been sound asleep in a comfortable railway compartment, now I was listening to the temporarily forgotten throb of the little Austin engine coping valiantly with that range of the Andes which separates Arequipa from the Pacific Ocean. For a few days the journey across Argentina and up the Atacama Desert had become like an unreal dream. Now Cuzco, Machu Picchu and the mysterious lake were abruptly cast into the world of unreality in my mind, before the shatteringly real spectacle of mountain roads, rock-scattered and with gaping cracks from the recent tremors. I experienced a new and sudden sense of continuity with the earlier part of my journey. Before long I had accomplished the climb, with rather less difficulty than usual, and was descending again to the road junction at Vitor and taking a fresh stretch of road across the desert towards the sea. There was in fact very little in the way of human habitation in the thousand kilometres between Arequipa and Lima. It was a tough prospect and the condition of the road for the first couple of hundred miles along the coast was very dubious indeed. For the first part of the route across the desert the road was excellent and unaffected by the earth movements. My first trouble arose through lack of signposts. The excellent tarmac road suddenly split in two, and two equally excellent roads lay ahead of me. The map showed only one and I had no idea which fork to take. There were three sinister-looking characters in ragged clothes standing at the junction wanting a lift, and since I had no room whatsoever I thought it best to race past them as quickly as possible. I just managed to catch sight in the mirror of one of them waving either a stick or a knife at me. At a glance I was unable to decide which, but whichever it was I was not sorry that our acquaintance had been no closer.

I kept wondering as the kilometres went by if I was on the right route. There was neither man nor beast on that barren road, from whom I might inquire. Sand and rock alone skirted the long black tarmac route on which I was racing. At last as I started to climb down into a valley the rock not only skirted the road but also formed a great barrier about four feet high. It was a minor crisis. I thought I might possibly get over it in the downhill direction, but I would never be able to climb uphill over it, and supposing I was on the wrong road! I couldn't stay still so I was forced to

gamble on it. It was a double gamble really because I wasn't at all
sure that I wouldn't either get the car stuck on the ridge of the
rocks or even break it in two on them. In a moment I was on the
other side and just beginning to proceed when I heard the noise
of a heavy engine in the distance. I stopped and way down towards the bottom of the valley I could see a lorry moving steadily
up in my direction. I waited until it arrived and asked the driver if
I was on the right road to Lima. When he told me that I had to go
back I wanted first to distrust my translation of his Spanish, but
when he pointed in the direction I'd just come from, I couldn't do
that any more and began to want to believe that he was just an
ignorant lorry driver and was mistaken; but both he and the man
he had with him were insistent that I must return and take the
other road at the junction where I had seen the three sinister
characters. I think they saw the doubts in my mind written on my
face. They did not try to convince me, but went to the back of
their truck and made a pleasing selection of the delicious fruits
they were carrying—oranges, lemons, figs, peaches, melons, etc.
—and proceeded to put it in my car. They seemed to sense that
this would (*a*) give me confidence in them and faith in their
advice, and (*b*) help to compensate for the mistake I had made. I
knew that I had to turn back, but not until they had helped me
over the pile of rocks did my new Peruvian friends wave good-bye
and leave me to retrace my tracks seething with a sort of inward
anger that was constantly soothed by the thought of that delicious
pile of fruits in the back of the car, even though I couldn't eat
most of them. It was their psychological meaning that did so
much for me and began to rebuild my confidence in truck drivers.
It was never what it had been in Chile, but I never again had the
same needs. I revved up to the maximum as I saw the three
suspicious characters still trudging wearily along the road, but
this time they took no notice of me because I was travelling in the
wrong direction for them.

I was once again on the Lima road after wasting an irretrievable
sixty to seventy kilometres. I was determined that the next time I
came to such a road junction I would just sit in the middle of the
road until something came along to determine the correct route. I
passed through more sand and rock and through several rocky
gorges before reaching the coast. I saw what the American A.A.
handbook meant about dangerously unguarded roads and what

the Foulkeses had said about the Peruvians being reckless drivers on their splendid new roads was amply demonstrated. It was surprising how far I was able to travel at a fair speed and without encountering any severe obstacles that could be ascribed to the earthquakes. Only in the valleys were a few rocks scattered about the road and occasionally one or two came hurtling down just in front of, or just behind me. As I climbed along the small range of hills by the edge of the ocean I was perturbed by the poor running of the car, and it was some time before it struck me that this was due to the poor quality Peruvian petrol. A long way farther on I was able to buy a gallon of high-octane petrol imported from America. The difference in performance was instantaneous and startling.

It was very late afternoon when I reached Ocoña where the real trouble began. The road ran into a newly built tunnel. A barrier across it barred all traffic from entry. The next section of the road along the coast was a spectacular engineering feat which had just been completed by the Peruvian government and now in one blow from the depths of the earth had been destroyed. I passed through the village of Ocoña and over a bridge in the valley. A little truck driver's restaurant and bar stood at the roughly blasted entrance to the tunnel, so I pulled up there to make inquiries. Traffic was certainly coming through from Lima. There was a bus-load of people. They had come by an inland diversion on an old trail over the mountains. They were embarrassingly curious and so were the local people who drifted in for drinks. The proprietor made it clear that I shouldn't attempt the journey that night and, after I had unloaded most of my fruit on him, suggested that I should sleep in the car outside his establishment. Meantime he advised me to sit in my car in case any of the people who were probing about it should steal anything. It was exceedingly embarrassing and I felt quite unable to make any kind of contact with anybody in particular. I merely sat there like an animal at the zoo while everybody had a good peer in through the windows at me.

Later the bus went away and many of the local customers began staggering home. In particular I noticed the children gradually disappearing. I was apprehensive about what the night would bring forth and I was glad that my luggage, which was already pretty shabby, had had to be packed in old cardboard boxes etc.

after the episode in the river in Chile. I looked like a motorized tramp. As the night went on and only the poor lights in the restaurant illuminated the surroundings, I could see the last few confirmed drinkers sitting within. An Indian came out, held on to the frame of the hood of my car as he squatted on the ground to use the dusty earth beside me as a lavatory. I wondered at first what he was up to when he started to run his hand across his throat and jabber rapidly in Spanish. For a moment I thought he was preparing to attack me there and then with his knife, but then he pointed to the mountains. He was warning me not to travel over the mountains until morning because of the bandits who were attacking the diverted traffic. He then most politely asked if he might make use of a piece of dirty rag which lay on the ground. He wondered if it was mine and if I wanted it! Having readjusted his dress, he insisted that I should accompany him into the bar and have a drink with him. I sat there for some time drinking a solitary bottle of plain soda water. I had a feeling I might need all my wits about me before the night was out.

Gradually the last staunch customers drifted away, and I went out to sit in the car for the night. The landlord fetched the dogs in and put some rough wooden shutters over the open front of the restaurant. One by one the lights went out until the last glimmer was gone. As I grew accustomed to the complete darkness I could just make out the forms of a small group of men huddled up against the entrance to the tunnel. At such moments one cannot help wondering to what lengths poverty might drive such vagabonds, and I kept one eye open throughout the night to observe any uncertain stirrings. I had a few scares but eventually the first welcome glimmers of dawn appeared. As I checked and replaced the oil and water, two lorries began to ascend in convoy. I followed close on their tails and was glad to hear the sound of traffic coming up behind me in the distance. The word track was scarcely applicable to this abandoned trail which had now been opened as an emergency measure. It was even bumpier than most of the other mountain trails I had followed but, apart from that, it offered no especial difficulty. Soon I was on top of the Crest Lima and the sun's first broad rays of early morning were shining across the Andes. By nine o'clock I had covered the whole ninety kilometres of the diversion and was bumping down to the edge of the Pacific again. I had been travelling much faster than I usually did over such roads in an endeavour to keep fairly close to the lorries.

The coastal road was paved once again but it had been badly gashed and shaken in many places. At one place I saw one of the two lorries sway right over and almost fall down into the sea immediately below. The sun was now shining fiercely on the awful completeness of rocky desert. To the eye, at least, the absence of all living things was as complete as on some planet without an atmosphere. I had not had breakfast and I had to find somewhere where the rocks would provide a little shade. It was like looking for a place to picnic in the immediate environs of a great city and it was some considerable time before I came to an entrance to a cave near the road. There I stopped and set up my camp kitchen and bathroom; and after a good wash and a meal felt like a giant refreshed. I washed away the dirt and the horrid memory of the previous night and set my course through the rest of Peru. Long weary miles of desert followed. The sea beat constantly on the shore and was seldom far away. No animal life was visible but very occasionally habitations of human beings, similar to those in Chile, appeared. The few sticks and bits of seaweed seemed to signify an even deeper poverty, though how this was possible I hardly know. At one point a hill of sand had been shaken down on to the road by the earth movements and a gang of about half a dozen Indian workmen were posted in readiness to help the traffic through. It was by such expedients that the Peruvian lifeline between its two largest cities had been kept open. The poor car was subjected to a fierce five minutes' 'assistance' through the fine powdery sand which I thought must certainly have penetrated into every moving part of it. I feared this as I had feared it in Chile and I took similar precautions: a quick application of the grease-gun to a few of the most vital parts. This of course served the purpose of pushing out the sand and grit.

After passing through the area of the earthquakes, I came on to a stretch of poorly paved road which led me through the fishing-village of Puerta Chala, a remarkable village where, for some reason I was unable to determine, the church and the houses were picturesquely constructed out of heavy timbers, almost as if some large galleon of old had grounded there and provided material for the building of a whole village. Another very odd thing about this part was that one noticed the occasional cow strolling about among the sand and rocks. Did they feed them on seaweed? I did not stop to ask but raced on, hoping to reach the town of Nazca before dark. The scene of endless rocky desert continued as the road turned inland. At a small restaurant I obtained a lunch which had come up out of the sea; its name had no meaning for me, its substance fortified me for a long drive during the afternoon. The sky was lit up by the vivid colours of a desert sunset as the sun itself approached the western horizon and prepared to plunge my half of the world into night. Daylight disappeared just as the lights of Nazca came into view. The last few miles were difficult. Sand drifted on to the road, and the boundary between deep sand in which I might easily become stranded and the hard surface of the road became almost undetectable. At last I reached the town itself, another rather typical Latin American town of fair size. That was how it appeared as I entered the poorly lighted plazas. I had read in Woodcock and other writers that it was the centre of one of the ancient civilizations of Peru, that it was famed for its ingenious farming which it achieved by using the heavy dews of the desert and that it produced great art to decorate its pottery, examples of which I was later to see in the archaeological museum in Lima. Today it is inhabited by a very varied population which adds negroes and zambos—descendants of Indian and negro interbreeding—to the Spanish and mestizo population. I had forgotten all that I had read about the town, but the wild behaviour of bystanders as I entered soon reminded me that I was in a different sort of place from any that I had been in previously. Here was something of the wild spirit for which Latin America is famed. When I asked for a hotel I was at once directed to the tourist hotel and advised to get there as quickly as possible. I feared it would be expensive, but since I had been travelling solidly for fifteen hours and had had next to nothing in the way of sleep on the previous night I was in no condition to do anything but indulge myself.

It was my first visit to one of the nationalized tourist hotels of Peru. In an atmosphere of palm leaves, fountains and coloured lights, I had my dinner brought to me by elegant waiters in formal dress. My room was lavishly and fashionably appointed in modern style and a private bathroom was attached. In that setting of tiles and chromium plate I was able to strip and wash away the last vestige of the dust of the long, bleak, desert coast of Peru.

Next morning I was off again early after paying a bill for about thirty shillings. I had filled up with petrol and gone only a few yards out of the town when one of the back springs suddenly collapsed. I had been a little slack about checking over the car before leaving because I was now on the busy main road to Lima and help would not be difficult to obtain. Back at the petrol station again an odd character who was lounging around jumped sharply at the chance of leading me to his repair shop. It turned out to be his own backyard. It will suffice to say that he was a hopeless mechanic, that he had about half a dozen rusty spanners and a few relics of abandoned lorries among which the chickens scratched and that it was difficult to get away from him because he seemed at least to mean well. Some dusty little children ran out to look at my car and a woman worked in a seemingly industrious manner in the slummy shack on one side of the yard. A whole morning was spent mending a spring, a job that would have been done in an hour by a good Chilean mechanic. I was fuming inwardly at the man's clumsy handling of the job, but he refused to let me soil my hands and made a very modest charge for his services when the spring was finally mended and replaced.

It was midday before I could start off again and I knew that I had very little chance of reaching Lima that day. I raced ahead, however, passing through Ica while most people were still having their siestas. A wind blew up on the desert road to Lima and a kind of small sandstorm arose. Sand billowed across the wide level plains, reaching a height of a couple of feet occasionally and penetrating the interior of the car. That night I turned into Chincha Alta, realizing that there was no point in trying to go any farther. I could have travelled in the dark, but I wanted to see the approach to Lima in daylight and in addition to that I was not anxious to arrive in the middle of the night when all my personal contacts in the city would be fast asleep. I pulled up outside an American car agency on the way into Chincha. The Austin aroused immediate interest and a garage was at once found for it. The proprietor drove me in his own car to find a hotel. The only reasonable hotel in the town was either full or didn't like the look of me. I was forced to stay in one of the really cheap hotels where one paid about half a crown for the night. Clayton was in my thoughts as the apologetic proprietor helped me in with my baggage. No food was supplied but a little dark attendant took my money and then led me to a small room at one end of a long green corridor, grimy but looking as if it were hosed out daily. On the outside of the bedroom doors of the village hotels in Latin America one usually finds a couple of rings like those put in the noses of bulls, and it is customary to put your padlock through them when you go out to ensure the safety of your belongings. In my compartment I put a groundsheet over the bed and made use of my own camping equipment. I only wanted a rest and, after fixing the padlock and wandering round the town for a short while, I went to bed and slept soundly till morning. The toilet arrangements contrasted fantastically with the individual privacy of the previous night in the tourist hotel. They can be left to the reader's imagination. I was getting a bit fed up with the long dull journey along the monotonous coast of Peru, but I still had plenty more of the same kind of thing ahead in the north. I was really looking forward to Lima, however. It should be full of interest; everything would be put right in the great city.

The man in the tiny restaurant next to the hotel, where I had breakfast, provided me with what I wanted in a most pleasant way, and I brought in my own pots of jam and so on to add to the dry bread and coffee he supplied. The charge was small and I was soon on the big main road to Lima once more. Villages and wayside restaurants become progressively more elegant as one approaches the rolling sandhills along the coast on the way in to the city. The traffic also became quite severe. On one occasion I pulled in to the verge for a few minutes and found myself stuck in the sand. In a matter of minutes a small truck stopped and the driver came to my help. On another occasion a little farther on an incident occurred for which I could never fathom out the reason. A large American car was coming down at high speed towards me on the other side of the wide highway. I took little notice of him until he suddenly swerved out in the road directly in front of me and forced me on to the verge again. If the climb had not reduced my speed the car would almost certainly have rolled over and brought my journey to an uncertain end. I could hardly believe my senses. Was it the same instinct in the rich Peruvians that had led them to hunt Indians as a sport? Was tipping a little car like mine off the road a sort of sport, really?

By lunchtime I had reached the poverty-stricken outskirts of the rich capital of Peru. In the city itself the streets and avenues are handsome and amongst the cleanest of any capital city I have ever visited. Labour is cheap and the Indians are used to keep the roads spotlessly swept. The behaviour of the traffic in the city struck me as being relatively mild. Its behaviour is gentle compared with Buenos Aires or Mexico City. The reason for this, I suspect, is that bone-shaking concrete humps run across nearly all the road intersections except on the main avenues. Drivers have a choice of reducing speed to about five miles an hour or breaking their cars to pieces on the spot. Quite an effective disciplinary measure! These concrete ridges are also used extensively in the vicinity of schools in many of the countries of Latin America.

I do not propose to give a detailed account of the great colonial city in whose cathedral the bones of the controversial Pizarro lie embalmed, a city built by the Conquistadores to avoid setting up government in the old Inca capital in the mountains. There is an endless amount that could be written about the expansive and beautiful city of Lima. Its avenues display elegant palm trees, and its buildings are splendid. It has the air of an important metropolis today but its riches lie fallow in a few hands and the mass of the population leads a life that is desolate and poor in the extreme. There is great poverty elsewhere in Latin America, but I saw none to match what I found in Peru and nowhere else does there seem to be the same positive will to retain it. Everywhere in Chile, for instance, there are signs of slum clearance and in education there are signs of a great attempt to eradicate the slums of the mind. It seems inevitable that the situation in Peru must one day explode and on that day I would not envy the fate of luxurious Peruvians.

I lived in comfort and visited the museums and places of interest in the city. I was taken round like a tourist. I found the museum of colonial history, with its long gallery full of forgotten presidents, extremely dull, but the great archaeological museum left me with quite the reverse impression. It was potentially just about the most exciting museum I have ever visited although its contents are badly and inadequately described. I began to get a real feeling of the great variety of the fantastic civilizations that have flourished so remarkably in the sandy and mountainous land of Peru. I saw the pottery of the Nazcan, Moche and Chimu civilizations. I was able to compare their advances in agriculture and art, and their knowledge of the seasons and of the movements of the heavenly bodies with the knowledge and advancement of the Incas. It is quite impossible to relate it all here, but in my mind there was one all-pervading impression, the thought that I was in the land of the Kon-Tiki. Only a few miles from where I was standing the Indians had sailed off on the rafts on fishing expeditions, and perhaps on that great journey to the South Sea Islands itself, guided only by the knowledge of navigation they had learnt in these sandy wastes north and south of Lima. Fifty miles from here and only a few years earlier the Kon-Tiki raft itself had set out from the port of Callao. I was racing through a wonderland to which I determined I must one day return to examine its mysterious exhibits at leisure. I knew unfortunately that I had little time to spare. Ecuador and Colombia were calling urgently to me and before long the rains would be falling up in the Andes, the same rains that almost thwarted Thor Heyerdahl and his companions. It still remained a question whether or not they would thwart me.

One evening I visited the Country Club of Lima with the manager of a British company in the city. I met many of his Peruvian friends and saw a dazzling sample of the beautiful girls of Lima. I doubt if they have the character of the Chilean girls but for beauty alone they are widely held to be rivalled by none. As soon as we had finished our dinner, my host and I quickly found ourselves surrounded by Peruvian members of this exclusive club, mainly the mothers of the beautiful girls who were dancing on the floor beside us. 'You are not here for long enough,' they said, addressing me, 'for us to introduce you to the beautiful daughters of Lima. You are not married? You must come back again for several months and we will promise to find you one of the most beautiful women in the world for a wife!'

I learned several lessons the following day on the beach of Miraflores outside Lima. My host of the previous evening had taken it upon himself to look after me while I was in the city. He regretted that his Argentine wife had flown to her parents in Buenos Aires after a severe car crash in which they had both been involved, but he transferred me from my hotel to his house and made an excellent job of making my stay as enjoyable as possible in the circumstances. My health was about to do its worst to frustrate his kind efforts. While we sat on the beach under an enormous coloured umbrella to shade ourselves from the sun which was already concealed behind cloud as it is for eight months of the year, various friends came round and we began talking. I started talking to a very pretty little sixteen-year-old schoolgirl daughter of one of Mr. James's friends. Her name was Rosita, which means little rose, and I learnt from her that Peruvian girls have high ambitions in the world of thought. They have little scope left in the world of beauty. Rosita's ambition was to go to Buenos Aires to study philosophy. I naturally asked her why she wanted to do that and she replied in a long preamble about the importance of knowledge. I could not help pointing out that the greatest of the Greek philosophers, Socrates, thought himself wiser than other men only by virtue of the fact that he knew that he knew nothing! She was thoughtful. Perhaps her thinking became dialectical from that moment! Another force was at work preparing to teach me another lesson while I was talking to Rosita. I had allowed my feet to stick out for a foot or so beyond the shade of the big umbrella. I felt nothing at the time but before evening both my feet were swollen to a great size and badly burnt, and that by a sun I couldn't even see shining. It was a very painful and impressive experience. Mr. James had warned me that the lack of moisture in the atmosphere caused the sun's rays to have an amazing effect within a few minutes. I had failed to take his warning absolutely literally. Had I stumbled on a training-ground for astronauts who will have to face the cosmic rays on other planets?

I don't know if that experience was in any way connected with another painful one that was about to trouble me. I had suffered considerably from boils since my illness in Chile and on that night one of them contrived to come up under one of my teeth and caused the most violent toothache I have ever known. The next day the abscess under my tooth was still throbbing painfully. I was advised to go to the dental clinic of a Dr. Worthy, an American doctor of very considerable note in the city. To begin with he rather made light of the matter, but when he returned with the X-ray photograph he exclaimed: 'By God you really do have something like an abscess here. It runs right down one side of the tooth and right up the other. I've never seen anything like it before.' He took the tooth out but was unable to stop the bleeding. He expressed even greater horror, in the most graphic terms, at the state of my blood. He assured me that if any provincial dentist had had to deal with my abscess I would most certainly not have been alive, and he warned me that if I had to have an operation or cut myself badly on the rest of the journey I would probably bleed to death. He had had to use three times the prescribed maximum of some special preparation sent down directly from the United States for emergencies, to make the gum heal at all, and throughout the day it had to be opened up at intervals of a few hours to clean out the festering poison which still remained. On the following day I had one of my other teeth filled. Two more precious days had been wasted. Dr. Worthy was brusque but very kind and, when it came to paying him, he replied, 'I guess you'll need every cent you've got for that journey of yours, just leave me a photograph of yourself and the car. I'll keep it to remind me what you looked like after you've gone.'

I had some doubts about setting off into the north of Peru. I had decided to set out early on the following morning but was delayed by an error discovered at the last moment in my Colombian visa. The various jobs that were necessary had been done to the car, in particular a new pulley had been machined to save me from having to cut out bits of the old tyre to keep me going; I had bought various capsules which Dr. Worthy had recommended and at last I was ready to drive through the slummy outskirts of Lima on to the big highway leading north. The road was long and straight and in wonderful condition and the kilometres slipped away rapidly. I stopped for lunch at a little wayside restaurant and the little waitress who served me said that I hadn't eaten enough for her to charge me. I had to press her to take a shilling for it. Once again I was travelling along a sandy coastal region past more of those little ports from which the Indians must once have set out on their pae-paes, balsa rafts, to go fishing and on trade expeditions to Ecuador. Just as it was getting dark I saw a small version of one of the tourist hotels outside the village of Huamey. The manager had heard about my journey in the previous Sunday's edition of *La Prensa*. I was the English writer travelling through Peru? I was most welcome to his hotel, and so forth. I asked for the most 'economical' room and, although in those small hosteleries as they are called the rooms are all one price, I noticed that all the normal extras were crossed off when I received my bill on the following morning.

There was every convenience: a private bathroom and a lock-up garage for the Austin. I was still feeling quite weak after the abscess and my swollen feet and I was glad to lie down in luxury.

The rest of the journey through Peru was simply a matter of covering ground as rapidly as I could to reach the Ecuadorian frontier before the rains descended. I hurtled regretfully past the end of a small road leading up to the sugar plantation of a Hungarian baron whom I had been invited to visit; I went less regretfully past an island that seems to consist solely of the droppings of the sea-birds which since Inca times and earlier have been preserved on account of the value of guano in providing fertilizer for the arid and sandy land; I flew past Trujillo, saw its dirty industrial exterior, recalled that it was traditionally the city from which popular uprisings in Peru began; past the lumpy remains of the Chimu civilization whose gold was long ago plundered and whose pottery I had seen at the museum in Lima; and arrived finally at Chiclayo by nightfall. Again I was off early in the morning. The next stretch of the route lay inland and was hillier and more cultivated. It was Saturday and I was hoping, within a few hours, to reach the hacienda of a friend of Michael Westcott's at Chulucanas. James Macdonald whom I was hoping to meet had returned from Cambridge with Michael Westcott. His father had gone out to farm in the north of Peru over thirty years earlier. His mother was Peruvian. I had to go ten miles or so off the main road to reach the village and from there a dirt road in extremely bad condition ran for the last few kilometres to the Macdonalds' house. The real rains had not started but there had been a few wet days. I was able to recognize James at the gate of his father's bungalow, and when I told him who I was he jumped up and sat astride the bonnet of the Austin and together we drove up to the front door.

It was only eleven o'clock on Saturday morning and there was no point in reaching the frontier before the following Monday morning. I could relax for the rest of the day. Unfortunately, James was just on his way down to Lima and could only wait for a few hours to tell me a little about his own journey; and indeed he gave me the most hopeful picture of the rest of the route that I had so far received. He seemed quite confident about Ecuador and Colombia, but was sure I would have to ship the car round the jungle gap in Costa Rica as well as the Darien. I thought afterwards that he definitely underestimated the mountain work ahead of me in Ecuador, but I suppose that was because he had done it the other way round in a rather different sort of vehicle. My immediate problem was a small gap into Ecuador which was due to be closed for the rainy season. The rains were overdue according to James and his father, but since they hadn't already come they knew from the phases of the moon that they wouldn't start in earnest before the following Thursday.

On Sunday I crossed the Sechara Desert which Tschiffely had also crossed in an old car to get money from the bank in Pirua, while his horses waited at a point on the inland route he was intending to take into Ecuador. Farther north still I came to the region of the oilfields of Peru. This, I thought to myself, is where all that bad petrol comes from. By nightfall I was in the tourist hotel in Tumbes. James had warned me to indulge in the last bit of comfort I was likely to experience for a long time. My main worry was that Ecuador was not on the list of countries which appeared on my international carnet. I wondered if I would even be allowed to take the Austin in, or if I would have to do the rest of the journey on foot!

VIII

Jungle Terrors in Ecuador

After passing through the Peruvian customs with little or no difficulty, I came to a small wooden bridge with a slatted floor. A rough notice on an archway above it indicated that I was entering the Republic of Ecuador through the frontier village of Huaquillas. The whole place was bustling and full of commotion. Men of all colours and types rushed around with barrows full of tropical fruits. Money-changers rushed up to me to try and snatch the first opportunity of doing some business. As I had missed the bank in Tumbes, I was forced to accept their rates and was pleased to learn later that they were in fact very reasonable. I needed no one, however, to warn me of the dangers ahead. I sensed and almost smelt the jungle in front of me.

The village of Huaquillas consisted of a single earth street with a row of shacks on either side, of which one or two were shops and most of the others government offices. I found the guards and officials extraordinarily kind and practically helpful, as was generally the case with people who had the jungle at their back door. Once again the change of accent tended to make communication difficult. I had to go to four different offices and on each occasion someone was sent with me to show me the way. When it came to documents for the car, I was feeling extremely anxious. It was clear that the official had never seen anything like my international carnet before, and he admitted as much but said that he saw no reason why he shouldn't accept it. I kept quiet about the only reason I knew why he shouldn't, and was amazed once more to see how *expected* problems can suddenly vanish into thin air.

The change from desert to jungle, from the civilization of Peru to the primitiveness of Ecuador, is almost unbelievable; the human mind, with its limited ability to take in changing situations is baffled. There was a thirty-kilometre track running through a finger of jungle that stretched down to the coast. No road ran through it, but animals and occasional vehicles had formed a kind of track with deep ruts, which was being constantly invaded from either side by the undergrowth. I trundled over the first eight or ten kilometres fairly satisfactorily. It was dry and by slow and careful manœuvring I was able to prevent the wheels from sliding into the ruts. After an hour or so I reached a small military outpost with a few wooden houses, set up on poles four or five feet above the level of the ground to keep the occupants dry during the rainy months, and a wooden church. The guards looked at my papers, and told me that the next twenty kilometres were almost impassable as they had already had several afternoons of heavy rain. And as one of them raised the barrier he said, 'Tomorrow, Señor, this barrier goes down for the last time until the next dry season.' I had reached Ecuador with only one day to spare! 'A day later,' I thought to myself, 'and my whole schedule would have been wrecked.' For a little while I felt a sense of elation at what I thought was my good luck, but shortly muddy patches began to appear in the track and I was running axle-deep in mud. I thought I had been clever in negotiating several of them and hoped that I had got over the worst when the track improved somewhat for several kilometres. Suddenly as it wound round through a particularly dense patch of jungle with high towering trees and the huge leaves of wild banana trees, I saw lying in front of me a veritable quagmire, between five and ten yards in length. Only one of the old Argentine carts with wheels ten feet high would have stood much chance of getting through it. As I looked I noticed a tree-trunk lying the full length of the waterlogged track a couple of feet from the undergrowth. If the ground beneath it were still firm I could hack the undergrowth away with my machete and drive over the hazardous stretch with two wheels on the log. I hacked away for some time, hoping I wouldn't disturb the afternoon siesta of the jungle animals and that I wouldn't frighten any snakes under the bushes I was slashing at. I learnt the truth of what Clayton had told me. I could hear various creatures rustling and slithering away from me, but I saw nothing; for the animals of the jungle are experts at camouflage, whether they are running away from you or moving up into a position for attack.

When I had cleared sufficient of the bushes I began the precarious crossing. It all seemed to be going well until about halfway, when the rear wheel suddenly slid off the moist log. I emptied the luggage out and tried every conceivable way of restoring the wheel. I put boards under the car and tried to jack it up, but the entire boards just sank down in the mud. I tried lifting the car, but I could get no firm foothold myself. Although the military outpost was several miles away, I knew there was nothing for it but to walk back and beg for assistance. Picking up the spare axle half-shaft I had with me in the car, for protection, I started to return on foot. Apart from an odd bright-coloured bird flitting across the path or an odd rustle in the bushes, the jungle seemed almost unnaturally quiet in the torrid afternoon atmosphere, and I was developing quite a confident jaunty pace, wishing it had been as easy in a car as on foot, when I heard a crashing noise among the trees as though some large animal were smashing its way, bound by bound, through the undergrowth to reach me; at least that's what it sounded like to me at that moment. To someone in a steadier frame of mind it might have sounded like a man hacking away vigorously with a jungle knife. For a couple of moments later a wild dark-looking man a little over five feet tall, in tattered clothes and waving an enormously long jungle knife in the air, jumped out on to the path. He was quickly followed by a little boy carrying a cloth filled with berries and fruits. I went straight towards them giving a friendly wave and a smile and soon we were walking together towards the village.

Ducking underneath the road barrier, I proceeded towards the hut out of which the guards had emerged on my first arrival. A dog covered in sores and scabs lay at the door but took no notice of me. Inside the hut seemed dark and dirty and a couple of men lay snoring on wooden bunks. I made a few taps and bangs with my half-shaft to wake them up and went on to apologize to one of them who started to raise his head and ask what the matter was. How much my words were responsible for what happened next I don't know, but I suspect that a recollection of the chap who passed through in the odd little car suddenly came back to his mind, for he seemed all at once to comprehend the situation completely. There was no one in the village that could help me and they, the guards, couldn't leave their post. There was only one hope. Roughly what he told me in Spanish was that the last weekly bus of the season was due to pass through in a couple of hours' time and that he would find me a pleasant place to sit down in the shade while he continued his own siesta. One thing in particular worried me. I had stupidly left my traveller's cheques in one of the bags lying in the bushes beside the car. It was not likely that anyone would pass that way, but it left me with a nasty anxious feeling and made the two hours seem like an eternity. In any case was it even sure that the bus would really turn up? After some time the guards began to stir. They reassured me that the bus would definitely be along and gave me some bananas to eat. Later a little girl came out of one of the houses with a trayful of cakes for sale. I preferred the bananas.

I was thinking about Tschiffely's entry into Ecuador farther east on the Loja road, with a band of pleasant smugglers, when the noise of an engine in the distance made one of the guards exclaim, 'El camion.' Within a few minutes a very high old truck with bench seats in the back and a faded canvas awning for a roof pulled up at the barrier. The guard explained my position to the driver and accepted a few bottles of something or other from him. I was told to jump in among the passengers who shoved over a bit on one of the seats to make room for me. The guard lifted the barrier—the last time for four months!—and we trundled on towards my car. We had not gone far when the bus suddenly halted. The boisterous passengers began to cheer the driver as they pulled parcels from under the seats and from behind a sort of old bathroom mirror, which was in fact the driving-mirror. Silk stockings and other articles of women's clothing were prominent among the goods that suddenly appeared. They were in fact bringing luxury goods in from Peru to sell at a high profit. Amidst much joyful noise they passed bottles round and each had a substantial swig to celebrate the successful passing through the guard-post.

I breathed a memorable sigh of relief as we turned in to the spot where I had left the car and I saw it again, untouched. No 'tigre' had eaten it! I jumped off the bus and like a flash of lightning half a dozen men had charged into the mud. I threw the luggage into the back and was going to help push it through, but they told me to jump in and carried me and the car straight through. It was a matter of moments before I was on the other side, and when I pressed the starter button and the engine roared immediately into action they let out a hilarious cheer, joined by the rest of the passengers of the bus. The bus remained behind me and the driver bellowed out instructions every now and again. I would probably have found them difficult to understand in English, but in Spanish I found them impossible. After I had got stuck once or twice the driver held a conference with the passengers and one man, who held a special Ecuadorian taxi driver's licence and turned out to know the track like the back of his hand, volunteered to stand on my running-board and guide me. The inside of the car was full of the badly packed luggage. The skill with which he piloted me through that jungle track will always remain vividly in my memory. He seemed to know the exact depth of every mud patch. At one place he would say keep to the right and full speed ahead, and would wave his arm forcefully indicating that I must rush it fearlessly. At another place that might look innocent enough to me he would tell me to stop and look for a spot where the undergrowth was beaten down a bit. 'It's a diversion, Señor.' I had no choice but to follow his instructions while creepers and small bushes tore away at the underneath of the car and an occasional tree-stump hit the back axle or dented the floor. Once or twice we had to lift the car over tree-stumps that were exceptionally big, but apart from our breaking the battery holder, which we tied up with wire, knocking off the pulley for the speedometer drive and leaving several nasty dents in the floor, the car suffered no serious damage; and by early evening we were in the town of Arenillas, thanks to the genius and incredibly detailed knowledge of an unforgettable Ecuadorian driver.

I duly reported to the guard and after having my papers checked asked if he could advise me of a hotel in the town. After a few moments an officer of the guards came out of a nearby building to look at my car and satisfy his curiosity. He would be happy, he said, to arrange for my car and any luggage I might care to leave in it to be put in the charge of a sentry for the night and if I cared to take out the things I needed he would send one of his soldiers with me to a hotel. I felt sure I could trust him and was greatly relieved by his offer of assistance. The streets of Arenillas were plain earth formed into whatever shapes the activities of humanity happened to have imposed upon them. The houses were shabby and badly needed painting, and like those around

9a. A girl in local Panamanian costume at fiesta time

9b. Indians on the coast of Panama

10a. One of the thirty-four rivers crossed in Costa Rica where help was available

10b. A small stream in the same area where I found myself alone

the military outpost were made of wood and set a few feet above the level of the ground. The balconies and sun-shutters in the glassless windows reminded one of this dingy town's distant connexion with Spain. It looked as though it had probably seen better days. But today the paint was fast flaking off and leaving the wood to rot, or at best had taken on a dirty grey hue. Pigs and chickens wandered about the streets and apparently inhabited the space underneath the houses. The shops were open-fronted and primitive in the extreme. Great bunches of green bananas, potatoes and various tropical fruits and vegetables were strewn on the floor and thus displayed for sale. There were one or two bars which I wandered into later and grocers' shops with bread and shoddily wrapped goods from the few factories in Ecuador and from foreign sources who knew upon whom they could foist their rubbish.

We tramped through several dirty streets until we reached a wooden building with a notice, 'Hotel', over the door. We stepped down into a dirty little grocer's shop next door and the soldier began to talk with an old woman who sat on a stool behind a very old wooden counter. The floor was just the natural earth and space for the shop had been obtained by digging out the earth underneath the house where the chickens and pigs were normally kept. The one thing that really took my fancy was an old pair of brass scales. The old woman said she had a room and that her price was twenty sucres for the night, which the soldier indicated was about right. We went up to see it. It was one in a long corridor of wooden cells, with bars round the top eighteen inches of the walls to circulate air and light. A sheet lay at the end of a couple of boards raised above the ground. I accepted at once and the old woman handed me a rusty padlock made in Japan, to hang through the usual two rings outside the door. The soldier having accomplished his mission returned to his barracks. I sat on my bed, opened a few tins of assorted foods which I quickly dispatched and, feeling very thankful for the luxury of safe surroundings and nourishment, decided to nose round and see what the rest of the hotel was like. The buildings enclosed a small courtyard filled with all kinds of junk and an old engine for generating the electricity for the establishment. Round two sides of it ran a rickety wooden balcony from which a little shed protruded. The smell that emerged from it made any inquiries about the location of the toilets superfluous, and a small basin was perched on the railing of the balcony with a few dirty soap marks around it as evidence that it was the place where people washed, and sure enough it was there I was guided when I asked the old woman for a jug of water.

Feeling much refreshed after I'd managed to splash the front of my face with cold water without tipping the basin over the top of the generator, I decided to go for a stroll round the town before turning in for the night. The new church in the plaza was half completed and one couldn't help wondering how poor Arenillas managed to pay for it. Some of the shops in the square were more interesting, for they sold cloths brought down from Indians in the hills. One even appeared to be a kind of tailor's shop. Although I visited one or two of the bars where old gramophone records were being played, and began several conversations, none of them developed into anything, owing to mutual difficulties on account of the local dialect and my still fundamental ignorance of Spanish. As I lay down on my wooden bed and flicked the mosquitoes away, I counted myself lucky not to be lying down with or even inside 'tigres' and snakes. What annoyed me most was not being able to turn the light out, for one dim bulb had to serve several rooms and simply went out when the generator was turned off. The generator made the whole hotel vibrate until about eleven o'clock when we were all suddenly plunged into darkness, catching the family in the next compartment before they were ready, to judge by the scramble that went on for the next few minutes.

Next morning I woke up early hoping to reach Cuenca, the third city of Ecuador, before nightfall. It was to be, I had learnt, a level road through modified jungle to a place called Pasaje, and from there according to the maps the road climbs about fifty miles up the Andes to Cuenca—that fifty miles, typical of the unreliability of the maps of Ecuador, turned out to be nearer to a hundred! I passed over a decent gravel road for some miles, through green bushy countryside that might almost have been English. At one point I met soldiers marching along in single file and setting out to raid the bandit-infested areas of the jungle lowlands. I had chosen a good day for highway robbers would keep well off the road while the soldiers were about. A thought suddenly struck me as one of the leaders of the soldiers was talking to me. I would not have been at all surprised if they were seeking for some of my good companions on the old bus of the previous afternoon! Tschiffely had found that robbers could sometimes be one's best friends in Latin America. I wondered . . .

At Pasaje I knew I was supposed to have some documents stamped, but I had no idea that I was meant to call in at the immigration office. I reached the outskirts after passing through several villages and areas with frequent jungle clearings, where quite well-built houses hinted at the wealth of the jungle by comparison with the desert that produced the miserable hovels and slums of Chile and Peru. As I was approaching the town I stopped to ask a policeman the way through on to the road to Cuenca, but before I had time to attract his attention quite a little crowd had gathered round me and were asking questions with eager curiosity as well as making various experiments with different parts of the car, such as unscrewing the radiator cap, seeing if the headlamps were secure, lifting the front of the car up and so on. Their intentions, I felt, were completely innocent but they attracted the attention of the policeman and prompted him to make a little speech in Spanish, which I found easy to understand and memorable for its naïve charm: 'This gentleman has travelled a great way to come to our country. We should be proud that he is so interested in Ecuador and treat him with good manners. Please move away a little bit.'

I was glad to be tackling the climb up to Cuenca at a reasonable hour in the morning for it was still only eleven o'clock. I had been firmly warned not to attempt it without reaching the city before nightfall. I pulled up at the first and only garage I had seen in Ecuador. I had been unable to get petrol in Arenillas but I was carrying a good supply from Peru. The first thing I noticed as I left the town was a signpost which read 'Cuenca 173 klms.'— double the distance I had expected! I duly showed my documents to the guards and continued on a level road for a couple of miles before it turned into a narrow rocky track that began to wind up the mountainside through severe jungle country. The large leaves and the high trees of the jungle swept down into great valleys of billowy green on one side of the track and heavy creepers hung over the other. I was soon passing through a tunnel of thick greenery, with occasional shrieks and cries of wild birds emerging to drown the noise of the valiant little engine.

Once over the brow of the first hill the road tumbled down into a valley and over an old wooden bridge under which the waters roaring down from a steep waterfall flowed tumultuously and seemed to symbolize the wild savage country into which I was entering. It made the Atacama Desert seem benign and settled as if its dangers were merely passive and unintended. Here it was different. By its very nature the whole countryside was wild and active, waiting to spring, it seemed, on the unwary traveller. Not very much farther on I was stopped at another military guard post. Had I had my passport stamped at the immigration office in Pasaje? Unless I had I couldn't possibly proceed. I believe the guard was very nearly as sorry about it as I was when he picked up the telephone to inquire if he could make an exception in my case, and it was not without the utmost apology that he obliged me to return to Pasaje.

Back in Pasaje I quickly found the immigration office. It was run and organized by the army since the authorities were constantly concerned about the possibility of an invasion from Peru. A soldier took my passport and asked me to take a seat in a waiting-room while he went into one of the offices. Some little time elapsed—and I was feeling impatient about every minute wasted—before a young officer emerged and to my surprise began to speak in fairly fluent English. He apologized profusely for causing me the inconvenience of having to return such a long way and then came out to see my car. He was immediately delighted. 'The soldiers will do everything they can to help you, but you should have an Ecuadorian wife on your journey. The Ecuadorian women make wonderful wives, they are not so sophisticated as the women of Peru and they would work hard to help you on your journey.' I promised to give the matter my serious attention, but had I listened to everybody's advice, I would have a nice little collection of Latin American wives by now.

Although considerably soothed by the young officer's kind attitude, I muttered things to myself every time I realized that my wheel had passed three times over the same road and that I had gone altogether nearly forty miles out of my way. Basically it was my own fault, and it was the only piece of inconvenience I had over documents during the whole trip, but I vowed I would take greater care in future. I decided to try and make up for lost time by being a little less gentle than usual with the car, and I was soon back at the point from which I'd returned and was once again heading into fresh jungle. For some time human habitations were quite plentiful. Jungle houses thatched with banana leaves, round which dark-skinned children played while their parents were probably having a siesta within, made their frequent appearance. Large gourds stood outside filled with water, and fat bamboo canes, also used to keep the family's water supply in, lay in the shade. I had no time to stop but merely replied to the children's curious stare with a friendly wave. Later in the afternoon as the climb continued the billowy rolling jungle began to thin out. Although the engine was boiling as in the mountains elsewhere, it was no cause for concern because I was continually coming to springs in the rocks at the side of the road. At some of them the women from the huts were doing their washing, and as I pulled up at one a woman fled for her life, leaving her washing behind. I realized that she could not have been accustomed to meeting wholly pleasant personages travelling along these routes, and I felt I would like to have known exactly what fears should have replaced my sense of dark foreboding uncertainty.

Without fully realizing the transition I found that the jungle had ceased and I was on coarse grassland resembling that on the altiplano in Peru. What was worse was that the frequent presence of water earlier on had caused me to be somewhat careless about ensuring that my spare containers were full. The relentless climb continued and not a trace of water appeared. I had nothing left but the drinking-water I carried for myself when a van became visible in the distance, the only vehicle I'd seen on the open road since leaving Pasaje. I stopped him boldly and asked for water, but he only advised me to go back in spite of the interruptions of his wife who seemed to think that he should give me some. He was adamant, but assured me that there were only twelve kilo-metres more to the top of the mountain. 'To hell with going back a second time,' I said to myself as he drove off, and I decided to risk it on my drinking-water. I came to a halt once near two enormous bulls which were grazing by the roadside. I wondered if they'd attack me as I filled the radiator with my diminishing supply of drinking-water, but they took absolutely no notice. I had been told that bulls only attack men in civilized countries where through frequent handling they lose their fear of them, and this was an opportunity to test it, though their great size made me feel that it was an experiment I would gladly have left untested.

I reached the top literally on the last dregs of the second container, and from there rolled downhill towards the world of the mountain Indians of Ecuador. These Indians, descendants of the Incas, are peaceful farmers and to be sharply distinguished from the savage Indians of the jungle. At the bottom of the hill where the road began to level out and I realized that I must at all costs obtain more water to avoid doing irreparable harm to the engine, an Indian was standing with his donkey and a couple of women. The women were frightened and moved away, but the man knew a few words of Spanish and immediately led me to a spring where I filled my containers. I liked him. He seemed an ordinary human being, he smiled pleasantly and was free of the cowed resentment from which the poor Indians of Peru suffer. Although Ecuador is an extremely conservative country and its governments give very little encouragement to change, it must be admitted that they have retained many of the good features of the bygone Inca days. Not only do motor-vehicles still have to trundle over the old cobbled roads of the Empire of the Four Directions, but the farming villages of the Indians have also remained largely undisturbed and seem much happier and more self-supporting than those in downtrodden Peru. As I continued I saw the neat whitewashed houses of the Indians. Their farmlands were carefully laid out; and their attitude to travellers struck me as peaceful and friendly. The colours of their clothes were similar to those of Peru but in general a little gayer and certainly cleaner. I stopped in one of their villages and looked into the general stores where potatoes, beans and produce of the farms were for sale. The shop had acquired certain commodities of the civilized world such as matches, made in Ecuador of course, and the ubiquitous bottles of mineral waters that have flooded Latin America, though usually made and bottled in the country in which they are sold. I was glad of them as they saved all risk of contaminated water. I asked the old woman who ran the shop for a bottle and began drinking it on the spot. Not caring very much for its flavour I didn't finish it. The old woman insisted that I must either have a bottle of something I liked or else I mustn't pay. The simple unaffected honesty for which the Inca's people were famed still lives among their descendants.

Farther along still I came to another larger village. Crowds of men and boys stood around in the street. They seemed in a festive mood and ready to give me a rousing welcome. When I stopped I felt that they were in too good a mood to leave the car with them while I went to get another drink. As they all talked and chattered and asked questions, I picked on one, handed him some money and ordered him to get me the drink. I was to learn a little later, after experiences that seemed to last for an eternity, the reason for their festive mood. One question asked by a young Indian really did stick in my mind as being more original than anything that had cropped up on the journey so far. In all seriousness he inquired if my Austin was the latest kind of motor-car. Perhaps it was hardly surprising in a land where only a few jeeps and trucks are seen outside the cities.

Evening was drawing on and Cuenca was still a very long way off. Away in a valley I could see a small town with the twin towers of its church rising above a collection of indistinct houses. It happened at that moment that a jeep was approaching me along the main road. I put my hand up and stopped the driver to ask his advice: 'The rest of the route to Cuenca is easy. The road is good though it climbs up a little and passes through a small jungle region. And if you do not reach Cuenca you can stop at Giron which is only forty kilometres away.' I have always felt a twinge of regret that I never visited the town across the valley, set mysteriously in the evening mist.

I would not have called the road good. The rainy season had just begun in the mountains, and although the route was classified as an all-weather surface, there were long stretches several inches deep in mud and once or twice I nearly got stuck. As I began to climb again the radiator started its old habit of boiling away furiously and suffering from fits of excessive thirst which sometimes brought me to a temporary halt. I liked it less here than anywhere else, because before beginning the present climb I had descended once more into jungle country and the hot steamy atmosphere was no help to the situation, nor did I like the rapidity with which darkness seemed to be falling. The jungle wasn't too bad in the afternoon but with the fading light one suddenly gets the feeling that its most savage inhabitants are stirring themselves into sinister life. Shrieks which probably only come from vivid-coloured parrots, superimposed on the croaks of thousands of frogs and the metallic rattle of innumerable rattlesnakes, strike an inconceivable sense of terror into the lonely traveller. Darkness became complete and clouds of baffling mist rose up from the undergrowth and sometimes reduced visibility to a few feet. Occasional pairs of eyes gleamed out from the bushes at the side of the road, in all probability from some member of the cat family. Large fireflies flitted around. It was in fear and trembling that I was compelled to pull up every now and again to replace the water that had left the radiator to add itself to the misty jungle clouds. Each time, before getting out of the car, I gave the running-board several hefty clouts with my machete in the hope that the loud metallic noise would frighten off wild beasts that might have got the idea of making me into their supper.

I caught sight of a little glimmer of light in the distance. At such moments the mere thought of a human habitation is sufficient to exclude any notions of what dangers it might contain. I pulled up to put extra water in the radiator and walked towards a form that was standing in the doorway in the light reflected back from my headlights by the clouds of mist, and I was able to see dimly the yellowish features of a transfixed Indian countenance. I could not tell whether it was a man or a woman. It looked like some terrible sexless being out of Coleridge's *Ancient Mariner*. Three times I implored it in Spanish to tell me how many kilometres it was to Cuenca, but neither a sound nor a flicker of movement came from it and I was forced to turn away. Doubtless the poor creature was far more terrified than I was, and understood only the Quechua tongue imposed on their forefathers during the Inca rule. Had I realized then what dangers might lie in human habitations in those parts, I should not have greeted that light flickering in the darkness with such unwitting joy.

What it feels like to be alone in the jungle in an Austin Seven with a badly boiling radiator can only be left to the reader to imagine. There were indeed not many times on the journey when I felt sheer terror, but for a couple of hours that night I experienced it to the full, and it left an indelible impression on my mind. The wisps of mist grew worse as I climbed and for stretches of a few hundred yards at a time reduced visibility to almost nil. The jungle noises, however, receded into the distance and I seemed to edge my way upwards inch by inch. At last the headlights illuminated a white notice: 'Giron. 2,224 m. above the sea.'

Jungle Terrors in Ecuador

The guards were asleep in their post when I knocked at the door, but they soon came out and with typical Ecuadorian friendliness welcomed me into the town out of the jungle night. One of them volunteered to come with me to show me a hotel a mile away while his partner looked after the post.

The car quickly attracted the attention of the local town youths, and soon I had a rather boisterous following that I would have preferred to have been without. Having fixed me up at the hotel, the guard returned to his post on foot and left the young men to show me the way to a small garage where I might leave the car. The poor car had to sustain a terrible hammering because the cobbled streets were incredibly rough and a couple of young men insisted on riding on each running-board. The garage was closed and I decided that the only thing to do was to leave the car outside the hotel and hope for the best. As I was driving back up again one of the young men suddenly jumped in front of the car and started doing what looked like a mad war dance right in front of me. I had to swerve violently to miss him and muttered a string of rapid curses to myself about the riff-raff of Giron. I only realized how mistaken I was when one of them beckoned me out of the car to see a large uncovered manhole in the middle of the road. The poor chap I was cursing had risked his life to save me going into it! They warned me to be careful of that kind of hazard because it was a fairly normal practice to steal the covers from the manholes in the towns of Ecuador.

My feeling towards the young men certainly warmed up somewhat after that incident; whatever strain they might have put on the car, they had certainly saved it from a much more disastrous fate. When one young man from the back came round and quietly asked me to come to his house and leave my car there for the night, I agreed. To get into his backyard I had to drive over the site of a demolished house and through a narrow gap between two big mounds of earth. After shouting much guidance, the young men left me alone with my new Ecuadorian friend. An electric light shone out of the window of one of the rooms to which I was immediately directed. Inside, a group of people sat rather stiffly round the room on upright chairs. I was introduced to each one in turn. After that I was shown to the bathroom, quite a nice modern one, and given soap, flannel, towel and so on. The young man explained that his family had had dinner, but that he would take me to a restaurant in the town, the only one open. It was run by two Indian women in traditional dress and consisted of a row of tables in a narrow passageway. At the far end they were cooking savoury-smelling concoctions over a half-open fire. I settled for soup and bread and coffee. As might be expected in a country where Spanish hospitality prevails, I was not permitted even to think of paying for the meal. The young man's hospitality went even further, however, and I encountered the saying 'Mi casa es su casa,' carried to its limit. So that I should not be worried about the safety of the car my Ecuadorian host wanted to move out of his own room which had a French window opening into the yard where the car was parked, in order that I might sleep beside it and personally ensure its safety. Though I didn't accept the offer, I felt quite happy that the car was in safe hands when I returned to the hotel.

On the following morning the young man arrived at the hotel at six o'clock and we walked up to his house together. He told me that he knew about Austin cars, that there were quite a number of them in Cuenca and that there was an agency for them there. I set out for Cuenca with a special interest in mind. One of the fascinating things to do during travels is to compare what one sees with what earlier travellers saw. Tschiffely had taken special note of Cuenca and prophesied that when the railroad reached it it would become one of the finest towns in the Republic. I believe that that prophecy has been remarkably fulfilled.

Cuenca was about twenty-five miles away over a gravel surface road in exceedingly good condition. Although I didn't set out until half past eight, I had arrived at the Inca walls on the outskirts of the city by ten o'clock and was trundling along the cobblestones towards the centre. The market was situated in one of the central plazas and was literally humming with life. Indians from all around had brought in their wares, finely woven and colourful cloth, Panama hats with frayed edges, for which Cuenca has long been famous, and an inexhaustible variety of other goods. At the lower end of the plaza the small Austin agency was situated. I contrived to approach it against the one-way traffic around the plaza, but even the police didn't seem to mind, since one of them struggled both to direct me into the agency and to keep back the horde of Indians who had slipped over from their stalls to peer at the curious newcomer. A woman was in charge of the shop and stores and I had to wait for an hour until the manager returned.

When Alberto, the manager, arrived back he combined a charming welcome with a shrewd business assessment of the value of my visit to his agency. The car was whisked off for immediate cleaning and checking and before lunch-time a film of my car travelling through both the old and the new quarters of the city, past the new university as well as along the Inca walls, had been made. It was to show in the cinemas of the city on the following week. We then had lunch together on the balcony of the theatre in Cuenca. Indeed the restaurant which operates there during the day-time is the most select in town. For once I forgot about diet and enjoyed a marvellous meal as Alberto ordered each new dish. I remember particularly a bowl of freshwater prawns in a most deliciously spiced sauce, a speciality of that part of Ecuador. The school of painters in Cuenca is of international reputation and their remarkable murals, combining Christian and Indian tradition, decorate not only the new cathedral with its rich gold panelling, but are to be found also in the theatre. What provincial English town patronizes the arts like this? And how many theatres have the ingenuity to make themselves pay by transforming themselves into elegant restaurants during the day? Alberto was very proud of Cuenca. 'We are anxious', he said in Spanish, 'to use all the industrial advantages of America, but we do not want our people to become mechanized. We admire the good things of the United States, but we think that we in Latin America have a chance to learn from some of their mistakes and to show the world how to avoid some of the pitfalls of industrialization. In Cuenca we had the first automatic telephone system in Ecuador and we have the most modern waterworks. After lunch I will take you to see it.'

On the way up to the waterworks just above the city, we stopped and went into a hat shop in one of the back streets. 'This', said Alberto, 'is where some of the genuine and most beautiful Indian work can be bought,' and he selected a light fawn Panama hat, bordered with delicate Indian embroidery in a pattern made with threads of silver and gold, representing, of course, the deities of the sun and moon. In other streets Indians worked on large wooden frameworks outside their cottages. They were bus bodies which when finished would be fitted on chassis imported from Europe or the U.S.A. We finally reached the water-works, which was indeed a fabulous establishment, presided over by a board of a dozen doctors and chemists. Under a glass-roofed building a series of about half a dozen containers, each of which looked like a large swimming-pool under yet another covering of glass, were set a step or two below each other and filled with sparkling water. In each one different stages of purification were being carried out and, according to Alberto, there is no city in the world that has purer water than Cuenca, a claim that no one who had seen the waterworks would ever consider questioning. At the far end one could see the Indians who had flocked from far around, queueing with their containers to obtain pure water.

At tea-time, after Alberto had shown me sufficient visible proof of the fulfilment of Tschiffely's prophecy, I started to ask him about the route ahead. The prospect was formidable, he told me: in many places the road climbed to well over 14,000 feet, and despite all its civilization, Cuenca had living within twenty miles of its outskirts a tribe of headhunters, and he warned me that sometimes bad men in the villages murdered travellers and took their heads to the Indians to be shrunk. It was completely illegal but impossible to put a stop to altogether. He later showed me a couple of heads. The man had a beard. 'They like getting them with beards,' he said. 'They are more of a novelty to sell to American and European tourists! The Indians if left to themselves are only concerned with shrunken heads as trophies of war. It is your fellow Europeans and Americans whom you have to thank for your head being in danger, but you will have no trouble if you take care where you stop.' The conversation proceeded, but owing partly to the completely different pronunciation of the letter J in Spanish, it took me some time to realize what Alberto meant when he started talking about jaguars. He warned me about them not only on account of their speed but also because of their intelligence and cunning. Unlike most animals that are merely afraid of motor-vehicles, jaguars seem to be able to assess their chances of picking off a man in the back of a truck and making off with him at high speed. These were not at all pleasant thoughts to start off with through the rest of Ecuador.

I passed through a string of Inca villages when I had left Cuenca, still much as they were four or five hundred years ago except for the prominent addition of a Catholic church. Just after leaving Azogues I caught sight of one of the most curious and horrible creatures I saw on the whole journey, one of the deadly poisonous bird-eating spiders of Ecuador, which I thought I identified by its hairy body and the raised angular position of two of its rear legs, giving it a slight resemblance to an enormous grasshopper as it scuttled across the road immediately in front of the car.

Then there was a terrible climb up to 14,200 feet before the road descended to the small town of Tambo. This time I had no weather forecast or help as I had had crossing the Andes in Argentina. All I knew was that it was the rainy season and I could well expect the famous electrical storms for which the Andes are famed. Both the car and I were gasping desperately before we reached the top of that bleak mountainous country. Nothing, as far as I could see, inhabited it, but my imagination was prone to a slight preoccupation with the tales of headhunters and jaguars that Alberto had told me on the previous day. The effects of height and lonely isolation tended to play on my mind, and if an aeroplane had happened to pass over on its way to England I would have been a ready passenger. Just as I was leaving Tambo, I noticed a branch track going off to the right, with a signpost which said that Guayaquil was 134 kilometres away. A thought suddenly occurred to me. If I made straight for Guayaquil and got a boat to Panama, I could make Central America before the rainy season. The route wasn't marked on any of the maps I'd either had or seen and was probably a hellish jungle track, so I continued on for Quito but debated the alternative in my mind. I had already heard that the road into Colombia was closed, and at the rate I was going I probably wouldn't reach Quito before the Easter Festival, which I had been warned was a horrible affair and would probably lead to the destruction of the Austin at the hands of the drunken crowds. All the respectable people locked and barred their homes and left the city for the week. As I continued farther, violent storms began and lightning streaked around the mountain tops. Then I came to a point where I was unable to climb either in forward or reverse gear. With patience, in decent weather, I would have coped with it somehow. The prospect seemed hopeless and the next village was nearly a hundred kilometres away. I made up my mind on the spot that I'd try to get to

Guayaquil somehow or other, and turned back to try the trail down the Andes from Tambo.

It was mid-afternoon and again I decided to put my foot a little farther down on the accelerator than usual, or, to be more correct, I let the car roll at quite a fair speed over the bumpy track as it zigzagged steeply downwards. For some way it was misty and cloudy and then all of a sudden I seemed to plunge beneath the cloud to gain from the edge of a steep precipice a breathtaking aerial view of the billowy jungle which lay between the bottom of the Andes and Guayaquil. It was a scene such as I had only seen in books before. Rivers ran between the masses of tightly packed greenery, and looked like the sinews of some fierce monster lying asleep in the glistening sunshine.

I had little idea into what I was descending, but gradually I realized that the jungle was beginning to creep up the mountainside. Huge leaves spread almost like umbrellas half-way across the track. I passed the grass dwelling-places of some of the jungle savages, one of whom, about five feet tall and with wild bushy hair, jumped out on the track stark naked and jumped quickly back again when he saw the car. I wondered if I should expect a shower of poisoned arrows as I passed his home, but nothing came. Farther down I came to homes of a more civilized kind where people had made small clearings for themselves in the jungle, had built wooden houses and lived on what the jungle provided. A jaguar skin and some smaller skins of wild cats were stretched to dry on the wall of one of the houses at which I stopped to inquire about the road ahead. 'It improves considerably, Señor,' the man of the house replied in tolerable Spanish. 'In about two hours you will be in Guayaquil.' I found his prediction fairly true about the road but not true about the time. I had arrived on the foundation for a new road that had been begun between Guayaquil and Cuenca. One village I passed through was crowded with negroes who work on the sugar and cocoa estates around Guayaquil.

The sun descended and, as happens near the equator, darkness was coming on very rapidly, when an ominous and indistinct form emerged from the side of the road. It looked like a large savage animal and it started to move towards me and caused my heart to palpitate violently, but it turned out to be nothing more than two negroes on a bicycle. I continued on in the darkness and at last the lights of Guayaquil began to glimmer welcomingly in the distance. I came on to a paved road and began to increase speed when without warning it ended and I literally fell on to a gravel surface that must have been six to ten inches lower. The light lured me however and I soon ceased wondering how many parts of the car might have broken with the jolt. What I did not know then was that Guayaquil lay on the farther bank of the River Guayas at the point where the Babahoyo and Palenque (down which the balsa logs for the Kon-Tiki floated) join it. This was a piece of ignorance that was to bring me to the verge of the worst disaster of the journey, just at the moment when I expected the light and the signs of humanity to welcome me in from the jungle. I turned into Duran, a shack town on the east bank of the river, and instead of asking for Guayaquil I asked for 'El Centro'. I was directed over rough earth roads past open-fronted timber dwellings. Fires blazed on the floors of many of them and their unfortunate inhabitants seemed to be about to begin a mighty orgy. A former British Consul in Guayaquil, who had travelled extensively throughout the world, described it as being entirely unparalleled in his experience for savagery and debasement of every description. Now at the immediate approach of the Easter carnival it was a seething cauldron of savage emotion. I caught only fleeting and confused glimpses of the disgusting scenes that flitted past my eyes on either side, and it was not long before a wild mob was streaming behind my car. Then suddenly two men from either side sprang on to the running-boards and two more on the luggage grid and smashed it off, or rather left it trailing behind on the ground. Hands came in on either side and all the loose small articles with the luggage disappeared. I knew that if I offered the slightest opposition I would be knifed on the spot, so I made the car struggle on. I promised one youth on the running-board that I would pay him if he would show me the way to Guayaquil. He shouted at the others but for some way they took no notice. He then guided me towards the ferry going over to the city. On the ferry itself, which was exceedingly expensive, he told me that I was approaching a city of robbers and that his father had been a sailor and travelled to all parts of the world and that it was his ambition to do the same thing.

In Guayaquil he led me to a pretty rough hotel in the centre of town and refused to leave until I had paid him a handsome sum as well as his fare back. At least what was left of the luggage was safely in. I breathed once more and set about phoning Mr. Stacey, the owner of the large Austin agency in the city. He came round to me within a few minutes, and I was surprised to find that despite his name he spoke only a little English. We went straight to one of the elegant sidewalk cafés in the city, and clapping his hands to fetch the formally attired waiter he ordered a large plate of toasted chicken sandwiches and several bottles of beer. I attacked them like a cave-man pulling at a leg of meat from over his cave fire after a perilous hunt. The elegance of modern Guayaquil seemed entirely out of place, but I enjoyed it nevertheless just as I enjoyed Mr. Stacey's enthusiastic interest in my journey. 'People in Europe have no conception of what travelling is like in Ecuador. The height of our mountains and the roughness of our tracks can hardly be equalled anywhere.'

It was proposed that I should change my hotel on the following day, but in my rush to try and find a boat stopping at Panama, I failed to do anything about it. I was desperate to try and get off before the carnival began, otherwise I would have to imprison myself in some hotel for a week. Late on the Friday night the British Consul managed to contact a representative of a German shipping company which had a cargo-boat calling in on the following morning. I was to visit the office at ten o'clock the next day, Saturday. 'We leave at twelve o'clock promptly,' the German official informed me, 'and the fare for you and the car will be two hundred dollars.' The car had to be delivered to the docks, luggage and equipment had to be packed and taken to another part of the docks, the immigration authorities and five other offices had to be visited. It seemed impossible, but Mr. Stacey put a new Austin and a wizard of a driver at my disposal to call round the various offices and lo and behold at twelve o'clock I was on the deck of the s.s. *Saarstein* with plenty of time to regain the breath I had lost during the previous couple of hours. Soon I was watching the towering Andes as we moved slowly along the coast of Ecuador and Colombia. I shall never forget the fantastic height to which they seem to rise in the sky when seen from the sea. They were indeed like the mountains of one's imagination in childhood, appearing to rise right up to the sun. It was fitting and awe-inspiring that with such a memorable sight of the Andes I should be bidding 'adios' to South America. My heart was very sad, but

11a. An example of one of the finely painted ox-wagons of the small farmers in Costa Rica

11b. In the little village of Somoto in the north of Nicaragua

12a. The tough little Indians of Guatemala trudging
over the mountains to sell their wares

12b. The most colourfully dressed Indians of all were in the regions around
Quezaltenango

as I had time to think of all that I had been through I felt inclined to agree with the captain, who had sailed many times up and down those coasts and expressed the opinion that the only kind of vehicle he would have done the journey in was a tank.

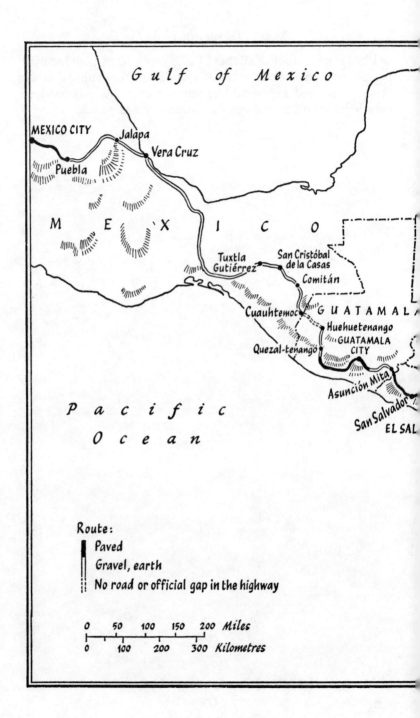

Route:
Paved
Gravel, earth
No road or official gap in the highway

0   50   100 150 200 Miles
0   100   200   300 Kilometres

Colón
Cristobal
Panama City
Balboa

Caribbean

Sea

DURAS

...el
...caro Gilan
Somoto
NICARAGUA
...anagua
Lake
Nicaragua
Rivas
PeñaBlanc
La Cruz
Las Cañas
San José
COSTA
RICA
Cartago
San Isidro del General
BuenosArries
Palmar Sud
Villa Neilly
La Concepcion
Remedios
David
Santiago
P   A   N
A
M   A
Penonomé
D

IX

Thirty-four Rivers to Cross

It was several days before we caught sight of land again, and then very early one morning I awoke and looked out of the porthole of my cabin to see numerous ships lying at anchor and waiting for their turn to pass through the Panama Canal. Central America lay ahead with its jungles and numerous rivers without bridges. I remembered the film Michael Westcott had shown me in Chile and, with my recent experiences in Ecuador still frighteningly vivid in my mind, I felt more than ever that I just couldn't face any more jungle in the Austin. At no moment did I feel more tempted to give up the journey and return with the *Saarstein* back to Europe. The expense, however, would have been prohibitive for me and I would always have to look back on the journey as a failure. I knew that if I could once get over that stretch of approximately a hundred and fifty miles the journey from there on would be relatively straightforward, with the exception of a bleak and dangerous region in the mountains in the north of Guatemala, where landslides are of frequent occurrence.

Later on in the morning, when I had climbed up to look out from the upper deck of the *Saarstein*, I could see the jungle on one side of the canal and the gleaming American buildings on the other, and I was just arguing in my mind the pros and cons of carrying on when a small motor-launch drew up to the side of the ship. We were due to dock not at the Panama City end of the canal but at Colon on the Atlantic side. The captain asked me if I would like to return in the launch that had brought out the pilot. If I went ashore it would give me an extra day or two to make my plans in Panama City and, as the days until the rainy season were running short, it seemed a pre-eminently practical thing to do and my debate with my fears seemed momentarily to subside. I agreed and soon I was in the little boat bouncing over the choppy waters towards Balboa, the port of Panama City.

A day later I was travelling by train along the banks of the canal and on the causeway across the Gatun Lake towards Colon. The names of Colon and Balboa reminded me that I was in the cradle of America's history. Colon reminds us of Colombus's first discovery of the Americas and Balboa of one of the saddest fates that befell an honest man in a part of the world where rivalries and personal ambitions went utterly unbridled for many years. Here as in South America the best and the worst elements in the Spanish character exhibited themselves dramatically side by side and tales of human villainy and heroic goodness abound. Not far from the very lines the train was running along chained slave gangs of Indians and negroes had carried gold and pearls and died in hundreds under the lashes of Spanish whips. Balboa was among the Spaniards who treated the Indians well and lived quite simply and frugally among them himself, but fate had it that he was tried and executed by a jealous governor at the time when the King of Spain had sent out a decree making him a governor himself. It is certainly a part of the world with a history of miserable as well as heroic deaths, and still today death appears to hold a fair sway over Central America as I was to learn later in some of the native villages.

At Colon I was met by a representative of a firm that imported spirits. It was associated with the Austin agency in Panama and its representatives, so I was told, were skilled at handling the sort of problems that might arise with the Austin at the customs. When all the documents were fixed up (the car wasn't due until some time the next day), the representative took me to a rough restaurant in the Panamanian quarter of the town. He pushed a couple of dollars into my hand, told me that it was the best place to get a solid meal and apologized for disappearing to keep another engagement for which he was already late. Meat and rice and tropical vegetables, all highly spiced and in substantial quantities, to be washed down with tins of American beer, made up the solid meal I was promised. I intended to visit the British Consul after lunch but decided that at least I'd better get a haircut before doing so. There was a small barber's shop opposite the restaurant with lurid Latin American magazines lying about on the floor. The general atmosphere of that quarter made me wonder if I'd get my throat slit, but I doubted if I looked worth killing and the cries of 'Fidel Castro!' from the children made me feel sure that I didn't fit the pattern for a local victim. Very much the reverse, I thought—and it was a fact that was to be of much more importance to me farther on in Central America.

At about two o'clock I knocked at the door of the Consulate and spent some time over cups of tea talking to the Consul and his staff about the route ahead. They didn't know the actual gap in the highway but as a result of their visits to the west of Panama they were able to add a new danger to the list that already existed in my mind. Herds of wild hogs were liable to be charging around and woe betide any small car that happened to get in their path! Another plan that I had in mind was to find out the address and telephone number of the Panama Yacht Club. Clayton had stayed there with a friend of his called Wally Gillis. Knowing Clayton, I might expect anything. When I spoke to Wally over the phone he told me unhesitatingly that he'd just been expelled from the club on the previous evening but that he'd find some member with a yacht for me to stay on and he'd be round to the Consulate straight away. We had just finished our tea when the Consul looked out of the window to see a couple of the shadiest types imaginable walking briskly up to the main entrance. One was wearing an old pair of jeans, an old shirt and a battered French sailor's beret and sported a small stubby pointed beard on the tip of his chin. 'These'll be your friends,' said the Consul with a slight smile; and I rapidly took my leave and hastened downstairs to meet them before they had a chance to make a closer impression on the staff.

In the club Wally introduced me to the most amazing variety of people I have ever met, voyagers of all kinds and descriptions who had come from all corners of the earth in little boats. Then he seemed to think it essential for him to beat as hurried a retreat as possible, and the last I saw of him was in a small yacht sailing away from the canal to God knows where. It was generally agreed by the company of wayfarers that I was a kindred spirit, prompted by the same urge for adventure as themselves—and only by chance had I chosen a different medium. I found myself settled for the first night in the bunk of a luxurious yacht and I never quite discovered who owned it. I heard numerous tales of famous expeditions and sea-folk, of little craft which had performed marvellous feats and then gone off never to be heard of again. I met a German with a wooden leg, who had crossed the Atlantic alone in a 25-foot cabin cruiser, and felt bitter about his feat never having been properly recognized. He believed himself to be the first German to have crossed the Atlantic alone in such a boat. I met another strange group of voyagers who were taking a yacht from New York to deliver in California, and became involved in a controversy between the captain and his crew. The captain had acted in a peculiar way during the trip down and was refusing to get in vital provisions because he was making hurried arrangements to rush his pregnant wife back by air to California. I learnt later from the newspapers in America that the man had gone mad on the journey and that his first mate's papers had been forged. He had attacked members of the crew when the yacht was becalmed for several weeks and the whole party arrived in San Francisco on the verge of starvation.

The captain and his wife became involved on the following Sunday in an event that concerned me and which constituted another of those ancillary adventures that happened in places where I thought I should be secure and undisturbed. On the day after I had slept in the yacht I was introduced to an American couple who evinced a keen interest in my journey and insisted that I should stay at their house over the week-end, since I could do nothing in Panama City until the Monday morning when the car, which was still tattered and torn after its trials in Ecuador, would have to be repaired and carefully checked. On Sunday afternoon the Americans insisted that I should go out in their yacht with the mad captain and his wife. The sea was choppy and not another sail was visible out in the ocean that afternoon, nothing but the occasional fin of a shark and a few steamers were to be seen. As we went farther out to sea the wind was gathering force and the sail at times was skimming the water. Controlling the boat might have been easier if the American couple had not brought their three-year-old child with them, which caused an intense argument between the mother and father. The mother was desperately anxious to look after the child and afraid herself. The father was equally afraid that anybody should show fear to the child in case it developed a fear of the sea. I have to admit that I was pretty scared myself and didn't fancy my chances if I had to swim around for long in those waters. Amid the general pandemonium I shall always remember the captain's wife regularly affirming, 'This is really living!'

Early on Monday morning I clattered along the fifty-mile concrete road to Panama City, with a broken chassis, two wings nearly falling off and a luggage grid tied up with string! Work began quickly at the Austin agency under the supervision of myself and Juan Barb, the serious-looking bespectacled foreman of the agency's workshop. The actual work was carried out by a couple of negroes. At lunch-time Juan asked me to come for a drive round the city with him. I learnt that despite his quiet and studious exterior he was a pretty firm supporter of revolution, for pointing to bullet marks on the outside of the presidential palace he commented that they helped to keep presidents and governments in order. 'We believe in showing them every now and again that they're not the rulers.' He also told me that Panamanian drivers didn't like parking-meters and periodically went round with sledgehammers and smashed them up. Here at last I had come up against the traditional picture of the Latin American character, and indeed I was to see many signs of revolutionary fervour throughout Central America as well as maiming and scars on the bodies of individuals who had suffered imprisonment and torture at the hands of tyrannical rulers.

I made many endeavours to contact overland vehicles which might be attempting to cross the gap from Concepcion in Panama to San Isidro del General in Costa Rica, but all were in vain. Absolutely nothing seemed to be travelling that way. I decided after consultation with the Austin agency to travel to David in the west of Panama and to make further inquiries there from an associate firm of the agency, who were distributors of jeeps. But before setting off on the three-hundred-mile road to David, about a third of which was paved and the rest a track of varying degrees of roughness, the sort of thing that bitter experience had taught me to regard as good, I had to get my Costa Rican visa. The Consul of that country on hearing of my intended trip asked to speak to me personally. He warned me that it was madness to attempt it alone and said that he would try to find a Costa Rican who would risk it with me. He was unable to do so and his anxious efforts merely added to the apprehensions I was already feeling.

It was not until lunch-time on Wednesday that the car was

finally ready for me to leave. I bade farewell to Juan and his friends at the agency and made my way through the hot tropical city towards the bridge over the canal. Like Tschiffely I have often been asked how I managed to cross it. One has the choice of a bridge or an excellent ferry. To begin with the road passes by the houses of wealthy Americans and Panamanians. Gradually as the afternoon wore on the houses thinned out and the countryside began to give signs of impending jungle. A narrow shave of a kind that could only happen in civilized areas occurred as I was driving along the concrete highway. A large American car driven by an opulent-looking business man came racing up behind me and, I presume for amusement, cut in so finely as he overtook that I was forced on to the bumpy grass verge and narrowly avoided overturning. The heat of the afternoon was subsiding somewhat as I entered jungle country once more. A wooden notice at the side of the road simply had the one word, 'Tigres', on it and was sufficient to warn motorists not to stop unnecessarily. I was just wondering about the advisability of carrying a gun when a truck filled with cheering workmen raced by. They sent a few shots up in the air as a salute. As the bangs resounded across the countryside I couldn't help wondering if my decision not to carry a gun had really been wise. By nightfall I reached Penenome where I found quite a decent little hotel.

Next morning I was back again on the stony rocky tracks. I passed through the shanty town of Santiago, where posts were set up outside the stores to tie one's horses to, and on to a stretch of road rather different from anything I had experienced previously, being made up from large oval stones out of the river-beds; they play havoc with the underneath of fast-moving cars, but to the little Austin trundling along at a very limited number of miles per hour they were no greater problem than the corrugations. Nevertheless it was a long, hot, difficult drive that day; and when, at about two o'clock, I pulled in at a wayside stores in a particularly remote part, I was delighted to be asked by the proprietor to come in and rest myself in a hammock tied between palm trees and beneath a bamboo and reed awning. The air seemed refreshing and cool. Chickens and domestic animals wandered around and the bits of old junk that such people collect lay about in an adjacent yard. It was not long before the proprietor's wife and daughter appeared with a pleasant meal and an abundance of fruits from which I selected with care the bananas and oranges. Once more I was a guest.

I found it odd how villages marked on the map simply didn't exist any more. To ask about one village I stopped later in the afternoon at one of the roadside Indian dwellings, constructed principally of grass thatch and bamboo. The owner had simply never heard of the names I read out from the map, but bade me sit down and brought out a liberal supply of bananas and large juicy oranges. When I had eaten all I could he packed more into the car for the journey. In those parts oranges are eaten in a curious way. One first peels off thinly the outer part of the skin as one would peel an apple, and then makes a hole at one end cutting into all the segments. The juice simply flows out and the peeling of the outer skin prevents the rest from cracking as you squeeze. I know of no more delicious way of eating, or should I say drinking, oranges.

I had seen very little of snakes, but I always took the precaution of tapping the car with a stick before opening up the bonnet in snake-infested areas. The countryside became rolling and more cultivated and I was soon to see the sad and terrible effects that the venomous creatures which inhabit it can have. As I was chugging along a couple of frantic parents waved at me from the roadside. When I stopped they took me to see a small boy in a contorted position with an enormously swollen foot. I gathered that some kind of snake had come down on him from a tree where he had been playing. They begged me to get him into the nearest town where some sort of medical assistance might be available. Indeed for such troubles as snake bites the best help is often available in primitive villages. I gave the boy some of the preparation I had with me and was about to clear the car to make room for him and his parents, when a jeep appeared and relieved me of the task but left the little boy's fate unknown to me for ever.

I came on to an unexpected stretch of paving not marked on the map. It was rather dilapidated but nevertheless good enough to make a big improvement in my speed. I was now in rather primitive farming country and felt a good deal safer than in the jungle. It had not been anything like Ecuador, though one can never judge the dangers by one's feelings in such parts of the world. Over a hill in the distance I could see the outline of a figure running at high speed across the fields in the direction of the road. He was trying to catch a vehicle that had overtaken me a little way back but was unsuccessful. When I arrived he waved at me. I felt that he was a genuine worker who had been with the herd all day and had just failed to get an expected lift. I felt I couldn't very well leave the poor devil after he had put up such an amazing performance to reach the road, so I fitted him in and drove him into Remedios, the next town, where as it had grown dark I intended to pass the night myself. Once again it was just another wooden shanty village. I made some inquiries about where I could safely leave the car and find a hotel and was advised to go and see the judge. When I at last found the judge's house he was out. Two fairly respectable characters were standing about in the road so I struck up a conversation with them. One seemed predominantly Spanish and the other was a pure Indian. Oddly enough it was the Indian who spoke a little English.

The Indian was emphatic that the car would be safe anywhere in the town. The people were honest and would steal nothing and liked to be trusted. We talked for a little while and then went off to the hotel together for dinner. I wandered through the restaurant, which bore many resemblances to a rough truck driver's café in England, and carried my luggage up the back stairs to a room on a long wooden veranda overlooking the town.

'Come and have dinner with us,' said the Indian, ordering numerous dishes and quantities of drink. As he became increasingly intoxicated he found a great many faults with my English and the fact that I often found it difficult to follow him caused him to doubt if I really was English! The main question that had been on his mind even before he started to drink was why I wanted to travel, or rather why European and American people generally wanted to travel. That was an urge, he told me, that the Indians simply did not feel unless the pressures of life forced them to it. Perhaps, I suggested, it was the same thing that forced some of his race to heavy drinking. The Indians are interesting and basically more honest and straightforward than Europeans, but when drunk they are curiously dangerous. The Spaniard sat rather silently trying to keep the Indian calm and also plainly aware of the dangers which might arise. When the waiter asked for the money he turned to me and said rather abruptly, 'The Englishman will pay for this.' I did not object to doing so, of course, although the table was littered with hot spiced dishes which I'd neither ordered nor eaten. When that was settled the Spaniard wanted to say good night and get him quietly away. 'Isn't the Englishman going to buy me a drink? I've been buying him drinks all night!'

Things were brewing up to a situation where a gun might have been advantageous. That I knew from Tschiffely's experiences, since the Indians and some of the mestizos are skilled and fearless with knives, but terrified at the sound of bullets or the sight of a gun. The reverse, as Tschiffely noted, seems to be the case with Europeans, which is odd since both can be equally lethal, and it shows, I think, that it is not danger that we fear but unknown danger. A small unknown danger will often frighten us much more than a great danger with which we are often so familiar in our daily life that we hardly notice it. Our own roads offer one such example. To return to the Indian, however, who seemed to be looking for some cause for a quarrel with me, I settled the matter quickly by buying a couple of drinks and simply slipping out before finishing my own. I leant over the rail of the balcony and looked down at the slight activity in the street. A few truck drivers were attending to odd things around their vehicles in artificial lighting, a policeman was on his beat and my car was standing safely beside a couple of big lorries. Shortly the Indian went tumbling up the street guided by the Spaniard. I took the opportunity to slip down and have a word with the policeman. He promised to keep his eye on the car during the night but refused the odd couple of shillings I offered for the service.

Next morning I rose early and hurried along the dirty veranda to see if the car was still safe. For a fearful moment I thought it had disappeared but then realized that another lorry had parked in front of it. As I was going downstairs to get some coffee before departing I noticed that the proprietor's sitting-room door was open. I peered in and was surprised to see a pleasantly and comfortably furnished room decorated in the prevailing style of Panama City.

The road on to David was through farmlands and was mostly paved and without any particular snags. By about half past eleven I reached the outskirts of the town which is of considerable size and importance. I later found it to abound with American troops carrying out surveys in the jungle areas around. I had many interesting conversations with them and learnt more about the hazards ahead from tales of their experiences with snakes and wild animals, told in a plain and unexaggerated way. I telephoned the company connected with the Austin agency but discovered it to be closed until after siesta time in the afternoon, which in that region meant about three o'clock. My first contact, an entirely accidental one made in the street, was Herman Castro, a Costa Rican representative of an American agricultural company, who travelled round various parts of Central America advising farmers and estate owners about fertilizers. I merely stopped him by the roadside to inquire but he immediately took it upon himself to guide me to a hotel. It was a small pension owned by a Chinese couple. The place was spotlessly clean, the food excellent and the price reasonable for those expensive parts. But the atmosphere was hot and stifling. 'After lunch,' said Herman, 'I am going up to Boquete in the mountains on business and will visit some friends who have a nice house with a swimming-pool. I will be happy if you come with me.' I agreed readily provided we could call round at the agency on the way.

I was in for another unexpected adventure. Boquete is several thousand feet up in the mountains past the still active volcano, El Hato, and is one of the favourite holiday resorts in the republic: the hotel charges forty dollars a day! I found that so hard to believe that I had to verify it personally. We set off in Herman's jeep. Grey clouds overshadowed the sky to the right and smoke was belching out of the volcano. 'It's becoming active again,' said Herman, 'but it's nothing to worry about yet,' as he sped on at breathtaking speeds up the twisting mountain roads. They were paved but dangerously unguarded at the edges, and just as I was wondering what would happen if something appeared in the opposite direction, a brightly coloured sports car came flashing towards us. We swerved, wobbled and slid along within inches of the precipitous edge. When we reached Boquete Herman called in at several houses and then went off to see the overseer of one of the estates. We had to walk for some distance through fairly high grass and since Herman was wearing snake-boots he led the way and I followed a few paces behind. An occasional rustle through the grass indicated a fast-retreating snake, for few snakes have positively aggressive tendencies. We reached the small bungalow where the overseer lived. The veranda and most of the rooms were strewn with the roots of dried-up vegetables. Much conversation ensued which I was unable to follow.

'Now the work is done we can go for a swim,' said Herman and
we went to the house of his friend. He told me that it was one of
the most luxurious homes in the Republic. It was mainly American in style with one or two Spanish touches. The door, for
instance, had a little grill to peer through at the person knocking.
Herman knocked and an astonishingly beautiful maid opened the
door. Within a few moments Herman had taken a flower from his
shirt pocket and fixed it tenderly in her hair. Inside we were taken
to an old lady who was the mother of Herman's friend. She
explained that he was away and told us to enjoy the pool. In a few
minutes the maid arrived with towels and swimming-costumes
and we went into tiled bathrooms at one end of the pool. The
place was fabulously appointed and we both enjoyed the swim
although the water was in fact slightly chilly. When we got out
Herman began to double himself up. The cold water, he said, had
affected his stomach. We must go quickly and get something for
it. The chemist he selected was one of the elegant bars in Boquete
where he swallowed down several whiskies in rapid succession. 'It's
better now,' he said, 'I'm ready to drive back to David.' It is
scarcely necessary to describe the experience of the return journey. Back in David, Herman pulled up outside a fashionable shop.
A pretty girl was just closing the door. Here we parted with
Herman saying confidentially, 'In Costa Rica we believe that man
needs women.'

My principal concern was to get across the gap in the highway
ahead and I discussed it fully at the jeep agency on the following
morning. They could offer no help, however, and I dithered
around the town trying to find anyone willing to attempt it with
me. Herman almost decided to accompany me in his jeep if I
would stand the expense of the journey, but he became a little
uncertain and, I could tell, regretted having suggested it. As I was
trudging round getting rope and extra bits of equipment that I
thought might be useful, I happened to meet a large Texan in a
broad-brimmed cowboy hat. He was interested in my journey and
gave me a lot of advice about how to get through Mexico. 'There's
two mountains you'd better avoid with that car of yours.' 'I very
much appreciate your advice,' I said, 'but what am I going to do
about the immediate problem of getting into Costa Rica?' He

thought for a moment: 'You'd better go and see Ed Cummings, boy, he's the road engineer.' That was a wonderful piece of advice and the beginning of the solution to my problem. Ed was one of those fine Americans who have slipped through the net of civilization: he had a preference for the jungles and wild places, although he and his artist wife had a pleasant air-conditioned luxury flat in David. 'If you don't get anything better fixed up, I'll take you as far as the Costa Rican border and get you across the Chiriqui Viajo on Tuesday morning,' was the response I got when I presented my problem to Ed. I had learnt from the jeep agency that from there on I would have to travel for thirty or forty miles along a track running through several small rivers to reach a clearing known as Villa Neilly. There a gentleman known to the manager of the agency had built a small village whose only communication with the rest of the world is a small railway line running from the port of Golfito on the coast to a United Fruit Company plantation in the Costa Rican jungle. From there on I knew not what to expect. I only hoped that Señor Neilly would come up with some good idea.

Tuesday morning arrived, and I had found nobody to make the crossing with me and had accepted Ed's offer. Ed followed me in his jeep from Concepcion onwards. The surface of the road was actually much better than any of the other dirt roads I had been on. It was used by very little traffic. As we drew to within a few miles of the frontier we came to the first of the bridgeless rivers of Panama. It was fairly shallow and I would probably have got through with the magneto off. My experience of the river in Chile, however, had made me a little too cautious. I should mention that Ed was in Panama as an adviser to the Panamanian road builders. The bridge, which was nearly complete, was in the hands of a national company. The director of the work happened to be about and, when he saw Ed and me at the water's edge testing the crossing, he came over to see what was going on. He was certainly enthusiastic about the whole venture. 'You'd better wait here and I'll send off for a large truck and we'll load your car on it and get it safely through. We'll forget about work on our bridge today. It's not often that a thirty-five-year-old car passes through this way.' Ed and I waited for some time and we were shortly joined by a small native boy who said nothing and sat and looked on with patient interest to see what was going to happen.

Thirty-four Rivers to Cross

The heat of the tropical day was coming upon us in its fullness and a little way up the river we could see a group of native women bathing naked in the refreshing water. It seemed like a South Sea paradise and I should have liked to have done the same, but Ed warned me that people who are not natives are very liable to contract skin diseases on the feet, and I felt I should run no unnecessary risks that might make the unknown stretch ahead even more hazardous.

The truck arrived. The director ordered that it should carry me through this river and two other small ones and then through the large Chiriqui Viajo. 'We will leave you at the Costa Rican border and then you'll be alone and have to take your chance.' That was certainly not a pleasant thought, for the route runs through thick jungle and the map showed several rivers before the route came to the point where Villa Neilly was supposed to exist. Still, as usual I lived in the present and enjoyed Ed's company and conversation. At lunch-time we pulled in at one of the native villages near the frontier. At one end of it there was a restaurant. One section was pretty rough. The truck driver went in there. I was about to follow but Ed touched my arm and led me through a passage into a cool pleasantly decorated room which I had never suspected could exist in those surroundings of primitive native huts. 'They've learnt to lay this kind of thing on for us. It's more expensive, but it's safer for you and me and there'll be a good supply of cool beer put aside.' The meal began with a dish of soup made of jungle vegetables including a root which is extremely poisonous when raw; when cooked its pink flesh-like substance tastes delicious in a savoury-smelling soup. This was followed by chicken—Ed had a suspicion that it might have been iguana which is often served as chicken—accompanied by uncooked bananas of an unsweet variety tasting almost exactly like potatoes. Sweet bananas and other fruits followed and seldom has beer seemed so excellent to me as it did then, even though it was tinned.

When we reached the Chiriqui Viajo it looked wide and fearsome and its current moved rapidly over some scarcely visible rocks near where the truck pulled up. A special pilot came to drive us through. At first we drove in at about forty-five degrees to the current and then at about half-way started to turn upstream against the current. The water was several feet deep and we drifted some inches downstream for every foot the driver was able to take diagonally towards the farther bank. At last the dripping vehicle in which the water had been lapping round our feet reached dry land again. We climbed up the river bank and came to a pole in the middle of the track. The Costa Rican national colours were painted on it to indicate the exact position of the nation's boundary. We found a guard in a small wooden hut who was anything but pleased to be disturbed. He insisted on the Austin being driven right up to the hut in spite of the fact that there was only a narrow foot trail leading between the bushes. When I reached him he made me unpack all my luggage and spread it out on a patch of dusty filthy ground. He was the only really unpleasant Latin American customs' official I met on the entire journey. As he was about to check it all minutely another guard arrived who appeared to be his superior and ordered him not to give me any further trouble. I felt sad and apprehensive as I said good-bye to Ed and went on alone.

It is necessary to give an accurate account of this gap in so far as I knew it at the time. I understood that an American firm had undertaken to build the road basis of half the gap and had nearly completed it. A Costa Rican firm were tackling the other half and were not nearly so far forward. The strange thing was that the Costa Rican government had made no contract at all for building the bridges. Thus I found to begin with that the surface was quite smooth, having a gravel finish that had only been disturbed by the road-building trucks and equipment. I had travelled about thirty miles, forded two small streams and was at the edge of a wide river from which I could see what I assumed to be Villa Neilly a short way off. The journey had been through pretty dense jungle but the work of the road builders presumably had scared away most of the wild life; I could hear and see parrots and monkeys, and innumerable iguanas scuttled across the road looking like miniature brontosauri. They are eaten by the natives and, as I had already discovered, taste pleasant. What is objectionable, however, is to see the natives bringing them home alive: a whole row of them spiked through their mouths dangle in agony from a metal rod with a pointed end. They are kept alive to keep them fresh. An occasional snake would slither away between pieces of rock left at the roadside by the builders.

It happened that, as I was waiting and thinking about the

crossing, a road machine with a kind of crane on the back came along. I managed to persuade the Costa Rican driver to hook on to my front axle and lift the front of the car up to get it through the water. With terrible splashing and jerking, which made it seem inevitable that the whole car should tip over on to its side and be ripped across, with God knows what consequences, we finally reached the farther bank. The river must have been nearly a hundred yards wide and it was not difficult to imagine that in the rainy season it turned into a raging torrent. Soon I was at Villa Neilly. It was really quite an elaborate enterprise, designed to make Señor Neilly the first to exploit the resources of timber and metal ore up in the Talamanca range which lay just behind the jungle lowland through which I was travelling. I tried first to find Señor Neilly but he was up in the hills and nobody knew when he would be back. The village had a hotel and two large bars in which Latin women lounged about in tight and fantastically inadequate dresses, waiting for the dancing and night life, which duly commenced when darkness had descended and went on until long after I had fallen asleep. There was nothing quiet or provincial about Villa Neilly. I fixed up to stay at the wooden hotel in the main street, and after putting my car behind some stout wire netting with a padlocked gate, where the pigs and chickens were kept, I began to wander round the village with a couple of Costa Ricans who had come down from San José with a jeep to sell aspirins and other patent medicines to the natives. They emphasized that they had come in a jeep and assured me that I would never get through with the Austin. They had only just made it and the rains would be beginning any day now. They were going down to Golfito on the little train that ran through the United Fruit Company's banana plantations; and wanted me to join them on the trip and then attempt the journey to San José together. They warned me again and again that I didn't stand a chance alone. I, however, knew the Latin American character and knew that they would think nothing of delaying until the next dry season. As we were discussing the matter a group of men came wandering down the street. 'That's Señor Neilly,' they said, pointing to a tall man in the group. I approached him with my letter of introduction and with high expectations of a warm welcome. He showed little interest, however, and merely asked me to see him in his office at ten o'clock on the following morning. I returned to the dirty little hotel to have some dinner and was preparing to retire to bed, somewhat dejected, when the sound of guitars and music struck up in the bar opposite. The night life of Villa Neilly was beginning. I must see it so I wandered along the wooden balcony to where it turned on to the side facing the street, and from there with my elbows resting comfortably on the railing I had an excellent view of the gaieties below. With characteristic vigour rumbas, sambas and cha cha chas went on far into the night. The women flaunted their sex as only proud Latin American women know how to, and drink, I judged, was disappearing in pretty substantial quantities. It was a hard working, hard living and hard playing community. I enjoyed the fun vicariously from the balcony for an hour or two before turning in. I was glad to find my bunk protected by a very serviceable mosquito-net, for although it was my experience on the whole that mosquitoes did not find me to their taste, some of the vicious brutes out there evidently thought I was better than the dark tough-skinned natives.

On the following morning I made my appearance at Señor Neilly's office at ten sharp. I had to wait some time until he arrived but when he did he was exceedingly affable and friendly, very different from the tired man I'd spoken to on the previous evening. He told me that the next seventy kilometres to Palmar Sur would not be too difficult. The road surface was good and although there were a dozen or so rivers to ford they were not deep. The really difficult part of the route was from Palmar Sur to San Isidro del General. That would be the real problem but I would have to find out about it when I reached Palmar. Señor Neilly showed me various parts of his town and then took me in his jeep to the railway station where some government official, who managed to combine his official work with work on the railway, stamped my passport and gave me various documents. Only then was I officially in Costa Rica, and later when I reached San José it transpired that it was my voyage that brought it to the notice of the Chief of Police that there was no immigration authority at the point where I had crossed the border. The stout and affable Chief of Police came out and looked at my car and said with a smile, 'If you crossed the border in that car we'd better hurry up and classify it as a regular point of entry.'

When I had seen the electric plant for lighting the village and one or two of its other amenities, I had a hurried bite of lunch consisting of a bowl of soup, some bananas and a bottle of soda water, and then prepared to extract the car from among the chickens and pigs, taking special care of the little piglets that were playing round its wheels. I had only gone a few hundred yards along the road from the village when I saw a group of men talking with a priest. They waved to me to stop to satisfy their curiosity and somehow or other the halting Spanish conversation wound round to wild animals. It looked as though I were just approaching a region of dense jungle so I asked if there were 'tigres' about. 'Only small ones,' somebody replied. 'Ah,' interjected the priest, 'it's the tigers with two legs that you need to worry about.' It struck me as a rather nice-sounding remark at the time but its meaning made no great impression on me. Somehow the sight of other members of my own species was a thing I could not help but welcome. A notable incident in the journey occurred after I had travelled four or five miles. I was driving through thick jungle listening to the sounds of brightly coloured parrots and monkeys jumping from tree to tree, when in spite of the bumpy road I thought I detected something strange about the steering. When I got out to investigate I found that the rear nearside tyre was flat, the only flat of the whole journey!

So long as I was on the road I was making quite good time. I even passed through several streams without much trouble, but when I came to a wide river I felt anxious once more and wished I had been doing the journey with a couple of horses. Luck was with me again, however, for as I stood hesitating on the brink of the fast rippling waters a native approached me. 'It's quite all right, Señor,' he said and when he saw that I would not easily be reassured he offered to wade ahead and lead me through a shallow passage in the river which must have been seventy or eighty yards wide. I was able to see the height of the water all the way on his legs and it struck me that he at any rate was not one of the tigers with two legs, especially when he gave me a most friendly parting wave from the farther bank. At the next big river I thought I was lucky to meet a road-construction machine and to be able to persuade the driver to tow me across. It was a rough crossing and the Austin was pulled into deeper water than I cared for. I had taken the precaution of putting grease round any places where water might get into the engine and I had taken the magneto off, but everything was out of my control once I was hooked on to the big machine in front of me. It must have looked rather like a giant leading an ant by the hand, or rather dragging it through the rocky bed of a river. The truck could not wait and once on the farther side he left me to reconnect the magneto and get myself going again. It can be exasperating to try and get an old car going in the comfort and security of one's own garage, but there is something odd about the experience when you've checked everything and everything appears to be in order and you just can't get going and you're in dense jungle surroundings. You wonder if the rustling you hear in the impenetrable foliage is a 'tigre' preparing to spring. I checked the timing. I checked everything over and over again with a sense of mounting tension, for the afternoon was now wearing on and I didn't fancy being left out there for the night. At last I gave it up and just went for a walk to calm myself down. It happened that another road vehicle was hidden behind some bushes farther along the track. On the seat a man was lying fast asleep. I woke him and with a good push we managed to get the Austin going again. A little moisture must have seeped in somewhere and made it difficult to start.

Some miles farther on I came to a small camp of the road construction company. An American sat behind a desk in the office. 'You'd better get along quickly,' he advised me. 'We're not allowed to accommodate any travellers in the camp, and if you can reach Palmar Sur tonight there's a group of British helicopter boys there who spray bananas for the United Fruit Company. They'll be glad to see you. You'll be back in a kind of civilization if you get on quickly. There's only one difficult river and that's a mile or so up the road and some of our boys'll still be there and give you a hand through.' When I reached the river I left the car on the road and wandered down the little track which led steeply down the river bank to the water's edge. Hanging creepers dangled down from the lofty trees overhead and a vehicle could just brush past the enormous leaves of strange tropical plants on either side of the track. There was no sign of another human being about and both the crossing and the steep ascent on the farther side looked extremely formidable. I decided to return to the camp since I didn't wish for a return of the trouble I had had in Chile. At least I was determined I must go through with the magneto off. Just as I was returning I saw a truck standing in the road with its bonnet up. 'We were on our way to the river,' said the Costa Rican driver, 'but our battery packed up on us.' 'I'll drive you back to get another battery from the camp,' I eagerly offered, thinking that one good turn would surely deserve another; and was sorely disappointed when I was told that the truck was not going to be allowed to cross the river that night.

During the course of the evening I began unburdening my feelings to a sympathetic American foreman. He told me that his company was wild with the few travellers who had passed through those regions and then written exaggerated and misleading accounts of them. They had made it seem as if no road had been built, whereas in fact his workmen had struggled under the most adverse conditions to build the foundations of a good road and had succeeded even through patches of the most treacherous jungle swamp. Few people realized what struggles and difficulties they had had, and when writers who merely travelled through said that their road was no good the company got very angry. They had been given a firm order from their H.Q. in the States to give no kind of assistance to, and to have nothing to do with, odd travellers who passed through that way. I promised I would stick scrupulously to the facts about the route as I experienced them, and I believe I have done so. I have an equally great abhorrence of exaggerated travellers' tales. My listener was a rough honest American of the kind that is a true ambassador of his country to the peoples of other countries, and he began to tell me stories of his experiences among natives both in those parts and in West Africa, where he had spent several years after the war. He had been brought up in an honest-to-goodness way on the banks of the Mississippi and hated above everything Americans who went out among other people with superior attitudes. He told me that whenever any group of natives accepted him as a friend he always felt it to be an honour, and only a few weeks earlier he had had a fight with an American in a bar. He had found the way his fellow American was talking about the people he was among so vile that he had been unable to control his impulses to violence. 'That kind of American shows what sort of a guy he really is when someone raises his hand to him,' he said in a southern drawl. He then spent some time telling me how he had taken several months trying to become friendly with a tribe in the West African jungle. At last he had been accepted by them. He felt triumphant, he said, to be a friend of human beings who were finer than many of his fellow countrymen who merely brought disgrace on the real America.

The railway ran through this encampment and where the train stopped the natives had constructed a rough hotel for themselves. 'I shall be quite happy to stay there for the night. I also have no high and mighty ideas about myself. I want a shelter and I'll eat their food, but can you look after my car for me in the camp?' He agreed and I settled down to the problem of getting my luggage over to the 'hotel' on the other side of the railway. Soon I was sitting down to a large dish of rice with the eggs of some jungle bird cooked on top of it. I was starving and it went down well. I often found it easier to speak with natives who had picked up a smattering of Spanish than with people of real Spanish descent. Our linguistic abilities were more or less on the same level! I chatted about my journey and I brought out a few coins to show them. Among my audience was a small boy who collected coins. One of his great longings was to have an English penny. I told him that if he cared to come and help me carry in my big case from the car I would find one for him as well as a few coins from some of the other countries I had passed through. He was delighted but as we walked through the long grass he warned me to be careful of snakes. An occasional rustle was the only indication we got of their presence as they slithered away. The little boy's conversation was remarkable. He went to school in a mud hut where the children sat on the floor and had only very few books, but he knew a great deal about Europe and England, far more than most English children know of Latin America!

Next morning I set off very early to the river expecting that something would come to help me across. There was sign of neither man nor vehicle. I was in a reckless mood. 'To hell with them,' I thought, 'I'm just going to drive straight through.' And I did. It was a struggle and I had to reverse up the farther bank, but within a matter of minutes I was trundling along the road as surely as ever, without the water having had the slightest effect on the running of the car. From there to Palmar Sur it was not too bad. I must have forded ten or twelve streams but my success in the early morning had made me bold. At about ten o'clock I drew up beside a helicopter hangar in Palmar Sur. A head popped out of a small door at the side and as it disappeared I heard it call out, 'Blimey, look what's here!' Within moments several pilots and mechanics appeared and I was given a roaring reception by a group of chaps who weren't quite sure if they should believe their senses. That night I was installed in a room in a modern wooden bungalow with fans to reduce the oppressiveness of the hot tropical air which was really intense. All day sweat had been simply pouring off me. It was the hottest part of the whole journey.

On the following morning I went with one of the pilots to see the local head of the road construction company, Ben Wallace. To reach his camp we had to be ferried across the Rio Grande de Terraba and then walk for about a mile until we came to the entrance of a camp that was surrounded by barbed wire and had an armed guard permanently on duty. We managed with difficulty to persuade him to let me enter alone. Ben Wallace was a brusque but basically helpful American. 'I've heard about your trip and I'm prepared to ferry your car across the river free of charge. But I can do nothing for you from here on. We've finished the rest of the road in our sector and there will be no one to help you along the route. If you get stuck we won't do anything about it. I'm going to warn you what it's like. The worst place is about ten miles from here. A steep track runs at forty-five degrees to the river's edge on both sides. There is a concrete cross there. Eleven of our people have been killed there recently. If you get over that alive you'll be over the worst. A couple of Chileans in an old Pontiac rolled over the side. I haven't seen your car but I've been notified about it and I don't believe you can possibly make it, but you can try if you like. If you break your neck don't expect us to come out and mend it or even help you. We're far too busy trying to get everything cleared up before the wet season. I'll give you permission to go through my part of the road. After that you have the section that the Costa Rican company are doing. They're way behind us in the work and they may not let you through at all.' This was bad news and I returned greatly depressed to discuss it with my friends at the bungalow. We got in touch with the Austin agency in San José by wireless telephone. They had a batch of new Gypsies arriving in a week or ten days' time and they would attempt it then, but they had nothing they could do it in immediately. By then the rains would have started and it would be impossible. I had to find some other way. There were some Chinese merchants who had an old jeep. I thought of paying them to come part of the way but everybody doubted if they were to be trusted. Murder and robbery were very common in those parts. Three people were chopped up and murdered during the three days I was in Palmar! The helicopter boys warned me to be careful on the next part of the route. The peasants, they said, are not quick-witted and will not attack you if you are moving, but if you stop beside one of the fields where they are working they will gradually realize that you are helpless and come out and murder you. They take a particular delight in chopping people up in pieces, cutting off the arms and legs before actually killing them. I pointed out that I thought that they were trying to frighten me.

After three days when all attempts had failed, I challenged my English companions. 'Look,' I said, 'I'll undertake this if any one of you will come with me. I'm not going to do it alone because I know that I'll get stuck in the rivers. If I have someone with me to put blocks of wood under the wheels, we'll get up somehow even if it's inch by inch on a slipping clutch or a stalling engine. We'll both push and steer the car from outside if necessary, but we'll get over this gap in the end.' David Harrison who was due for a few days' leave, felt obliged to respond to the challenge, but first he insisted on showing me the first few miles of the route in a helicopter that had just been overhauled. He wanted to test its air brakes. We noticed one or two bad landslides as well as the fatal river crossing. Nevertheless we set out on the Saturday morning. The landing-barge couldn't ferry us across until ten o'clock and so, before starting off, we packed all unessential equipment and sent it on by air to the capital.

We crossed the Grande de Terraba and approached the barrier at the closed section of the road. I showed a note from his boss to the guard, and the way into the unknown was opened by a man who obviously thought we were slightly crazy. He was probably right. After a short time we saw the concrete cross ahead. The road ended abruptly and a narrow precipitous track at one side led down to an almost empty stream below. Water at any rate would be no problem here. David and I went down to assess the difficulties and to work out the best way of tackling the problems. We decided we would get to the bottom and empty the luggage out there before ascending the other side, where I would keep the car to the inside of the track to turn the front wheels into the rock if it started sliding downwards. At the same time David would have a wooden block ready to put under the rear wheel as well as adding his own power to the energy of the engine. As we were returning to the car discussing the details we heard the sound of an engine in the far distance. We could hardly believe our ears. It was impossible that anybody could arrive at such an opportune moment. It was true, however, and within a little time a dilapidated old blue truck arrived with a couple of Spanish Costa Ricans in it. The vehicle had a four-wheel drive and the driver expressed his pleasure at having the possibility of helping us. Our worries seemed to be over. 'Get your car to the bottom and then I will fix this chain to it and in a minute you'll be up the other side.' That was more or less what happened. It was too much a lightning operation for me to have time to experience much fear, or at least to be conscious of it. A single splash and a few terrible jerks and I was through the water! A moment later I was up on the other side; whether safely or not remained to be seen. Could the poor little Austin's front axle have stood up to such vicious tugs and jerks? The best thing was that we hadn't gone over the edge. In a few moments David came trudging up and we could see no visible sign of serious damage, but the driver of the truck, who was going up into the hills to buy cattle to bring back to Palmar, promised to remain behind us for a few miles until his track departed from the main road. That was good because, in spite of his impulsive methods, I felt sure he would help us in real trouble, and perhaps, after all, those impulsive ways were the best for tackling the hazards of such country.

The driver remained behind us as he had promised and showed no sign of impatience, nor did any immediate trouble with the car materialize. Shortly we had to bid 'adios' to each other, and with his flowery good wishes David and I continued alone. How those Latin Americans love and admire adventure!—with directness of heart and without making too much of the risks or asking too many questions about the good sense of it. They seem to think it is worth while for its own sake and that in itself is good sense, in my opinion. After a few minor adventures at almost dried-up rivers and after crossing one of the parts affected by landslide, where we met a couple of natives riding on burros, we turned by a diversion from the new road into an area of sun-baked shrubbery. The track was narrow and stony and ran under an archway of desiccated trees. The bushes on either side were also utterly shrivelled up and looked as if they could never live again. Once more we could scarcely believe our ears when we heard the sound of a vehicle drawing steadily closer behind us. I was even more surprised when I saw that it was the aspirin-man I had met in Villa Neilly. 'We're made,' I said to David. 'We have this jeep van with us for the rest of the way over the gap. We'll be at the village of Buenos Aires in a couple of hours' time and perhaps even make San Isidro tonight.' It seemed easy. I felt it was a bit of a cheat in a way, but I needn't have done.

The driver of the van was a little dark Costa Rican of clear Spanish descent. He was delighted to see me and made me drive along while he brought out his moving camera which he exhibited as one of his most prized possessions. Together we trundled along until we came to the River Bruja. The road came to an end once more and an assortment of narrow tracks led down to the water's edge. The descent to begin with was so steep on the best of the tracks that we decided to fix a rope on the back of the Austin and David and the men from the van held on to it while I drove the Austin down with all its brakes on. Had there been a free run at the bottom or had I had decent brakes it might have been safe to descend without assistance, but there was a barrier of rocks a little way from the bottom over which the car had to be partly lifted. The River Bruja was wide and deep and there was no possible chance of fording it. We had to search round for some natives who, so we had heard, had a log raft. It was a rough contraption and a bank of stones to form a sort of tiny primitive jetty had to be built up to get the car aboard. Despite all my pleas and to my utter consternation it was tipped off when we were still ten or fifteen yards from the farther bank. I anticipated a certain repetition of my Chilean experience as I plunged through the water. The natives, however, proved right but by so narrow a margin, I was sure, that I dared not contemplate it. I was merely thankful to hear the engine ticking over on dry land once more.

We believed that the worst was over. We were now within fifteen miles or so of the little town of Buenos Aires and we thought we had no more significant rivers to cross. We began to notice, however, that we were coming into a region of lush green foliage. It was evident that the rains had begun here and when we came to the last river before Buenos Aires we found that its banks were slippery and treacherous and that the water in it was flowing fast. I descended the near bank in the same way as I had done previously but got stuck in mid-stream. It was decided that the jeep should try to make the ascent first and when it had reached the top we should join my rope to the chain they were carrying and in that way attempt to pull me out. The driver selected a point right in front of me to make his ascent. Charging through the river he set his four-wheel drive in motion and rushed at the farther bank. Half-way up, the vehicle suddenly slewed round sideways and wavered as if about to roll down on top of me. It was touch and go for some minutes and we all rushed up with whatever implements we could grab and started furiously scraping the mud away from the upper side so as to level the jeep before it slithered down and toppled over. It was a desperate rescue operation and all the time I could see in my mind the jeep rolling straight down on top of the Austin in the middle of the stream. Little by little, however, as we worked the jeep began to level up and we cut a passage out behind it to enable the driver to back down into the stream again. On the second attempt he chose a point farther down the river and was successful. We then carried out our plan with the Austin, which was also successful; although for several anxious seconds I felt it would almost certainly tip over on the muddy uneven bank, and I held one hand firmly on the steering-wheel while with the other I gripped the back of the passenger seat to save myself from getting squashed underneath should the car go over on the side on which I was sitting.

Soon we began to approach cultivated land and fields with quietly grazing cattle. We were coming into the isolated town of Buenos Aires which according to the maps has a population of over two thousand inhabitants. I had been through many towns that could be compared to Wild West towns but Buenos Aires was truly a living example of a cowboy town. The one main street had a row of wooden shacks. There was a large bar and a restaurant on one side and a hotel and another bar on the other. Outside were posts for tying up the horses and in fact before our very eyes the cowboys came galloping in down the main street and did so. The only thing that was wrong was that where one expected to read 'Sheriff's Office' one saw instead 'Comisaria de Policia'. During the evening there was music and noise and dancing and some drunkenness, but no serious fighting or shooting developed. David and I arranged to leave the car in the police station and then sought out a room in the hotel. It was rough by some standards, but it was a clean country roughness and I had long learnt to count it luxury to be able to lay my head down for the night and sleep. Both the jeep driver and David and I made various attempts to obtain permission to drive over the unfinished road to San Isidro, where the rough track which constitutes the Pan-American Highway begins again and continues in a more or less passable form all the way to the Mexican border—satisfactorily and often excellently paved roads ran all the rest of the way to New York.

We made a further attempt to get permission on the following morning, but it was quite clear that the local authorities would not give it; it could only be obtained in San José. David and I decided that there was only one thing to do. There were guards posted at three places along the road. We would try and bluff them. I had a lot of important-looking documents including one with a big embassy crest on it from Buenos Aires in Argentina. I guessed that would puzzle the guards and probably intimidate them into letting us through. It was with great reluctance that we had to say good-bye to our friends with the jeep; and with much apprehension about how we would fare alone at the still numerous rivers ahead. When we returned to collect our luggage a great commotion was going on in one of the bars. Two men had just been engaged in a fight. One was standing at the bar and two women were trying to persuade the other to come away. They looked as if they might have been his wife and his mother. Both men had shirts hanging loosely over their sunburnt backs and every time the two women succeeded in getting their man to the door, the other would hurl some apparently insulting words at him and he would wrench himself loose from the two women, shirts would fly off and both would glare menacingly at each other as though ready for the fray again. This happened so many times that David and I felt that we couldn't really wait to see the end of the encounter.

San Isidro was now about fifty miles away when we set out at about nine-thirty in the morning. We had to cover a five-mile stretch of road on which broken rocks had been roughly distributed, we almost got stuck in a boggy patch that had been affected by the rains and we contrived to get past slightly bewildered guards. The rivers and the descents into them and the climbs out of them were difficult, but not so difficult that with me driving in reverse and David pushing we were unable to negotiate them. I noticed one curious thing during the middle of the morning. When we had travelled for an hour or so after leaving Buenos Aires we came into jungle country once more. I learnt the difference between being alone and being with a companion in such parts. I was sitting quite relaxed at the steering-wheel as the Austin trundled steadily on through glades of tall trees with tropical creepers dangling down and the umbrella-like ferns on the ground seeming as if they were struggling to rival the great trees. I could not help recalling how tense I had been when travelling through similar places on my own. In Ecuador I had sat bolt upright and gripped on to the steering-wheel for hours on end, expecting some disaster to befall me at any moment.

At two o'clock in the afternoon we were rolling along the last stretch of the route into San Isidro. We cared little about the guards at the last check-point. We would have laughed out loud at them if they had tried to turn us back then. But instead they laughed and joked about the whole matter and, I am sure, perceived the trick we had played on their companions on the earlier part of the route.

There was an excellent restaurant in San Isidro, which catered for the adventurous tourists who came down from the capital and even for the occasional Americans for whom this was the last point in their attempt to reach South America. We had an excellently grilled steak and various vegetables, and although water was purified on the spot we preferred the pure orange juice that was supplied for a few pence a pint. We were not yet quite at the end of our adventures, for immediately on leaving San Isidro the road climbs 11,000 feet up into the Talamanca Range to the Cerro de la Muerte, the Hill of Death. Friction arose between David and me. He wanted to set out immediately for San José and, I think, thought me a little feeble for not doing so. I, however, had suspicions about what the climb was going to be like and refused point blank. 'We'll find a hotel here and settle down for the night. Tomorrow I'll prove to you that my decision is right.' We found a hotel in the main plaza run by an Italian. The building was made of wood but we got two rooms, each with a spring bed and a mattress in it. The doors of the rooms, which fitted badly in their frames, were painted with fresh pink paint and everything was clean and neat though crude.

Thirty-four Rivers to Cross

We collected the car from the Comisaria de Policia at seven in the morning and loaded it with bottles of orange juice and sandwiches which we bought from the restaurant as we were leaving. We had also filled up the tank and the spare can with petrol on the previous afternoon and the ascent into the Cordillera began immediately. The morning was clear and sunny and beautiful, and we reckoned we would be well up the mountains before the tropical heat became oppressive. The car seemed in excellent form as it wound steadily and decisively upwards, coping well with the severe gradients and the badly constructed mountain track. David was highly impressed but was beginning to think that he and not I had been right on the previous afternoon. At one point we drew in at the edge of a precipice and in the clear air and gorgeous morning sunshine we were able to see San Isidro below, and far away over the jungle regions beyond, through which we had crossed. It was a sight that David declared would alone have made his participation in the journey worth while.

Up as far as six or seven thousand feet all went superbly well, but after that the carburettor began to play various odd tricks which all the adjustment I made to the mixture did not entirely overcome. Round the steep bends David had to get out and walk with one or two items of heavy equipment while I continued in reverse with the Austin. The car's behaviour there was odder than anywhere else in the mountains, and once I got going I daren't stop until I reached a more level stretch. I would then have to wait five or ten minutes for poor David who would come panting slowly upwards lugging the pieces of equipment. I was full of apologies each time and explained that the near heart-failure I had suffered every moment on the bend was honestly as bad as his plight.

Near the top we ran into the heavy cloud for which the mountain is famed and from which it earned its name, the Hill of Death. Many have perished through running over the precipitous edges of its track. So we now had another peril. The mist became as thick as a fog on a November morning in England. Once or twice a vehicle passed with its lights on and we narrowly missed it. It was two o'clock in the afternoon before the road began to level out, and it still remained mist-bound. By this time David had become fully aware of the wisdom of my decision on the previous afternoon. 'It would have been no fun with darkness added to this sort of visibility,' I commented. 'Can you imagine what it would have been like up here last night?'

The next part of the drive was one of the major disappointments of the journey. For twenty-eight miles a famous skyline drive runs along the edge of the Talamanca Range. It is reputed to provide the most striking scenery of the whole Pan-American Highway. On clear days the two great oceans of the world are sometimes visible at once, the only point on earth where this is so. At last we descended gradually out of the mist and past mountains and volcanoes to the still high plateau on which the capital is situated. Finally after passing between peasant smallholdings and colourful Costa Rican ox wagons we saw Cartago, the old capital, in the distance. Schoolchildren in their white overalls thronged round as we pulled up to visit the ruins of the old cathedral. Its great thick walls now enclose a pleasant, cool little park where the inhabitants of a city that has suffered from constant earthquakes can now sit on the benches and meditate. We did not delay long but pressed on quickly over the new road leading to the present capital. We met an American car when we stopped for a few moments at the roadside. 'Say, where have you come from?' the driver asked. I told him Buenos Aires, Argentina. 'Hey, wait a minute. I thought that was impossible.' I gave my explanation which was accompanied by many colourful American exclamations. I was already feeling quite on top of the world but when he said, 'I've just come down from the States, you've got your journey made now,' it set the note of triumph on which the rest of the trip proceeded, and in a context tinged with triumph I drove into the capital cities of each of the Central American Republics except one, into Mexico and finally into New York. Indeed I felt I was already on its doorstep and could see its towering skyscrapers although it was still nearly five thousand miles away.

13a. Descending the Talamancas towards Mexico

13b. One of the last trails of the Pan-American Highway before reaching the
good roads of Mexico

14a. 'They stood some twelve feet high and eight or nine feet wide.'

14b. The Maya village of Chamula in the south of Mexico. The cross was an ancient pre-Christian symbol known as the tree of life and its form is governed by the concept of the four points of the compass

X

The Wisdom and Follies of Costa Rica

T he builders of San José had learnt their lesson from the recurrent tragedies of the old capital. The new city that sprang up is composed of low light-structured buildings which are not affected by the frequent tremors. The inhabitants sleep peacefully in a city that has earned itself the title of 'the city of cardboard and lace'. Living at a fair height they experience a climate which is never too hot, and are on the whole hard-working and temperate in mind. The city is planned in small blocks and the Costa Rican drivers, even when they are drunk at three o'clock in the morning, stop religiously at the halt signs at every intersection. Costa Rica is probably the most interesting country in Central America and its history makes it almost unique among the Latin American republics. It has not experienced a revolution since 1861 and it claims to be the only country in the world with more schoolteachers than soldiers! Education is widely available and there is little serious poverty in the developed parts of the country. Any Costa Rican is entitled to apply to the government for a house and a smallholding. He receives these for nothing more than a contract to do his best to work the land efficiently.

I arrived at the Austin agency in San José just in time to rush round to the British Embassy to collect the mail that was waiting for me. My car was greeted with amazement and my claim to have crossed the gap almost with incredulity. It happened that I arrived just at the same time as the English doctor in charge of a large clinic in the city, Frank Freeman. I collected my letters and a conversation ensued in which Frank took a leading part. When I had explained various points about my journey, Frank suggested

o   *209*

that I'd better come straight out to his house. I still had an old pair of sailing-trousers and an old grey sweater on and I apologized for looking somewhat like a tramp. 'That's all right,' said Frank, 'that's just what you are really.' I felt he'd somehow completely understood me and we were at once on free and easy terms. 'I can't give you a room in my house. Half of it's being rebuilt at the moment and all the kids are bunched up in one room, but if you don't mind camping in the hay barn above the stables, you're welcome to stay with us while you're in San José.' The cost of living is extremely high throughout the cities of Central America, higher even than in the United States, and I told him exactly how welcome his offer was.

The next day was spent in making numerous minor repairs and adjustments to the Austin. In the evening Pedro, the Costa Rican representative of a British firm, took it into his head to show me what life was really like in his city. We drove out first to his house in one of the new, wealthy, residential districts. The striking designs and the highly colourful decoration showed that Costa Rica also was trying to participate in her own way in the bold new architectural revival of Latin America. It was not very difficult to appreciate that the moral climate of the Central American republics was very different from Europe and indeed from South America and Mexico also. We drove with a friend of Pedro's through the city, past the Central Plaza where the evening promenade was taking place. I remembered Tschiffely's account of this event, how the young women promenade round in one direction and the young men in the other, only the engaged men being allowed to walk in the feminine direction in the company of their fiancées. I could not but agree with Tschiffely's judgment: 'I have rarely seen so many exceedingly pretty and well-dressed girls as were parading in this plaza.' Unlike Tschiffely I did not approach this event alone and unforewarned and I did not get involved in the embarrassment of finding myself travelling in the wrong direction. Indeed we passed by quickly, for the event has declined in these days with some decline of class distinction, and, I imagine, a drastic change in moral outlook.

We arrived at the first night club that Pedro had planned to take me to. It was a rather large hall with subdued lighting and a bar at one end. 'It's too early for anything to be happening yet, but we can have a drink and a chat for a while,' remarked Pedro.

He began to describe graphically the kind of parties and orgies that Central Americans indulge in, and explained how one notorious governor of the city had failed miserably to impose morality on the Josephinos, as the inhabitants of the city are called. 'There are some prostitutes in these clubs, but here in San José the girls have equal rights with the men. A girl from a good family can come out to one of these clubs if she wishes.' He went on to tell me the story of the governor who planned a comprehensive raid on all the night clubs of the city. It turned out that his own wife was spending the evening in one of the clubs and was among those arrested. 'Since that time,' Pedro emphasized with some delight, 'our city governors have occupied themselves with looking after their own wives and have been content to leave us to look after our own morals!'

After a while a few girls began to arrive and Pedro asked a couple of them over for a drink with us and began to jabber away to them in Spanish about my journey. Behind us a rather pleasant-looking girl with auburn hair was sitting alone. 'Why don't we invite her across?' I suggested. 'She looks lonely.' I was amazed to find that she spoke fluent English and had had part of her education in the United States. We had a delightful conversation for an hour or so while Pedro and a friend of his chatted away in Spanish to the other two girls. After a little while a row occurred between them and Pedro came over to me and announced that we must all leave immediately. I was sorry to conclude my little tête-à-tête with the brown-eyed señorita, but as she caught my hand and asked me to return later, I knew there was little chance since I was due to leave the city very early on the following morning. What a revolution towards the equality of the sexes, when a well-bred young girl can go out for a night's adventure!

From there we went to another club. This time it was very Parisian in style. A predominantly male gathering was eagerly watching a dark-eyed señorita strip off alluringly as she danced on a small intimate stage. Pedro ordered a table and whispered a few private words to the manager. What bribe he was offering I don't know, but within a few minutes of the end of the dance the girl who had just been naked was sitting fully dressed beside us at the table. 'She is a very sophisticated girl,' remarked Pedro. Unfortunately she left me stone cold and I began to grow extremely bored as Pedro and his friend talked away rapidly in Spanish. I threw out hints that I needed to leave to be ready for the following morning.

I feel rather like one of the blind men of Hindustan, who went to see the elephant. Each got different impressions on account of getting hold of different parts of the beast. My impressions would have appeared even stronger if I had recorded all that Pedro told me or described all the arrangements he suggested making. I have refrained from doing so because I do not want to produce a one-sided picture of the remarkable city and its inhabitants.

I set out early in the morning from San José and passed along a fairly narrow but well-paved road leading out through a string of up-to-date suburbs. Neatly painted black-and-white notices indicated the name of each one, as well as the distances to and from other places and the route number of the road on which I was travelling. It was some time before I reached more countrified parts. The climate and the scenery except for a few characteristic things might well have been some hilly part of England. The small towns were Spanish in style and the numerous colourfully decorated ox wagons made me aware all the time that I could only be in Costa Rica. The true Latin artistic spirit is put into the bold and beautiful designs on the wheels. The old folk art still persists, like the work of the Neapolitan fishermen on their fishing-boats, but the invasion of the motor-truck is very noticeable and all the main roads north of the capital are well paved and have anticipated Costa Rica's mechanized future.

As I drew near to the coast after a long steady descent, I began to feel the return of the oppressive tropical heat. The atmosphere, however, was still dry and, as in so many other places in Central America and Mexico, the leafless trees and shrubs awaited the approaching wet season to bring them to life again. I stopped at a small wayside restaurant, not far from Puntarenas, the country's main port, and learnt that an Austrian girl on horseback on her way to South America had just spent the night there. It was always a disappointment to just miss meeting someone who had also obviously been caught by the same spirit of travel and adventure as myself. The thought of horses brought Tschiffely back to my mind as I travelled along the long hot level road to the Nicaraguan border. He had commented that Nicaragua was a hot country both climatically and politically. Owing to a revolution

which was then in progress he had been very reluctantly compelled to go by sea from Puntarenas to La Union in El Salvador. I
was more fortunate. There was no actual revolution going on, but
I ran into the forces preparing for one on the borders of Honduras.

It was early afternoon when I reached the town of Las Cañas,
the ducks. I was to look for the hacienda San Luis, which was
owned by a Canadian from whom Frank had assured me I could
expect hospitality. I suppose if a man leaves Canada to start up a
farm in the wilds of Central America, he is not likely to be too
amazed at another man happening to drive up from Buenos Aires
in an ancient car. I don't think he bothered to welcome me in
words, but before I knew where I was my bags were on their way
into his bungalow and the afternoon was spent visiting his farm.
He had built a road ten kilometres long through it. It was constructed of a whitish volcanic material. There had been a whole
hill of it on his farm and he showed me where more than half of it
had been carted away. It made a magnificent hard surface without
developing the corrugations that occur on earth and gravel roads.
I was to experience it later in Honduras and the speed with which
it enabled me to pass through that country saved me from a great
deal of bother with documents. The Austin was to be turned to an
unexpected use that afternoon. A new cattle-weighing machine
had just been constructed and it was necessary to test its accuracy.
Since we knew that the Austin weighed eight cwt. we merely
drove on, looked at the indicator and made the necessary con-
version to the metric system. I continued looking right over the
farm. A complete village of pleasant Canadian-style wooden
houses had been built for the native workmen and their families.
The main crops of the farm were sugar and tobacco and my host
took me into the barns where great quantities of tobacco were
drying. 'Careful as you enter. Yesterday as I went in the head of a
coral snake was dangling from the lintel of the doorway. I was
slightly blinded by the contrast from the sunlight and didn't
notice it until I was only inches away. They're deadly brutes;
there's no cure for their bite and they abound in vast numbers
round here. The men usually manage to avoid them but I frequently lose cattle.' I walked round cautiously between the
bunches of tobacco leaves hanging from the ceiling and every few
seconds I thought I saw the deadly red stripes on the coral snake's

head dangling in front of me and about to strike. I was extra careful about opening up the car on the following morning.

I should have liked to have delayed awhile in many places in Central America but I knew it was imperative to reach Mexico before the beginning of April. It was especially important to get over the gap in northern Guatemala before the rains fell, when landslides would almost certainly block the route in the great descent between walls of mountains known as the 'Corkscrew'. I therefore departed early in the morning loaded with a large picnic lunch that the Indian maid had prepared. I expected paved road all the way to Managua, the capital of Nicaragua. I also knew that I had to move pretty rapidly because according to the handbooks it was only possible to spend three days in Nicaragua without special permission which was complicated to obtain and in the circumstances not worth the bother. Before reaching the frontier I climbed up again into hilly green farm country and then descended to the border village of Peña Blanca. The formalities were quickly over, but I noticed now that the Paysanos, the peasants, looked sour and vicious and I felt immediately that I was in a country whose people had suffered oppression and hardened themselves to political murder. The contrast with the friendly Costa Ricans was something I could feel without even stopping the car to talk. I took much greater care to make my own waves and greetings even more friendly in outward appearance and I only stopped to inquire about the route when I came upon one of the large road-building machines. I learnt from the driver that the southern section of the Interamericana in Nicaragua was under construction and that the old paved road had been ripped up for a stretch of eighty kilometres to build the foundation of the new four-lane highway. For some distance I was diverted on to an old road which ran along the shores of Lake Nicaragua. The waters lapped up almost to the edge of the road and reached so far out of sight that it was hard to believe that I was not beside the sea. In the distance I could see the dim outline of two volcanoes rising out of the water on the Isle of Ometepe. As I glanced through my binoculars it seemed even more like a great sea for every here and there I could see the vicious fins of sharks pointing up above the wavelets. Nicaragua is the only freshwater lake in the world where sharks are found. Their presence poses many problems for geologists and geographers.

The Wisdom and Follies of Costa Rica

The full heat of a tropical afternoon beat down on the little Austin and it was little wonder that its thirst needed quenching every now and again. I was on paved road once more when I stopped to attend to the radiator. Just as I was getting into the car a peasant approached me from behind some trees. He was bare to the waist and wore an old baggy pair of trousers and a filthy greasy sombrero. A sharp machete dangled loosely and unsheathed from his belt. How different from the rather neatly dressed Costa Ricans! I was just about to get my lunch out when I noticed him, so I decided to continue, offering him some bread and a couple of hard-boiled eggs which he accepted with delight. In that way what might have been an unpleasant incident was easily avoided and we chatted about the route as we picnicked together. I was to hear many unpleasant stories of murders by peasants when I reached the capital. Nicaragua today is in a rather strange condition. For many years it was held under tyranny by the dictator Samosa until he was assassinated several years ago. Today it is run by his two sons: one who controls the army and is reputed to have a tyrannical outlook, and the other who heads the government and is attempting to make the country more liberal by introducing free elections and the various concomitants of democracy. As evidence of this I noticed that almost all the police and military control posts were out of use and somewhat dilapidated—a good sign, I thought.

It was about four o'clock when I pulled up outside Casa Cross, the Austin agency in Managua. The car was put safely into the garage and I was taken into a big modern office on an upper floor. A group of business men were seated around drinking cups of tea in a truly English fashion. Could I really be in Central America? I wondered. It seemed much more like London when I was going round preparing for my journey. My arrival, however, was expected at any time and in spite of my trampish appearance I was quickly brought into the afternoon ceremony. A room had been reserved for me at the best hotel in the city and, as the week-end was just approaching, Mr. Cross had planned a trip round the lakes in his launch. The last important European visitor he had taken out, he told me, had been the King of the Belgians. This time, I suggested, he would have the privilege of taking out a kind of king of the tramps. I had not ceased to be fascinated by the idea of myself in this role since my meeting with Frank in San José.

The Wisdom and Follies of Costa Rica

I was of course shown the sights of the city, including Samosa's infamous castle. A great fawn-walled fortress is perched on the edge of the gaping crater of an extinct volcano. I was told of the medieval torture chambers and dungeons that lay beneath its bright wall, where until a couple of years earlier unspeakable atrocities were the order of the day for Samosa's political enemies. I was warned again to proceed with the utmost caution through the rest of Nicaragua; especially in the villages I was to take care not to touch anyone with the car, even when moving very slowly, for the villagers were likely to take sudden offence and were looking for opportunities to lynch anyone whom they might associate with the old ruling order. But dangers came not only from the rebels. Preparations were known to be going ahead for a new revolution in the wild country around the borders of Honduras. The fear was that some officer of the guards would associate me with Castro on account of my beard and have me shot. People were sometimes shot on the merest suspicion in that area and the Crosses were concerned on my account. I said that I thought my excellent documents would see me through the guards and that my beard might well be my best passport through the bandit country. I was not mistaken in this judgment.

After tea I was led round to the hotel. The car was put into the back patio where I was assured it would be watched and guarded by the cook. The hotel was cooled by fans and was a pleasant change from the heat I had experienced during the day. It was constructed along the usual Latin American lines, but was much more luxurious than most of them. Vines and tropical plants spread their cooling influence over the courtyard at one end of which meals were attractively served in the open air. My first impression of the guests came as a real surprise. A priest was speaking rapidly in English to a couple of rather odd-looking Irish characters. I guessed I'd be seeing more of them later and sure enough they approached me after dinner to join them in the bar. They were two brothers according to their story. The elder brother was addicted to drink. The younger one strongly disapproved of it but, since, as he explained, he had been brought up to bow to seniority, he could do no other than accept his brother's orders to drink, while struggling to use all legitimate means short of open rebellion to bring his revered brother to a sober and better way of living. They had a story, they claimed, that would beat all adventure stories ever written if they could only let it be known to the world. My own adventures were mere child's play beside their story (I'd scarcely told them anything about mine, but that didn't seem to be very relevant). They had been washed up ashore on the coast of Nicaragua as the only two survivors of an Irish vessel which had foundered during a great storm. All their papers had been lost and, although they had struggled to make contact with Irish diplomatic sources in Washington, Ireland or her representatives had simply rejected two of her suffering sons. The British Consul, they said, had been unable to do anything for them. In desperation they had struggled to escape from the tyranny of Nicaragua into Honduras where they hoped they might get help. They had travelled through jungles, had been almost starving for weeks on end, had been chased by bandits and finally after weeks of struggle had been caught by the military guards at the border. Their only hope then had been to try and work to gain enough money to buy Nicaraguan nationality. They needed quite a lot of money and for a year they had worked on a sugar plantation with the natives until they could bear the brutal work and heat no longer. They then made another attempt to escape, this time into Costa Rica. Now they were back again and getting some help from the priest and they crossed themselves as they spoke reverently about him. Their immediate need, however, was whisky and as I was determined not to waste my money on more than one or two rounds we fairly quickly bade each other good night.

The following evening I went round to the house of one of the representatives of the agency for a drink. I was rather struck by the sight of several dead men lying about in the street, of whom nobody seemed to take the slightest bit of notice except to avoid tripping over them. I supposed some street cleaner or the dogs or buzzards would dispose of them before they began to decompose and stink too offensively, and went on my way fairly sharply of the opinion that human life was regarded even more cheaply here than in other parts of Latin America. Mr. Cross later assured me that they were only dead drunk, that it was indeed the natural thing on Saturday nights and that nobody would take any notice of it.

There had been an American poet at the party, whom I had noticed at the hotel, and on the following morning we found ourselves deep in conversation. He had left the wild scramble of life in New York and built himself a home far out in the peace of the jungle of Nicaragua. I expressed my spontaneous sympathy with his plans and outlook. Indeed I would have gone far out of my way to visit him had he not been intending to spend several weeks in Managua gathering together a few of the products of civilization he thought he would prefer not to manage without, for he was no fanatic. He began to read me some of his poetry about the rats scurrying about New York. Unfortunately the rats didn't publish it when he sent it to them, about which I felt he was slightly hurt. I was afraid that I also considered that it was definitely not good poetry. I nevertheless felt that he might have written good poetry, as he began to speak of the native people of the village where he lived. He particularly disliked civilized women, I remember. 'Even these Latin American women who appear so gentle are tigresses at heart,' he declared positively. 'But the people out in the jungle where I'm living are nice,' he added introducing an odd softness into his voice. 'They are honest and kind and uncomplicated. I can get on with them and trust them. Sometimes I have to speak sharply to my cook but not often.' Where he lived was as near to heaven as any place on earth could be. It was barely accessible by jeep for just a few months of the year. The rest of the time he was absolutely cut off from the vileness of the civilized world.

On Monday morning I set out again on my journey to the north of Nicaragua. It was a dull day's travel through hot uninteresting countryside. The villages were dirty and the people for the most part had a rough hostile look. About thirty miles of the route was unpaved; the rest was excellent tarmac, and by late afternoon I had reached the little town of Somoto about twenty miles from the border of Honduras. During the last few miles the road had begun to climb through greener and slightly more fertile country. I noticed occasionally that children would emerge from the houses and shacks by the roadside and wave to me while the parents sometimes gave the sign of the revolutionary forces. It was plain that they took my beard as a sign of association with Fidel Castro, the figurehead of all revolutions in Central America. By evening I was settled in a small unfinished hotel in Somoto after reporting to the guards and receiving friendly and helpful treatment.

The Wisdom and Follies of Costa Rica

The following morning I delayed until a little after seven o'clock. I knew that the customs would be closed if I arrived too early and that a good paved road ran right to the border. I was now coming to one of the last unpaved sections of any length in the whole journey. The ninety-seven miles of the Interamericana through Honduras is unpaved all the way. I proceeded with some inner uncertainty in the fresh early morning air and sunshine. I guessed that the bandits and rebels would treat me all right unless they were in desperate straits themselves. After half an hour or so, having left behind the houses from which I sometimes got the revolutionary sign, and having arrived into wild hilly country, I noticed a small group of men galloping towards me on horseback. As they came closer I could see that they were armed to the teeth with guns and knives. As the leader rode up towards me I leant out of the side of the car and gave him a very friendly greeting. It was mainly the sight of my beard, I believe, that brought him to a sudden and respectful halt. I think he must have thought I was Castro motoring around to visit the revolutionary forces. I was totally unable to understand his rapid outpourings in Spanish apart from gathering that they contained strong expressions of political opinion. Rather than reveal my ignorance of the language, I made off with a speedy 'Adios, Señor, good luck,' which I could manage in authentic accents.

There were several cars at the border when I arrived. The formalities were brief and by twenty to nine I was ready to start off on my way across Honduras. My papers had not been quite in order but I gathered from the semi-literate official that if I left Honduras that same day I would be permitted to pass through without the visa which I had been unable to obtain. A large American car, whose driver glanced somewhat snootily at my Austin and obviously regarded me as one of the impoverished vagabonds who sometimes make their way down from the States to Central America, set off at the same time and soon went racing ahead of me. I pottered along at my own steady speed over a wide road constructed of the volcanic material I had met earlier on the hacienda in Costa Rica. For many miles the road was wide and good, passing through wild bush countryside with only very few signs of habitation. A certain amount of farming was attempted around the village of San Marcos, the odd-looking Brahmin cattle that I saw through much of Central America adding to the picturesqueness of the scene. Now and again I would disturb a group of reluctant vultures gathered around some half-eaten carcass. One or two of the bravest would remain so that as I passed by closely I was able to get a good view of their vile red heads and bloody beaks.

The morning was passing steadily and so were the kilometres. I almost relaxed my cautious attitude a little too much in going down one hill, and as a result of the bad camber of the road and undue speed, I nearly lost control of the steering and all but tipped the car over the steep edge of the hillside. The height of the Austin off the road was an indispensable factor on such a journey as mine, but it had to be paid for in terms of a high centre of gravity which made it surprisingly easy to tip the car over on some of the rough and strangely cambered roads, even at low speeds.

As I descended towards the hot lowlands in the central part of my route across Honduras, I noticed the superior American driver I had set off with in the morning trying to repair a badly burst tyre. From this point of view the Austin's limited speeds were really practical over the rough roads. I saw many a fast car in Central America stopped because a piece of rock or stone had flown up and hit its radiator or cracked its sump or back axle. There was little now that I could do for the stranded American, but I felt it must have taught him a very salutary lesson to watch the little Austin chugging on ahead like the tortoise in the race in Aesop's fable.

By eleven o'clock I could see Choluteca ahead of me, the first fair-sized town in Honduras. The road had been really good and was the width specified for the Pan-American Highway. I was now nearly half-way across Honduras. I stopped at a petrol station to refuel but did not wait to visit the town. When I had filled the tank with petrol for which I paid in dollars, a man came out of the office and invited me in to have a bottle of beer. He told me that it was made in Choluteca. It certainly seemed excellent to me; one of those glasses of beer that will remain always in my mind, almost in my mouth, for the rest of my life. But perhaps at that moment a glass of water would have done the same. I gave a very brief outline of my journey and explained that I was English. My host for those few fleeting minutes attempted to use the few words of English he knew: 'They bad men in Nicaragua,' he said and showed me where his arms and legs had been in chains in Samosa's castle. The deep encircling scars which were visible round his legs when he raised his trouser legs were a sight that one could not quickly forget and set me thinking about the politics of those sad countries until long after I had waved good-bye to him.

Ten miles of road constructed out of stones from a river-bed, which formed deep furrows running with the road instead of corrugations across it, in sweltering tropical heat, was the ordeal I had to pass through for the next hour or two. An occasional truck would pass by sending a billowing cloud of dust over the flat bushy wilderness on either side of the road. The sun seemed to have dried everything to death. Once again there was not a leaf visible on the trees nor did I see the least sign of animal life about. Shortly, of course, I knew that all would be suddenly transformed. I hoped I would be in Mexico before that transformation took place, though I also regretted it. I passed through the town of Nacaome near where the road runs up to the capital with the delightful-sounding name of Tegucigalpa. Nacaome was just another shanty town, of little obvious interest that I could detect in my haste to reach El Salvador. Old boards, corrugated iron, donkeys and dilapidated trucks seemed to be its life and substance. The road improved again with a wide gravel surface as I began the gentle climb up the hills on the other side of Nacaome. Vegetation returned and huts of a native pattern appeared, and sometimes even bungalows with tiled roofs. Naked children ran around and disappeared quickly into their homes as I passed. Quite pleasant pottery decorated in quasi-Indian patterns was for sale at various points along the route, and of course farming was once more in evidence. The population seemed to grow much denser as I reached the border of El Salvador.

It was two o'clock when I reached the new customs house set against a barren hillside that I knew was in El Salvador. I had many thoughts about that little republic. The handbook of the American Automobile Association describes it as the most progressive in Central America. It has a network of good paved roads, it has many large towns, and every square inch of land that can be cultivated is exploited to the full. The first true sign of civilization I met was red tape at the customs. I was sure then that all the rest was true. There was no actual blockage but it took a couple of hours to get all the numerous papers and documents settled, and thus I was forced to banish all thoughts of reaching San Salvador that night. Ox carts and modern trucks as well as private motor-cars were much in evidence side by side along the roads. There were undoubtedly certain developments in this country, but the peasantry struck me as more exploited and de-pressed than in some of the more primitive regions of Honduras where the spirit of native independence still seemed very much alive. The bulk of the peasants in El Salvador work hard for poor wages for their masters on the large coffee plantations. Their homes seem desperately poor, their clothes a shabby version of those worn in America and Europe; and their children run naked and dusty round their dwellings up to quite a considerable age.

I turned off the main road into the town of San Miguel where I found a decent but rather expensive hotel. I had hardly settled in before a man from the local radio station arrived to interview me. I was rather surprised by this since nobody in the town had any foreknowledge of my arrival. I hadn't myself. Early in the morn-ing I set out for San Salvador. The men wandered along the verges of the road on their way to work and the women carried water-pots or bundles of washing on their heads. It was only eighty or ninety miles to the capital and by mid-morning I was driving along the big dual carriageway leading into the city. I found San Salvador modern and uninteresting but with many signs that it was in the process of serious industrialization. It had nothing of the Latin American splendour, not even small touches of colourful art to remind one of Brazilia or Mexico City. Three things only stand out in my mind from my visit to this city. In Central America one sees enormous wasps with two long thin spikes trailing behind them as they fly. I was driving in towards the city with my head out of the side of the car and my mouth open, possibly gasping for breath in the intense heat, possibly singing to myself or possibly just feeling stupid, when one of those formidable creatures suddenly shot straight into it. Perhaps I was preparing unconsciously for some seconds before its arrival to spit it out, but at any rate I contrived to do so with such rapidity that it hadn't even time to sting me. Nevertheless that nasty mouthful outlived most of my other impressions of El Salvador. My second memory is of a procession organized by the Austin agency. They had planned for me to drive round the city leading a procession which included every current model made by the Austin Motor Company, both private and commercial vehicles. The city traffic was dislocated and the event had been planned with the full co-operation of the city police. In return for that I had my hotel bills and entertainment paid for and arranged for me. My third impression is of a conversation with the British Ambassador there. He was one of the first people to sympathize fully with my refusal to carry a gun. He had travelled extensively on muleback through Ecuador and had had real experience of travelling in savage regions. He warned me, however, on two scores. First to be sure to have enough ready cash to be able to pay for an ox cart on the spot should I accidentally happen to damage one with the car. The drivers are terrified of their feudal masters and will kill motorists who don't pay up immediately. Secondly he warned me of the political situation in Guatemala, whose government lays claim to the territory of British Honduras. The argument was brewing up strongly at the time and it seemed possible that the Guatemalans might have a hostile attitude to anything British. A prohibitive embargo, for instance, had just been put on the import of English cars.

Thus I set out once more with apprehensions, for Santa Ana and the border of Guatemala. I hoped to make the whole journey to Guatemala City in one day. At Santa Ana I asked a policeman the route to the border and he asked me for a lift. By bundling large pieces of luggage on to his knees and squeezing the petrol and water-cans round his boots I managed to fit him in! I hoped he would speed up the formalities at the frontier for me and he did. After all I was in no position to carry passengers for fun, although I did carry a passenger who caused a good deal of fun later on.

After crossing the gap in Panama and Costa Rica, the rest of the journey through Central America had been rather dull. The real spirit of Latin America seemed to be missing. Whether it was the presence of the dollar or what, I just don't know. It struck me that the countries of Central America looked towards the United States with an envious spirit, their own seeming to have died. In Guatemala, however, it was different. There, once again, was the old enthusiasm that I had met everywhere in South America. I was stopped on the road, photographed on the road by passing motorists and made welcome in a thoroughly Latin American fashion, especially by a group of bomberos (firemen) of Guatemala City. I was given a note to the chief of the fire station and pressed to agree to stay there. It would save me wasting money on hotel bills, they said. It was a happy relief. I was expecting hostility and they gave me hospitality, more generous and more spontaneous than anything I had received from the people of any of the other Central American countries. I stopped for lunch and to buy petrol. A good restaurant was attached to the service station and the best lunch it could provide was served up. A chicken was roasted specially for my benefit. I feared a big bill but when I came to pay there was no charge.

Yes, I felt I was truly a guest in Guatemala. Perhaps it was this that caused me to be slightly overconfident when I reached the paved road that runs for the last fifty miles into the city. I happened to be running along close to a Land Rover and it entered my head to show its driver what an ancient Austin could still do. I put my foot pretty firmly down on the accelerator and the needle of the speedometer went jumping round in characteristic fashion towards the forty-five mark. Its readings were considerably low as I discovered later when I was checked as reaching fifty-five on the Bridgehampton race circuit outside New York. I had just overtaken the Land Rover and was wondering if I dared peep round to get a glimpse of the look on the face of the driver, when an unholy noise began to emerge from around the engine.

My mind went straight to the poor big ends which after all their struggles through mountain, desert and jungle, had now been pressed beyond their capacity. 'Oh, my God,' I thought, 'why the hell was I such a fool as to try and race it at this stage?' and I added one or two other colourful things about my own stupidity. The symptoms all pointed to the big ends. It was really madness to run the engine at all in that condition, so I pulled up to have a look. The Land Rover shot by, presumably without realizing my trouble. A few moments later a lorry pulled up and offered to take a note in to the Austin agency in the city. I was furious because I wanted to drive in triumphantly. If I had to be towed in I felt it would make the Guatemalans not only think that the British had no right to Belize (British Honduras), but that they weren't even competent to keep a little motor-car running. Nevertheless I thought I had no alternative but to give a note and a photograph of the sort of thing the breakdown truck was to look

15a. Arrival at my hotel in Mexico City

15b. The hacienda Molino de Flores near Texcoco

16. My first appearance with the car in New York after we had both washed off the dust of the journey

for. The lorry driver pointed out that if I could only get up the next ten miles the rest of the way was downhill. After further examination I decided that it was not the big ends that had gone, and so I could risk continuing to run the car. The point about big ends is that if they are caught in time they are relatively easy to repair with proper facilities, but if run too far after they have gone are liable to destroy the whole engine.

I crawled slowly up to the top of the hill, which was shrouded in mist, noticing once the indistinct form of a new Austin passing me by. I only hoped that it wasn't from the Austin agency. Although I was not in the best of moods to appreciate it, one certainly gains an impressive view of the city as one circles gradually down the mountainside of the great basin in which it is situated. I pulled up at the Austin agency at the very moment that a new Gypsy with repair equipment was setting out to meet me. I had not after all been missed on the road and I had arrived under my own steam! A twelve-dollar-a-night room in a luxury motel on the outskirts of the city had been booked for me. I was not much of a financial proposition for an agency that was finding it impossible to import British cars, but the manager explained to me that although he and most Guatemalans held that their claim to Belize was entirely justified and that the British government was absolutely wrong, they nevertheless entertained most friendly and cordial feelings towards England and English people. They believed, he said, that just claims were best achieved by friendly rather than hostile attitudes.

There is little of interest in Guatemala City although it bears all the signs of becoming a large and prosperous capital and the colourful mosaics on the university building were the first intimations of the remarkable architecture I was shortly to meet in the university city of Mexico. The designs were bold, realistic and modern, something of the old Indian traditions being conveyed by them: an almost brutal emphasis on the things of this world as opposed to the other worldliness of so much European and Asiatic art, for the Indians worshipped the gods of this world right up to the very doorsteps of the catholic church into which their forefathers had been reluctantly compelled to enter.

Sunday came round and I decided to go out for the day on one of the old buses running out to Antigua, the old capital of the country. It was a very ordinary bus and I bundled in with Indians and half-castes. I had hoped to look up an American painter whom Michael Westcott had met on his journey. I didn't know his address, and as soon as I reached the town I was assailed by guides who spoke English and wanted to show me round at prices applicable to an American pocket but certainly not to mine. One of them, however, knew the artist in question and took me straight to his house. He was out so I told the guide that I wasn't American and bargained for an abbreviated tour, mentioning my extreme dislike for any kind of guided tours and expressing one or two of my opinions about guides themselves. After that we got on extremely well and it was interesting to see the ruins of the thirty-six monasteries and convents which this town contained. One apparently specialized in baking, another in laundry and so on, so that the life of them all was closely interwoven. Despite all these signs of godliness, however, heaven had not looked down kindly upon them. The city suffered during the last century from so many earthquakes, one of which was accompanied by an inundation of disastrous proportions when a crack occurred in a mountain lake above the town, that the old capital was evacuated and the present capital built on a site less subject to such natural disasters.

Back in Guatemala City on the following day I made contact with a young Englishman, Mike Young, the motor-cycle racing champion of Central America. I was introduced to him through a contact of Michael Westcott's whose films and friends were indeed playing a very large part in my journey. Mike Young was a mechanic and ran a garage of his own. After discussing the matter for some while we decided to take the Austin Seven engine out of the car and give it a thorough examination. We were both amazed to see how little it had suffered from the countless millions of revolutions that had brought it up from Buenos Aires. We could attribute the noise that I had heard to nothing more than a small part of the braking system beside the gear box.

There was an unavoidable delay of several days, and when we were not working on the car we were flying round the city in a new British sports car at breakneck speeds. I found it a little hard to accustom myself to the change. On one occasion we went to see the large relief map made of concrete in one of the parks on the outskirts of the city. It was obviously designed to give the Guatemalan people a clear picture of what is theirs. The blue and white flag of Guatemala flutters fearlessly over what on most other maps is marked as British Honduras. As we flew back towards the city I recalled to mind Tschiffely's visit to this same map so many years ago. He had travelled on one of the city's old trams which had derailed itself on the return journey. After having responded to the driver's request to lift it back again, he had decided it would be easier to conclude his outing on foot. We were at the entrance to my motel before I could think any more about it.

The normal tourist from America takes the easy road to Tapachula on the Mexican border. There he puts his car on a train for a hundred and fifty miles at a cost that he can easily afford. There is another route, however. An old trail which is now being turned into the Pan-American Highway passes high up over the Talamancas and descends for nearly a hundred miles through dangerous and winding gorges down to the Mexican border. That was the route for me. It was to be the last real adventure of my journey. I could have fitted an extra one in if I had waited until the following week-end, when Mike said he would borrow an aeroplane and fly me over the Talamancas to Quirigua, to visit the extensive remains of the original capital of the old Maya civilization and one of the most interesting ruins in America. Mike had no pilot's licence but he'd had a couple of shots at flying a plane!

Owing to reconstruction work in the mountains I was advised to take the lower road along the coast of Guatemala through hot country where coffee and sugar plantations occupied most of the rich land. Soon after passing through Mazatenango I had to turn sharply up into the Talamanca range to get on to the Pan-American Highway once more at Quezaltenango, the second city of Guatemala. The road was paved and in very fair condition for all but nine kilometres. Those last nine kilometres were on a rough trail of incredible steepness and difficulty. I thought on several occasions that it would surely defeat me, but by manœuvring the car up in reverse I eventually managed it as I did in all the difficult mountain parts. I was coming into the real country of the Indians, without any doubt the most picturesque of any of the Indians I saw in America. I was not alone on my climb up this trail, nor was my method of ascent the most arduous or difficult. The heavily laden mules of the Indians struggled valiantly with their incredible loads, but even their endurance was overshadowed by the feats of the small Indian men I watched climbing with enormous frameworks fitted on to their backs, each wooden tier of which bore a row of at least half a dozen large clay pots—and each frame consisting of half a dozen tiers. The strength and endurance of those small bodies must have been phenomenal. I could really hardly believe my eyes. But it was not until I had accomplished the climb and was approaching a town which I thought was Quezaltenango that I saw the superb heritage of the old Maya art. The women wore shawls woven in colours and designs subtle and delicate in every shade and thread. It was a thrill and an artistic experience to look at them. I was fool enough to take my camera out in an attempt to keep the memory of it. But at the sight of the camera they fled like frightened rabbits with their little children scurrying after them.

I went on to Quezaltenango where I filled up with petrol, stayed at a pleasant hotel and set out on my journey through El Tapon early in the morning. The first few miles were over a level paved road until I came to the point where the basis of the new highway climbs still farther up into the mountains. The climb was steady but not difficult and the road surface was still relatively smooth, for it had been little used. It was incredibly dusty, though. Within a few hours I had reached the top and began to descend towards the town of Huehuetenango. Occasional villages still appeared and rolling barren hills spread out into a gentle blue haze in the distance. The landscape was like a strange dream. The barren rocky reality of my immediate surroundings contrasted with the etherial dreamy blue into which the bleak landscape gradually merged to make up this distant corner of Guatemala. Away over in front of me I knew that the same blue sky covered Mexico. Where, I wondered, would I be by the time night had turned all to shadowy blackness?

I was intending to top up my petrol tank at Huehuetenango before continuing into the wilderness of El Tapon. The climb into the town was steep and it was ten miles or so out of my way. The Austin did not take immediately to the task of climbing and I saw that coaxing would be necessary. I decided to risk it without the extra petrol and make straight for the Mexican border which was now only sixty or seventy miles away. A peculiar sense of leaving all human life behind came over me; this last venture into the desert seemed the last metaphorical straw. I had a kind of horrible premonition that something terrible would happen before I reached the civilization and security of Mexico. I felt sure that one of the famous landslides of this region would fall right on top of me. How could my luck hold out any longer? I was wrong, however, I wound steadily downwards through winding gorges, along rocky trails and over heaps of rock that had piled up on the road. It was very much like an old cowboy trail in the Rocky Mountains themselves.

Finally vegetation appeared again. Villages and people came into life once more. I was thirty, twenty, ten kilometres from the Mexican border, according to my calculations. I had almost finished with trails and tracks and difficulties, or at least I thought so. I felt like a schoolboy counting the days and hours till the holidays.

XI

A Picnic in Mexico

M exico is undoubtedly the most complex of all the Latin
American countries, both in regard to its history and its
present-day character. I had read of the Mexican revolution, I had heard wild tales about this adventurous country, I
had noted firmly in my mind that Tschiffely believed it to be the
country that best understood his ride, and I had seen pictures of
its flashy architecture. I knew there would be sunshine and sombreros of fabulous size. But it was not until I came to write this
chapter that I realized how little I know about Mexico. When I
crossed the border from Guatemala I didn't even know that. I
was just a pinpoint moving across a vast map of geographical, and
even more of racial mystery. It is probably just that racial mystery
that has given Mexico its fabulous distinction, that has created
the almost mythopoeic opinion which the world in general has
formed of that country.

In Mexico the Indian has not only survived but triumphed,
triumphed in a strange new world setting. Irene Nicholson in a
recent talk on the Third Programme ('A Revolution in Suspense',
printed in the *Listener*), said: 'Education without distinction of
caste or colour has had one side effect. It has brought the Indian-
ness of Mexico into prominence. Benito Juárez, hook-nosed
Zapotec, who presides over every Mexican schoolroom together
with the insurgent priest Hidalgo, is the prototype of today's
Mexican. It is chic to look like a low relief from Palenque, a
frieze from Bonampak. It is educated to pay respect to the god-
dess Coatlicue.'

In contrast to the little adobe hut in Guatemala, where I had to
wake up the official to get him to stamp my documents, I came,
not more than a few hundred yards farther on, to one of the most

modern customs buildings I have seen anywhere in the world. Its windows and its white walls and roof glittered brightly in the sunshine. Inside there were comfortable chairs for the weary traveller to sit on. There was a machine that provided purified iced water and hygienic cardboard cups to be thrown away after use. Free of charge, too! The documents were quickly and efficiently attended to. I was able to get petrol, although the new pumps at the petrol station on the border were not yet in operation and it had to come from enormous drums in a shed behind the garage.

I was now really in Mexico. A paved road began. It had some pot-holes for the first five or ten miles, but after that was excellent for almost all the journey through Mexico. I waved to the peasants along the roadside and got a spirited response from men whose hearts seemed sound but whose hands, I felt sure, knew how to spill blood. The black road still ran through a scene of arid wilderness. I had to cross a range of mountains, in which a few primitive dwellings appeared, before reaching Comitan, the first town of any size in Mexico and situated about fifty miles from the border. After travelling some thirty miles or so I stopped at a bungalow to make sure I was on the right route. The inhabitants, who had obviously been overdoing it on tequila, jumped instantly into their car and were going to lead me into the town. Fortunately they were rather too far gone to get it started and I felt quite relieved at not having to share the road with them.

As the sun was beginning to descend and the dry heat of the day to diminish, I arrived over the brow of a small hill and saw the town of Comitan nestling on the side of another hill in the distance ahead. It sent a sudden thrill right through me. In form and outline it was much like many of the towns I had already seen in South America. The twin towers of the church dominated the place, but it was altogether more colourful and showed a greater Moorish influence than anything I had seen hitherto. As its deep orange-brown roofs glittered in the horizontal rays of the setting sun, the view that my eyes actually saw seemed suddenly to correspond with the Mexico of my imagination.

As I came nearer to the town I could see the ejidos, the strips of communal land that came out of the revolution. I passed a garage and arrived at the entrance to a hotel. Vines and creeping plants entwined themselves into trellis work around a large courtyard and over a large baroque archway covered in orange plaster and fanciful ornamentation. My impressions were further complicated by the discovery that the establishment had just been bought by a German who spoke broken English. That he was making it into an excellent hotel was beyond question. I spent a very comfortable night there and was provided with good food at very reasonable charges. Several American couples were present and English seemed almost to be the prevailing language. Two young Americans who had been living in Mexico City were about to venture into Guatemala, and cross-examined me about the details of the route. I gave them an optimistic reply. I met them later in Mexico City and learnt that their car had been badly damaged in a landslide that blocked the road on which they should have returned and forced them to make the journey by train. Good luck had saved my finances and prestige by a matter of days!

An excellent road ran over the mountains in southern Mexico. The sun was dimmed by the building up of rain clouds and distant mists withheld many a spectacular sight from me. I had started off fairly early in the morning hoping to reach San Cristobal de las Casas in time to make a small excursion out to one of the two last remaining Maya villages, some ten kilometres or so outside the town. In San Cristobal the Indian market had been going on during the morning and the Indians from Chamula had been selling their wares. Many of them were returning on foot as I drove out along the rough dusty lane leading to the village. The men wore short tunics that hung rather like kilts from the waist downwards, leaving their legs bare from well above the knees. Their tunics were plain and simple and their sombreros wide, flat and shallow, with only a small rounded, bowl-shaped part for the top of their heads to fit into. The hats tended to sit on top of the hair. Their garments were mainly white or fawn in colour, but bright girdles and tassels hanging from their sombreros, of red and blue and other bright colours, indicated their rank or position in the village. They seemed on the whole very fresh and clean especially by comparison with most of the Indians I had already met. I was sorry not to be able to give them the lifts they constantly asked for, particularly since I was just about to take the pleasure of looking round their village.

A Picnic in Mexico

A few rough dwellings appeared but I did not seem to be arriving at the village. I therefore stopped to ask if I had by any change gone off the right track. I did this when I saw a couple of old women sitting under a tree outside one of the huts. They understood the name Chamula and pointed in the direction I was going. They added a great deal more in a language which was utterly incomprehensible to me. I had a feeling, however, that something was up and that I hadn't seen the last of them. One of the women was large and middle aged, the other was a lot older and enormously fat. I fancied that she was the mother-in-law of the younger woman. I wouldn't have given much for my chances, I thought to myself as I went on, of getting more than a few yards in the Austin with those two in it. Besides, they had three big baskets filled with mysterious goods and covered with cloths. The idea seemed like a joke to me as I trundled on towards the village. Soon I saw a collection of dark thatched huts without windows set on one side of the track. Curious wooden crosses were stuck in the ground around the huts. I imagined at the time that they were the result of the Maya's contact with Christianity, but I learnt later that the cross was a prominent symbol in the old Maya religion, indicating the four seasons in their calendar. I next attempted to photograph two little girls who were looking after the animals in the fields around the village. Like the Indians in Guatemala, they started to bolt at sight of the camera, but this time my chances were rescued by a herdsman who had learnt from American tourists that a camera might mean a few pesos. The Indians in general have the belief that when their picture is taken they lose something of their soul. If one judges by results in those places where the tourists have triumphed, their belief is perfectly correct!

I still had a long way to go during the afternoon and a formidable range of mountains lay across my route. I wanted to reach Tuxla Gutierrez before dark since my dynamo had ceased to charge and I didn't want to use the lights unnecessarily. As I trundled away from the village the two women were still sitting under the same tree. They waddled out into the middle of the track and gave me no choice but to stop. Despite all my protests and pleas, I was unable to prevail against them. Two of the enormous baskets were pushed into the back of the car and almost burst the hood at its seams, and the vaster of the two women squatted down on the passenger seat to the accompaniment of squeaks and groans from the flattened springs. Well, I thought, now they will see that I can't get anyone else in, no matter how much I might wish to oblige. But no, they were not to be defeated. The second woman simply forced the central portion of herself between the other woman's knees and the hood. Her legs and head and shoulders just stuck out of the side of the car while she clung on with one hand to the third of the enormous baskets and used the other to gain an artificial sense of security by grasping the door that swayed loosely on its little hinges. I then tried to make them understand that none of us stood much chance of getting anywhere unless they could clear enough room for me to operate the gear lever. My heart was with the underneath of the poor car which bore all the strain as we bumped over every yard of the rocky track, but it was the engine that found the solution and stalled when we came to a formidable incline. I resorted to an expedient that I intensely disliked using. The only way I could make them shift from the position they were in was by making them think I would pick them up again on the farther side of the hill. Still I consoled myself with the thought that they were probably a couple of tough-minded old battle-axes that had made many another poor devil in their own village suffer. I knew their type in our own society, which made me think how basically similar all societies are, an impression that was confirmed when I learnt the details of the rivalries of those last two remaining Maya villages. They were just like the petty rivalries between small villages in England.

With all the climbing of that day and the previous day I was nearly eleven thousand feet above the sea when I reached the brow of the last hill before descending the long winding road down into the hot plains of southern Mexico. Much of the view was blurred by the heat haze which spread out into the far distance. Nevertheless the impression of size and space, of great ridges of mountains criss-crossing each other on the perimeter of a vast plain evoked my first overwhelming response to the grandeur of the Mexican landscape. The road was excellently constructed and clear notice boards at frequent intervals stated the maximum safe speed for normal vehicles. I heard from visiting Americans that they are wonderfully accurate and if followed carefully make mountain driving speedy and safe. This is especially so on the motorway between Mexico City and Acapulco, Mexico's fabulous Pacific seaside resort.

I was making very good time and so when I got near to the town of Chiapa I turned off the main road to visit a newly unearthed pyramid. The Spaniards covered over these formidable stone structures from which the greatness of successive Indian empires shone forth in the garments of priests and warriors and in the deaths of numberless victims whose hearts were publicly extracted and offered as sacrifices to the gods. It is strange what a power such extravagant death has over multitudes of mild human beings. Even today the knowledge that these pyramids have such a history invests them with an awe that only murder can provide. Our hearts are still deeply imbued with reverence for violence. A little gate prevented me from driving into the field in which the pyramid was situated. Only the lower layers, with rows of fair-sized stones knocked somewhat out of line, remained. It wasn't the sort of pyramid to excite the ordinary visitor like myself. But for the archaeologist it held secrets and mysteries that waited to be unravelled. It was situated right on the borders between the Aztec and Maya civilizations. My chief interest was in Peru. The practical civilization of the Incas had always interested me more than the great artistic civilization of the Aztecs, which called for great spilling of blood to consecrate its megalomaniac dreams.

Tuxla Gutierrez is a large industrial city with something in the region of a hundred thousand inhabitants. When I arrived they were lining the streets in readiness for a procession to be put on by the Rotary International. I found the cheers and excitement I aroused more than a little embarrassing. I pressed on until I reached the hotel where I had been advised to stay. Of course it was full up on this occasion. All the other hotels too, I was told, would be full up. I eventually found a rather scruffy place to put up for the night at some absurdly low price. I felt justified in visiting the best hotel in the city for breakfast. It was a glittering modern palace of glass, of bright colours and splendid staircases. It could scarcely have been more up-to-date in its own Mexican way.

I was just leaving and about to step into the Austin when I heard the friendly accents of a Lancashire voice calling after me. I don't know who was more surprised: I, to hear a northern English voice in this rather remote part of southern Mexico, or Fred Whitehead, a mill owner from the textile city of Puebla, to see an

Austin Seven made in the very year he left England to settle in Mexico. He was just setting off with a party to explore a newly opened canyon. His party was just leaving. So in great haste he scribbled out his address and told me to be sure and call in at his home in Puebla. 'My sons are both car enthusiasts. I'd very much like them to see this car of yours.' I stopped at the Pemex station (short for Petroleos Mexicanos, the nationalized petroleum industry of Mexico). The attendants insisted on giving the Austin an immediate lightning shampoo, so that I left Tuxla in sparkling condition. It was just one little sign of the spontaneous enthusiasm that I felt existed everywhere among the Mexican people.

I drove for a couple of hundred miles through hot, dry country. The scenery could scarcely have been more uninteresting. Once or twice I was stopped at guard posts. With their automatics hanging down from their sides and rounds of ammunition displayed in their belts the untidy guards sauntered out inquiringly. They took no interest whatever in the documents I thought they were supposed to check, but really came to life as they brought out the drink to make spontaneous celebration for my successful arrival at the border of their province or wherever they happened to be. I felt that they were the true descendants of the men who had welcomed Tschiffely. Some of them, indeed, may have been the very same people.

Towards two o'clock I came to a large road junction some miles short of Tehuantepec. Both roads were wide and modern and in absolutely first-class condition. The heat was stifling and I was glad to see a modern service station with an attractive-looking restaurant adjacent to it. The dining-room wasn't very large, but it was clean, pleasantly decorated and colourful. Almost American; but somehow the chromium plating didn't hit you. I was struck instead by another typical example of Mexican extremes. Not more than a hundred yards away a few shacks where Indians lived had been constructed out of old junk on the bare dusty ground. Naked children and a few domestic animals played or scratched about in the sweltering sun. Old dried bones and bits of garbage lay unhygienically around those indescribably squalid dwellings. It was the sort of thing that made you wonder about the significance of the Mexican revolution. And yet in other places I was to see working people and their children neatly dressed, well fed and apparently happy and interested in life.

A Picnic in Mexico

After lunch I began talking with the manager about the best route to Mexico City. I had intended to travel via Oaxaca, but he strongly urged me to change my mind and turn immediately north to Vera Cruz. He assured me that at that period of the year the route via Oaxaca was hot, mountainous and extremely uninteresting. I was quite prepared to take the easier route. It was, however, a hundred miles to the nearest town and the afternoon was wearing on. I persuaded the manager to let me camp in one of the unfinished guest rooms at the back of the garage. Throughout the evening Mexican holidaymakers, usually in large American cars, came in preceded by their glaring headlights.

The road to Vera Cruz climbed up a long rocky hillside where I was warned to beware of sudden gusts of wind that sometimes cut powerfully across the wide black road. Later in the day I passed into a different climatic zone and reached jungle country once more. The difference this time was that I was able to race steadily through it. The native huts and the jungle itself were similar to much of what I have already described in Ecuador and Costa Rica. But the scenery underwent yet another surprising transformation in the late afternoon as I ran along the side of the hills that skirted the beautiful lake of Catemaco. I could almost have believed myself to have been in the English Lake District until I saw in front of me a typical Mexican town, brightly coloured, shining in the afternoon sunshine and nestling into the bottom of the hills at the water's edge. I might have driven in and spent the night there, but I wanted to reach Santiago Tuxla some miles farther on and in any case I liked the impression of the lake and the town just as I'd seen it. Going closer might have spoilt a dream-like memory.

Tropical villages, farming country and eventually suburbs made up the route to Vera Cruz. An apparently small thing, which was to have considerable consequences later, happened to the car soon after I had left Santiago Tuxla on the following morning. Excessive volumes of steam which reminded me of my experiences in the Andes blew up from the radiator and quickly brought me to a halt. I found that the leather fan-belt had come unstitched and also that it was impossible to fit another without undoing the engine mountings. The new pulley that I had had made in Lima had larger flanges than the old one, which it was thought would prevent any trouble from the belt tending to slip off. In England such a job as loosening the engine and raising it slightly on a jack would be simple and take not more than half an hour or so. I had really never allowed for the fact that in tropical heat such small attentions that the car might need can prove to be arduous burdens. I sat cursing in the car for some time before I finally hit upon what I thought was a bright idea. If it was only the thread that was gone, what was wrong with stitching it up again in position? After all, I had needles and thread with me. I am not quite sure what impression the natives or the passing motorists must have got when they saw someone leaning over the bonnet of such an odd-looking vehicle and working on it with a needle and cotton! However, it did the trick and I got to Vera Cruz.

Vera Cruz is the main port of Mexico as well as being a fashionable seaside resort. It was the week-end before Easter and it was like trying to get into a hotel at Brighton or Blackpool on an equivalent occasion. I was glad to set out as soon as possible to climb up into the Sierra Madre and make my way towards Puebla and Mexico City. In spite of the warnings I had received the climb proved to be nothing in comparison to what I'd already experienced. The hillsides were pleasant and green pastures and all the signs of agriculture prevailed for the first part of the journey. The Austin climbed without a murmur and I hadn't even to think about the complicated manœuvres which had been necessary in the really difficult mountain parts. I stopped to visit the fine archaeological museum at Jalapa, where I found myself quickly befriended by the young and charming Mexican director. He showed me every part of the museum's work and explained the difficulties facing historians and archaeologists in Mexico. My attention was arrested dramatically by the enormous heads carved in stone which were dotted around the grounds of the museum. They stood some ten to twelve feet high and eight or nine feet across. They were very realistic though somewhat fierce in aspect, they were the products of a pre-Aztec civilization and were dated to between A.D. 900 and 1000. Little is known about those earlier civilizations since they were harshly treated by the fascist Aztec régime. It was from such people that the Aztecs obtained the hearts they had to offer to their gods.

Once up on the Sierra Madre, one crosses long level plains of arid desert between the mountain ranges, where only the cactus and the maguey plant grow and extract the last vestiges of water and fertility that the dry sandy soil contains. I had often seen the moving pillars of sand that small whirlwinds raise into the hot air in desert regions. I had been within feet of one of them and I had seen low moving carpets of sand in the desert south of Lima, but I had never experienced a real sandstorm. A wind was blowing up now and from the mountains away over to my left I could see a brown wall rising up into the air and moving steadily across in the direction of the road. There seemed little point in turning back so I just kept going in the hope of progressing as far as possible before the full onslaught of the rocky particles hit me. I did take the precaution of putting up all the sidescreens, but I had not gone far before dust began to billow in through every crack and crevice. I stopped for a short time and tied a damp handkerchief over my nose and mouth. My worst fears, however, were for the car. Still I couldn't believe that there was any greater danger than there had been from the clouds of low sand that I had already driven through, and when the worst seemed to have passed over I started up again and forged on slowly through the mists of sand. At last I began to climb and, coming round on to the farther side of a hill, I discovered the air to be perfectly clear once more. From there on to Puebla was a fairly straightforward run through scenery of vast rocky splendour to begin with and then through dull country with all the ugly signs of human exploitation of nature. The journey on the whole was uneventful except that the needle and cotton episode was repeated in a much more inhabited district.

Puebla itself is a large industrial city with over a million inhabitants. It is the chief textile-producing city of Mexico, so that it was no wonder that Fred Whitehead found his way there after leaving Lancashire. I happened to ask a man on a bicycle the way to the street in which Fred lived. He led me the whole way across the city through a maze of one-way streets, until finally he waved in the direction of the street I was looking for and suddenly lost himself in the indistinguishable multitudes of cyclists pedalling home from work. The number I was looking for was Poniente 2,116. It turned out to be a pleasant old colonial-type house with a high white wall and a gate with strong iron bars in front. A balcony, with its ceiling and the upper part of the house upheld by a row of classical-style pillars, ran the full length of the house.

Vines and various subtropical plants gave it a sense of cool seclusion from the road. I rang the bell and within seconds a pretty face peered through the bars of the gate at me. She didn't understand English so I had to try to explain more or less who I was in Spanish. Within moments I found myself being interrogated on all aspects of my personal life by a bevy of Fred's pretty daughters. This, I thought to myself, is what he calls showing my car to his sons! However, both Fred and his sons turned up shortly and I spent a most happy week with him and his family visiting places of interest in and around Puebla. I saw the cathedral, the old university of Puebla and one of the new large schools, the last of which I found especially interesting. It was wonderfully equipped and housed in splendid modern buildings and, although this was holiday time, it was buzzing with activity. The children apparently found it a place they still wanted to be in the holidays! Another feature of Puebla's life is the excellent sports club—sports clubs in Mexico include not only swimming-baths and tennis courts and athletic facilities of various kinds, but libraries and reading-rooms also. Life is not divided into so many compartments as it often is in other parts of the world—an important sign of civilized vitality, I believe.

As I wandered round the streets with Fred, whose wife was Mexican and who seemed to have taken to Mexican ways like a fish to water, he would stop every now and again and after embracing some friend begin to explain about my journey. 'Ha venido de Buenos Aires en un Austin modelo mil novocientos veinticinco,' he would say in tones quivering with a sense of the incredible. One such friend he described as the Secretary of State for the State of Puebla. For Mexico is a group of federated states like the U.S.A. On its coins one reads 'Los Estados Unidos de Mexico'.

With the memories of one or two outstanding visits my reminiscences of Puebla must end. The first was to a convent which had operated secretly for nearly eighty years in the centre of the city, after the dissolution of the monasteries and convents. It was accidentally discovered in 1934 when, after an unsuccessful search by the police, one of the detectives slipped and fell against a picture which revealed a secret tunnel into the convent. It is now a museum and one of the big tourist attractions of Puebla. One enters it by that same small tunnel by which the young nuns entered it on their way out of this world, for no woman who once went in came out again alive. Even her bones were buried in its gloomy precincts. In its own way it fully lives up to Mexico's reputation for going to extremes. Gruesome pictures of Christ's sufferings line the walls and the heavy chains in which the nuns mortified their flesh, the leather straps with which they whipped out the last remnants of the lusts of their bodies from themselves, and the hair shirts which they wore next to their pale skin as they contemplated representations of the crucified Christ, give some idea of the self-torture, if such it all was, that went on behind the apparently normal exterior of a home for eight painful decades.

The other memorable visit was to Chulula, a small town just outside Puebla. Chulula is famous for a particularly ancient pyramid, now covered with earth and having a Catholic church constructed on top of it, for bloody massacres of Indians and for its innumerable churches. It is reputed to have one for every Sunday of the year. The murdering of the Indians seems to have outshone even the bloodthirstiness of the Aztecs themselves, and to square their accounts with God and their consciences the Spaniards, according to the story I was told, built a new church each time the number of murders reached a certain total. Inside these churches one sees the signs of Christian and pagan worship side by side, so much so that one writer has pointed out that it is almost impossible to decide whether the Catholic missionaries tricked the Indians or vice versa. Everything seems to be like that in Mexico whether it be Christianity, communism or anything else.

Even the Catholics were unwittingly following an old Indian tradition when they built their church on top of the pyramid. When an Indian civilization conquered another it did not destroy the existing pyramid temple, but crowned it with an additional layer to exhibit its superiority. It was so with the pyramid we were visiting. Many miles of a small railway had been laid through passages at various levels to clear out the earth—and the debris of time. We saw first the level on which the flamboyant pageants of the Aztecs had taken place. We then went lower and deeper through more and more primitive civilizations until we reached caverns whose walls were lined with primitive paintings of the early worshippers of the sun and moon. Long straggling interwoven lines of pale yellow and red ochre joined rudimentary faces of the same colours. Two crude circles of thick lines represented the eyes. The rest of the face was equally crude and uneven. Nevertheless, they had childlike primitive power, these symbols of life and death, and doubtless in their own time their magical power sent many a shudder through fearsome hearts.

One afternoon while I was in Puebla one of Fred's sons brought back his fiancée and two of her elegant cousins from Mexico City. They filled the car and demanded a ride. I succumbed to their charms but the misogynist tendencies of the Austin broke out again when we had travelled no more than a few hundred yards up the road. Pushing the little car back this time was a brief indignity by comparison with the incident in Chile.

On later examination it became evident that water was leaking into the engine; the trouble could almost certainly be ascribed to the constant overheating it had had to suffer and the two recent failures of the fan-belt had been the last straw. The local B.M.C. agent heard of my trouble and insisted on giving the engine a thorough check over. It was after some delay therefore that I finally set out for Mexico City. I felt all the time that Mexico was more than I could really digest. During the journey my eyes and mind had feasted on as much as they could cope with. Besides I was weary with the constant stresses and strains of the journey. I proposed facing the inevitable publicity that my arrival in the city would evoke, and then trying to snatch a few weeks' rest before entering the rush and bustle of the great United States. I had not long left Puebla to drive over the arid mountain ranges which surround Mexico City, once situated on an island in the centre of a great lake, when I noticed that the engine was once again beginning to fire unevenly. Rashly I made a mistaken assumption about its cause. I thought at the time it was still due to water entering the engine. I could not wait to investigate since I had an appointment with the representatives of the main agency in the city who were coming out to meet me at Kilometre Forty. I left the Austin, somewhat reluctantly, in the safe keeping of a restaurant owner and managed to get a lift to the meeting-place.

It was a deep disappointment to be driving along the splendid avenues of Mexico City in a modern car, and by having to return for the Austin I missed the opportunity of joining a party to Acapulco for the week-end. The splendour of the city was hidden from my eyes for some days. When I returned for the Austin I found that the trouble was due to the poor old magneto, which despite all its internal upheaval in Chile had done a magnificent job for well over six thousand miles through regions where, if it had failed, the consequences might have been drastic indeed. How could I be ungrateful to it? Perhaps if I'd been stuck I might have repaired it myself, but the representative of the agency thought it was best to go to a mechanic in one of the villages. His workshop was just a covered yard, but his mind understood the principles of electricity. He tackled the job in a way that would shame the average mechanic in England. There was no complaining that he'd never seen an Austin Seven or an Austin Seven magneto before. He worked from general principles.

The car had scarcely arrived in the city before the full blast of Mexican publicity struck me. The international news agencies wanted the details of my story, correspondents of several English newspapers as well as those of the main Mexican papers were present at a press conference organized by the Embassy, television and radio programmes were arranged and for a day or two my time was fully occupied. On the following day when I read my story I noticed on the same page part of a grand argument between two well-known newspaper columnists. Mexicans shrugged their shoulders about it when I mentioned it to them. 'There is only one way to end it in Mexico,' they all said; 'it is only a matter of time before they will have to fight a duel over it.' That was one side of the spirit of Mexico. The signs of physical death are ever present, though the outward signs of revolution are over and one can travel through Mexico without fear of assault. I found myself getting quite a spirited welcome from the people of the city. When I went out in the streets, children would flock round and ask if the Austin was the car they had seen on television, crowds would gather round in the streets more quickly and with more genuine enthusiasm than anywhere else on the journey, and on the main avenues the traffic, already lively, would forget itself while its drivers waved to me at our mutual peril. The problem was solved by putting the car on display in the British Industrial Centre in the Paseo de la Reforma, the chief avenue of Mexico City. It still looked very nice despite its hardships and trials, and a young naval commander was heard to comment from one of the upper rooms, while the television people were photographing the car below, that it was the same age as himself but in a good deal better condition!

A Picnic in Mexico

Immediately after the press conference I visited the new University City. It is bold, splendid and incredible. Colours, designs, vividness and power assail one from all sides. A large group of architects were let loose with plenty of money and materials to impose their will on a large area of volcanic wasteland, the only stipulation being that they should produce a university. There is nothing here of the pathetic mystery of so much modern art which to my mind is the product of a vacant civilization in which people are satisfied with queerness, mystification and clever techniques alone. The Indian awareness of the shapes and forms of this world, of the mystery of real life, is infused into the whole project of the University City and answers the riddle of where the unity and compatibility of its parts is derived from. Vast reliefs of human figures, greater than life and dynamically alive, decorate, one should perhaps say symbolize, the faculty of medicine. The colossal windowless library of the university is surfaced with a gigantic mosaic of different-coloured stones. One sees again the garments of the Indians at their festivals, symbols of their worship of life put together with a bold and delicate art.

When I returned I discovered that Irene Nicholson had left a note inviting me to join her and some friends for a picnic on the following day. One of our main purposes was to see a new road that was being built by students to join a remote village with the main stream of Mexican development. We sped out over the dusty basin in which Mexico is situated in a large American touring car. We were a party of five. I sat in the middle at the back, I think, and leant on the back seat enlarging upon the colourful incidents of my journey. They flowed out easily because they had been so real. Now as I think back I realize that as the wind rushed through our hair, often taking my words with it for no one but the plains of Mexico to hear, the spirit of this book was somehow born. We passed through the town of Texcoco, and out into an area of wasteland where only an occasional ruined hacienda remained from the days of the revolution. Eventually we found the spot where the roadworks were supposed to be going on, but as it was rather a special national holiday the students were away and we saw only the signs of a neatly packed-up camp. Close by was a small park in which there were concrete benches and tables for picnickers such as one finds along the highways of the United States. But the wine and the beer (and how excellent Mexican beer is!) and the roast chickens and the flow of interesting edibles that came from Irene's picnic basket were reminiscent of other times and places. The great feasts I recalled were Harrison Ainsworth's in *The Tower of London*. In fact we were lunching where the ancient Texcocan poet-king Nezahualcoyotl once composed his verses.

In a search that was now directed towards finding a newly unearthed pyramid, we passed many more destroyed haciendas. The question arose whether the peasants were really having a better life after having thrown off the chains of feudalism. On the whole the machinery for providing that better standard of life seemed to be going into action from Mexico City outwards, but the village we entered in our search for the pyramid was a drab place indeed. The adobe huts were tumbling down and grey, the villagers looked sullen and uninterested in life—perhaps they needed another revolution for their entertainment! The network of wires hooked up on primitive poles which brought electric light to the drab homes seemed oddly incongruous. The inside of the church I found the most depressing sight of all. Its very colours were a mockery. The priests had obviously persuaded the poor villagers to bring their paint to church. Garishly painted dolls with no traces of art or skill in their production were the objects they worshipped. The walls were also brightly painted with cheap colours. It was the last bit of colour in the life of the sad village.

In Texcoco itself we visited the Indian market which today is full of fakery put on for tourists, a clear example of the Indians losing their souls for dollars, but perhaps they had only left them at home. A long dusty trail on the other side of the town led us to one of the most beautiful haciendas that still remains more or less intact and is now being preserved as a museum. The hacienda Molino de Flores is a splendid example of romantic Mexico. One enters it by a fine archway, and notices the intricate designs on doors and windows which some nobleman travelling through seventeenth and eighteenth-century Europe decided to bring back and add to the general Spanish style of his home. At one end of a cobbled courtyard the cool waters of a fountain rise up in front of a delicately designed wrought-iron staircase, leading up to a balcony which runs the length of the building on one side of the courtyard. The uneven setting of attractive buildings around the courtyard gives a sense of infinite variety, like some romantic village on a sunny hillside in Spain. This charming hacienda, whatever its history, seemed as though it should have had a humanizing effect on those who lived within it. Perhaps indeed that was why it survived the others that lie ruined and forgotten.

It was some days before I began to form a picture of Mexico City. I had walked and driven along the wide Paseo de la Reforma with its splendid lines of trees, its roundabouts with golden statues and difficult Indian names, its skyscrapers, its commercial palaces of glass and its elegant shops. At the far end of this avenue on the only hill in the centre of an otherwise very flat city stands the castle of Chapultepec, where Maximilian lived, and whose name belies its fashionable European contents. At the other end of the same avenue, after having met such fiery names as Avenida Revolucion and Avenida Insurgentes, one comes to a fashionable shopping centre leading through to the Zocalo, the main square of Mexico City and as a city square surpassed in size only by Red Square in Moscow. It contains the cathedral and one is in the area of the old part of the city which is kept intact and separate from the new. It was the first of May. An enormous parade of workers passed through the square in the morning. It ran I believe into something like a million. Banners of all trades were carried and rather extravagant signs of respect for the President and for the Partido Revolucionario Institucional were shown. In the evening of May Day the old part of the city is floodlit. I knew nothing about it and was sitting talking to people in my hotel. Some Americans returned full of enthusiasm for the sight and, discovering that only I and a girl from Greenwich Village, New York, had not been to see it, pushed us both into a taxi. We grudgingly introduced ourselves to each other on the way and I learnt her name was Riki. When we arrived the lights were going off one at a time round the Zocalo. We were just in time to see the great red stone façade of the cathedral still lit up. Every nook and cranny in its massively and intricately ornamented structure was illuminated with breathtaking clarity. As the last light went out we started to walk back. Neither of us had enough money with us for a taxi, but we stopped at a small restaurant about half-way and had a cup of cocoa each. As we drank Riki began to explain to me what beatniks really were. The first and most important thing about real American beatniks was that nobody should even suspect them to be beatniks. They should dress elegantly and precisely as indeed Riki herself did. They should be firm upholders of every aspect of Victorian morality but at the same time be able to convey an intimate knowledge of the ways of the world.

By and large Mexico City settles down to sleep between ten and eleven o'clock. Its citizens are hard workers and they need sleep. After our cocoa we began an excursion on foot of the city looking for weighing machines until about four o'clock in the morning. The quality, character and personality of those unfortunate weighing machines hung entirely upon the shades of a gram they happened to register above or below a figure situated somewhere just over a hundredweight on our scale. Riki was an aspect of America. I should have liked to have introduced her to my poet friend in the jungle in Nicaragua.

The days passed by pleasantly in Mexico City. There is an infinite number of things that could be said about this most elegant and splendid of capital cities. I enjoyed gay, charming, sociable fiestas. I took a short intensive course in Spanish in a final attempt to strengthen my feeble grasp of that language, and I finished by promising to carry one of the large burros made of clay and crinkly white paper, which the Mexican children smash with sticks at Christmas time to release a shower of sweets and toys. It was quite a large creature and was like an extra personality on the expedition as it sat up in the passenger seat. It had come as the result of a request that I couldn't and didn't really want to refuse, but it was an added absurdity to the expedition and an added anxiety should the threatened rains suddenly release themselves and spoil its pretty white coat. I was given a strict warning to be particularly careful on the main roads north of Mexico City. The representative of an English company told me that he had seen a smashed-up Pontiac which had come up from Chile in a garage just outside Queretero. I never heard the end of the story of the two bus drivers from Santiago.

The main road north of Mexico City is a magnificent toll road for some miles and then a long straight road through what would be described as monotonous desert. I travelled on the first day to Queretero, a rather uninteresting town with a bit of Spanish, and a lot of dirty industrial architecture. I put up at a not too chromium-plated motel. It was characterless but comfortable. The next morning I set out on the longest single day's run of the whole journey, 355 miles from Queretero to Monterray. The road was excellent but grey clouds began to pursue me during the afternoon. I was approaching the mountain country in the north when they finally burst loose from the sky. Lightning flashed spectacularly in circles round a mountain peak immediately ahead. I climbed for some distance, entered a gorge in the mountains and, on emerging at the farther side, found the sun to be shining brilliantly again from a cloudless blue sky. The last fifty miles to Monterray was once more through mountainous country. but I nevertheless arrived before the shops in the industrial city had closed.

Monterray is the centre of Mexico's heavy industries. I was struck by nothing particularly except the numerous American tourists and the remarkable collection of model T Fords which are still running round the town as taxis, although it's normally assumed that all Mexican drivers tear the guts out of their cars after a year or two. I was now only 140 miles from the United States. By lunchtime I should be in Texas. The road ran through a scene of vast undeveloped scrubland. The heat was terrific. My journey not only through Mexico but through Latin America was over. Shortly people would be speaking English again. I was sad at heart as I stopped at the last wayside 'cantina' for a drink before crossing the Rio Grande and entering the United States of America at Laredo, Texas.

XII

New York at Last

It was seventeen minutes past twelve on 3rd June 1960, as I looked at the clock at the United States Customs' House. The officer smiled enigmatically as he firmly requested me to lay my baggage out on the platform for inspection. The poor old burro had to line up with the rest and received equal treatment with canvas bags and battered old suitcases. I was able to pick up the telephone to call New York and let the various people who had been awaiting my arrival know that I had reached the border intact. A solid stretch of paved road lay ahead of me for all the two thousand odd miles up to America's greatest metropolis. Admittedly the potholes in Georgia were often to remind me of South America, but on the whole the difficulties were of quite a different nature now. Driving a little old antique car with inadequate brakes, wearied and worn after a journey that would have torn the guts out of most cars, along the great superhighways of the United States, where enormous modern automobiles were hurtling along nose to tail at sixty miles an hour, involved its own hazards. They were probably no less great than those in the jungles and deserts, but no one is impressed by dangers in the jungle that we call civilization.

The scenery on the first part of the journey into Texas was much the same as the dry scrubland of the last few hours in Mexico. The same scorching sun blazed down on both, but the journey no longer held the same sense of strangeness and interest. On my journey through the States I felt on the one hand more than half at home and on the other I felt acutely conscious of the great differences between the various states of that mighty federation. I realized, for the first time, that the United States really is a collection of different countries, especially when I found Span-

ish spoken exclusively in areas of Texas and French in parts of
Louisiana. All my stereotyped views of what the 'Americans' are
like went west and I was constantly impressed by the enormous
human and material potential of the greatest of the Western
powers. Some English people told me that I should never try to
criticize Americans. Confidentially they would whisper, 'They
have no background or culture and they can't take it.' What
complete rubbish! I suspect that such stupid comments arise
principally out of petty jealousy over the present material pros-
perity of the United States, for they show all the signs of a
fundamental lack of human respect. On such occasions I could
not help recalling some remarks of H. G. Wells on the development of the English-speaking world: 'These differences in
method, pace and tradition are a great misfortune . . . We English
people do not respect Americans enough . . . We are disposed to
think they must be humoured at any cost; which is why we are
never so frank and rude with them as they deserve . . . Real
brothers can curse each other and keep friends.' I cannot begin to
describe the hospitality, the wit, the signs of great organization,
the tremendous qualities of the Americans, but there was one
flaw, it seemed to me, that ran through business and political life.
Everywhere I found people explaining the situation to me in the
same words: 'Here it's a case of dog eat dog.' This phrase betrays
the sign of deep-rooted social self-destruction, and it came not
from Moscow but from American business people themselves.
This is the sort of thing that calls for plain speaking between
brothers. Once again it would be easy to go on moralizing on
international relations for ever and forget that I am writing the
simple narrative of a vintage car journey.

I reached San Antonio and spent my first night in the United
States with the owner of the Austin Agency there in a luxurious
air-conditioned bedroom. We got up early in the morning and
had a hurried breakfast in a 'diner'. Diners were once the wagons
which served meals to the cowboys as they drove their cattle
along the trails of Texas. Today they have lost their wheels, have
become cemented into the ground and require a lot of chromium
plating. Across their shining stainless steel counters the most
appetizing of breakfasts are served. You can see them cooked
before your eyes, and marvel at the hygienic and colourful variety
of foods which these efficient chromium-plated cabins can pro-

duce. The burro was sent off to California in a big box, before I set out again. The next night I spent in Austin, the State Capital of Texas. Everybody I met was delighted by the coincidence in names and my arrival was accorded considerable publicity. The front pages of the newspapers spoke of the arrival of the Chummy Man and accompanied the announcement with an extra large picture.

From Austin I drove up to Fort Worth. I was expecting a rousing welcome but arrived late and could contact no one who was supposed to be planning my welcome. While I was trying to telephone from a service station just off the Expressway, a police car drew up. I was soon to enjoy my second spectacular entry into a city. This time it was not quite accidental. The 'cop' radioed in for an escort of motor-cycles to lead me to my destination. Whistles blew and sirens sounded as we rushed through red lights and all other traffic was brought to a temporary halt. It seemed like a royal welcome indeed and I felt tremendously important for a few minutes in a State where importance plays a very big part in life.

The next day I had to face a long interview by the director of the television news service and I had an opportunity to tell the Texans what their brothers in Latin America are really like, for it seemed to me that their view of the Latin Americans is as clouded by false preconceptions as is our own of the Americans. After a day of American hospitality and some inhospitality, my host accompanied me over the thirty-mile turnpike to Dallas where I would be welcomed by those friends of Irene Nicholson's, who had been on the unforgettable picnic in Texcoco. I wanted to see my interview, but I had arrived at a household, perhaps the only household in America, that didn't keep a television set! We had to visit the neighbours and eventually missed it by tuning in to the wrong channel. My visit to Dallas extended for a full week and while I was there my car was used to head a display of British cars driving out to one of the finest country clubs in Texas, where I lunched with Commander Whitehead whose beard has achieved fame in every American household.

From Dallas I travelled southwards again along the sun-baked expressways of Texas to the oil capital of that wealthy State, Houston. It so happened that I arrived just in the nick of time to take part in the celebrations for the Queen's birthday. The newspapers depicted my loyalty as leading me to drive madly over wild trails in the Andes, across blazing deserts, through dense jungles and over mighty rivers, all to reach Houston in time for this event!

From Houston I drove down to New Orleans, passing on my way through the great forests of Louisiana. I was now in the deep south where Bible religion and hard-headed racialism go hand in hand. In one restaurant a notice informed customers that swearing was not permitted, and another notice, obviously not meant to betray a sense of humour, read: 'In God we trust, all others must pay cash.' I broke my journey once more at Atlanta where I stayed with the Robinsons of the British Consulate and had the usual American hospitality and publicity accorded to the car and myself. I recall particularly vividly a precarious interview recorded as I was travelling along the downtown expressway at rush hour. Discussion about the lonely and deserted trails of South America was suddenly cut short by some strong exclamation and the whirr of an almost invisible modern vehicle cutting across my bonnet at one of the exits from the expressway. I was also rather amused to find myself referred to as 'that astonishing traveller', in the social column of one of the newspapers. I liked that adjective because in an odd kind of way the journey still astonishes me, and I still often find it hard to believe that it was more than an extraordinarily vivid dream. It is still somehow the impossible dream that I thought up when I was at school, but through both pleasure and suffering the concrete details have been filled in in a way which will never cease to astonish me.

I shortly found myself speeding up the U.S. highway 1 towards the Federal Capital. Washington seemed strangely different from all the other cities of the United States, a city rightly noted for its distinction and dignity which were aptly symbolized by the absence of skyscrapers and most of the other signs of modern American development. It took little notice of my arrival, being superior I assumed to the minor enthusiasms which afflict the rest of the country. Nevertheless I was given a fair share of publicity in the main newspapers and I was welcomed at the British Embassy. I was invited immediately with the Austin, of course, to a cocktail party just outside the capital. Those who saw the little old Austin being led out by the large new Bentley of *The Times* correspondent will hardly be likely to forget it, but however ridiculous it may have appeared being led through the main thoroughfares of the capital, it certainly looked fine on the lawn of a splendid country house and provided a topic for some stimulating conversation among a very international collection of guests.

Philadelphia was my next stop. I arrived late in the afternoon and tried to find the house of the captain of the boat in which I'd travelled to Panama. He had given me an open invitation to spend a week with him at any time when I might manage to reach Philadelphia. He said he didn't expect me to be able to give any exact prediction. When I eventually found the house in a rather remote country area about ten miles outside the city, I was disappointed to learn that the captain had gone back to his home in Austria before setting out on another voyage. Somewhat dejected, I drove off and eventually pulled up at a wayside restaurant where I sat eating a hamburger and gazing at the array of chromium plating around me. Motels are very expensive in that area; I sat there contemplating bringing my tent out for the first time during the whole of my journey. As I was thinking of how the car had had to carry it over the Andes and of all the times I had lugged it in and out of hotels and lodgings of various kinds, a man and his family came in and settled down along the counter. I thought he had a friendly-looking face and I suppose he must have thought the same about me, for we quickly struck up a conversation. I learnt that he was a young doctor and that he'd just come out for an hour with the kids. Shortly I began to tell him of my position and I asked him if he could recommend anywhere for camping. He guessed that his garden was as good as anywhere, and as he had to visit a friend before returning he gave me exact instructions to find the way to his cottage. I had to go past a big house and then down a hill to his 'little' cottage. Why is it that the reputation for understatement is reserved for us English? Our conversations that evening encompassed American and international politics and some lively things were said, things that would destroy for ever the stupid notions of those critics of America who imagine that Americans are not capable of self-criticism!

The following morning I motored down into Philadelphia again. As I halted at a traffic light I noticed behind me a man rushing in between the traffic in my direction. It turned out to be Henry Gerlash, the well-known antique car enthusiast. He had tried to chase me by car the previous evening but had more success that morning on foot! Through him I met George Norton, the President of the Antique Automobile Club of America, and Leslie Henry, a former President and now the Curator of the great Ford Museum in Detroit. Thus began a lightning tour of vintage car museums and numerous private collections which included Tom Marshall's famous collection of steam cars. When I arrived he was just adding to his collection an old Canadian locomotive, under which I made my first contact with the Marshall family. The whole history of the American automobile was presented to me with baffling rapidity. Another book could be written about what I saw but not by me, a mere ignorant traveller as I felt myself to be when I passed through galleries of antique cars, some of whose names I had never even heard of, and of whose specifications I knew nothing at all.

It was suggested that I should delay for a day or two and join in the Independence Day Parade in Philadelphia. The Austin was hurriedly added to a list of over a hundred antique cars and given a prominent place in the procession. Judging from the remarks of the children among the tightly packed lines of people which stretched for miles along either side of our route, I could have believed that I was on my way to a beatnik's coronation ceremony, my beard being the fatal symbol of that destiny. Once the procession was over, however, I nipped quickly off from the display ground after collecting a medal or two—one for having travelled the longest distance to reach the rally!—and started racing up the New Jersey Turnpike. It was a crazy thing to do, of course, at the end of a national holiday when all America seems to be struggling to pack itself back into New York. Nevertheless, it had the effect of redoubling the enthusiasm with which I got waved at, photographed and stopped all along the way, and in fact added chaos and danger to the most dangerously chaotic traffic situation that occurs annually in the U.S.A. At least it did so until a sensible traffic policeman pulled up and told me to get right off the expressway at the first opportunity and followed me to make sure I did so. Perhaps the worst danger had been from the ordinary American motorist who was interested but anxious not to show too many signs of unconformity. With him the pattern was this: his eyes would go straight to the mirror and his wife would turn round and stare out through the back window. She would then turn round again and a period of discussion would follow. Once off the turnpike I quickly encountered another police car. The driver, who had read of my journey in the New York papers, was extremely kind and helpful and set me going along a less congested route.

My problem now was that my official entry was not due for another two days. I was well in front, for once, of my estimated time of arrival and had to hide myself away in a New Jersey motel, slipping, nevertheless, furtively in to have a preview of my destination and to give a word of advice about how I thought I ought to be welcomed. Then on the morning of the 6th July, after the car had been polished and prepared for the occasion, it ran faultlessly and triumphantly over the George Washington Bridge and into New York City. As I made my way towards Central Park where a reception had been prepared for me, I passed by the Empire State Building, and almost imagined I heard the little Austin heave a sigh of relief when, recalling its memories of the Andes, it realized that it was not going to be expected to climb up it.

A representative of the Columbia Broadcasting System was at the reception. I was asked to avoid any publicity for a week so that I could appear on one of the major television quiz shows, To Tell the Truth, in which a panel of well-known personalities are faced with three people all claiming to have performed some feat, and have to guess, on the basis of a short period of questioning, which is the genuine claimant. While I was waiting I went out for a few days to visit Henry Austin Clarke, or 'Austie' as he is known to his friends, at his antique car museum at Southampton, Long Island. We travelled round a good deal together in the Austin, even taking it round the Bridgehampton Race Circuit at over fifty miles an hour while Austie indicated the points at which great racers had perished. Then one day as we were driving out of Austie's house we had to go over a nasty little bump. I approached it with the characteristic care I'd disciplined myself to observe throughout the journey (wherever such care was possible) and Austie remarked, 'I see now exactly how you got up from Buenos Aires in this car,' and I told him that it was one of the most sensible and perceptive comments anybody had made to me in America. We were on our way to the golf club to show the car to one or two people. We were having a drink when Austie said 'I'd like you to meet Henry.' A few words were exchanged and Henry was asked to come round the corner to see the vehicle in which he was told the fantastic journey had been done. We drove straight off when he'd seen it. 'Oh, by the way,' Austie remarked, 'Ford's that guy's other name.'

Thus I spent a week in obscurity waiting for the performance of To Tell the Truth, which I'd been lured into by the producer who had told me how much money I could win, how the programme went out from coast to coast to between thirty and sixty million viewers and how such great men as Sir Edmund Hillary had appeared on it. Two friends I had made in Washington, Frank and Joanna, were in the audience as the nervous moments passed during which I had to answer truthfully all the questions which the panel fired at me. There was a young man from Cambridge with me, who knew a great deal about Austin Sevens, and had taken so much interest in the university expeditions to South America that it was hard to believe that he hadn't been there. The other fake was a man from the Ministry of Pensions in Blackpool, whose only recommendation was that he had a fine sun-tan and looked like a seasoned explorer. I shuddered for a moment when he revealed that he didn't know what the Amazon was after the name had been pronounced distinctly twice, and began to stutter something about climbing its rocky tracks. Out of the panel of four, three plumbed for the Cambridge, and one for the Blackpool man. I wasn't even suspected. 'Was I all right?' I asked Frank afterwards. 'You were terrific,' he replied. 'Until the bell rang you looked as if you weren't capable of driving round Long Island, never mind up from Buenos Aires.'

Index

Index

Index

Index